15 Years of

ThisDay's
Thought
from theranch.org

Over 1700 Inspirational Quotes
Arranged by Categories

COMPILED BY GREG POTZER

ISBN 978-1-931760-45-4

About This Book

We are pleased to present this collection of Christian thoughts that have been shared over the past fifteen years of our ministry.

The various Christian quotations are organized in forty different categories to make them more easily accessible as one wishes to delve into particular topics, and some thoughts thereby appear in more than one category where applicable to their multifaceted messages.

We hope you will be blessed by these profound thoughts of comfort and peace, wisdom and guidance, wit and understanding.

And may God bless you in your continued walk with Him.

In His Love,

Greg Potzer and Eric Elder
This Day's Thought from The Ranch

Index of Categories

About The Bible

The true Bible is not the dead book, but the living reality, developed by the Spirit of God in the conscience of mankind. It is not a printed thing. The printed thing is the memorial of it, a souvenir of it, a mere chart; and a chart is not the ocean.
Phillips Brooks

The path of the Word and the path of the world do not run parallel.
Vance Havner

If it happens that you are well off, in your heart be tranquil about it- if you can be just as glad and willing for the opposite condition. So let it be with food, friends, kindred, or anything else that God gives or takes away.
Meister Eckhart

A converted Hindu who had been given a Bible and a clock said, "The clock will tell me how time goes, and the Bible will tell me how to spend it."
Unknown

Worry less about offending the people and more about offending the Gospel.
William Brosend

He who has the Holy Spirit in his heart and the Scripture in his hands has all he needs.
Alexander MacLaren

According to the values which govern my life, my most important reason for living is to get the baton- the gospel- safely in the hands of my children.
James Dobson

I can seldom read scripture now without tears of joy and gratitude.
Hudson Taylor

Of all the dispositions and habits which lead to political prosperity, religion and morality are indispensable supports. It is impossible to rightly govern the world without God and the Bible.
George Washington

Since 3600 BC the world has known only 292 years of peace. In that period, stretching more than 55 centuries, there have been an incredible 14,531 wars in which over 3.6 billion people have been killed.
John Ankerberg

More than fifty-five years ago my father told me, "The Bible does not belong on the shelf but in your hand, under your eye, and in your heart."
Martin Niemoller

I prayed for faith and thought it would strike me like lightning. But faith did not come. One day I read, "Now faith comes by hearing, and hearing by the Word of God." I had closed my Bible and prayed for faith. I now began to study my Bible and faith has been growing ever since.
Dwight L. Moody

An honest man with an open Bible and a pad and pencil is sure to find out what is wrong with him very quickly.
A. W. Tozer

By reading the scriptures I am so renewed that all nature seems renewed around me and with me. The sky seems to be a pure, a cooler blue, the trees a deeper green. The whole world is charged with the glory of God and I feel fire and music under my feet.
Thomas Merton

When a Christian shuns fellowship with other Christians, the devil smiles. When he stops studying the Bible, the devil laughs. When he stops praying, the devil shouts for joy.
Corrie Ten Boom

I try not to worry about life too much because I read the last page of THE book and it all turns out all right.
Billy Graham

The Bible grows more beautiful, as we grow in our understanding of it. *Johann Wolfgang von Goethe*

Nobody ever outgrows Scripture; the Book widens and deepens with our years.
Charles Spurgeon

The Holy Scriptures are our letters from home.
Augustine

The one use of the Bible is to make us look at Jesus, that through Him we might know His Father and our Father, His God and our God.
George MacDonald

Some read the Bible to learn, and some read the Bible to hear from heaven.
Andrew Murray

I study my Bible as I gather apples. First, I shake the whole tree that the ripest might fall. Then I shake each limb, and when I have shaken each limb, I shake each branch and every twig. Then I look under every leaf.
Martin Luther

I did not go through the Book, The Book went through me.
A. W. Tozer

We may be certain that whatever God has made prominent in his word, he intended to be conspicuous in our lives.
Charles Spurgeon

There was an old Christian woman whose age began to tell on her memory. She had once known much of the Bible by heart. Eventually only one precious bit stayed with her. "I know whom I have believed, and am persuaded that he is able to keep that which I have committed unto him against that day." By and by part of that slipped its hold, and she would quietly repeat, "That which I have committed unto him." At last, as she hovered on the borderline between this and the spirit world, her loved ones noticed her lips moving. They bent down to see if she needed anything. She was repeating over and over again to herself the one word of the text, "Him, Him, Him." She had lost the whole Bible, but one word. But she had the whole Bible in that one word.
S. D. Gordon

The more fully that the gospel is preached, in the grand old apostolic way, the more likely is it to accomplish the results which it did in the apostolic days.
Horatius Bonar

The words of the Gospels, repeated to a child, a workman or a peasant, do not surprise him in the least. Nothing is told with a view to effect. Not a word in the Gospels is intended to startle.
Ernest Hello

Read The Bible
It's User Friendly
Plus We Offer Tech
Support Here On
Sunday's At 10:30
On a church marquee

A man who loves the Word of God, a man who dwells upon what it says, a man who keeps a little text in his mind to think about as he is walking on his way, and that meditates upon it day and night, "Whatsoever he doeth shall prosper." If you can find a man who carries out this direction and doesn't prosper, you can doubt the inspiration of the first Psalm; but find the man first.
J. Hudson Taylor

The study of God's Word for the purpose of discovering God's will is the secret discipline which has formed the greatest characters.
James W. Alexander

The Bible as a book stands alone. There never was, nor ever will be, another like it. As there is but one sun to enlighten the world naturally, so there is but one Book to enlighten the world spiritually. May that Book become to each of us the man of our counsel, the guide of our journey, the inspiration of our thought, and our support and comfort in life and in death.
Thomas Galloway

I have found in the Bible words for my inmost thoughts, songs for my joy, utterance for my hidden grief's and pleadings for my shame and feebleness.
Samuel Taylor Coleridge

The Holy Bible is an abyss. It is impossible to explain how profound it is, impossible to explain how simple it is.
Ernest Hello

A young man who wishes to remain a sound atheist cannot be too careful of his reading.
C. S. Lewis

God's Word is an enemy for depression, an escape from temptation, the promise of the future, as well as a guide, hope and inspiration for now and always.
Al and Brenda Taylor

This Book outlives, outloves, outlifts, outlasts, outreaches, outruns, and outranks all books. This Book is faith-producing. It is hope-awakening. It is death-destroying. And those who embrace it find forgiveness of sin.
A. Z. Conrad

Disregard the study of God and you sentence yourself to stumble and blunder through life, blindfolded, as it were, with no sense of direction and no understanding of what surrounds you.
J. I. Packer

There is nothing in the Bible that benefits you unless it is transmitted into life, unless it becomes a part of yourself, just like your food. Unless you assimilate it and it becomes body and bone and muscle, it does you no good.
Henry Weston

Pre-eminent, supreme among the helps to secret prayer I place, of course, the secret study of the holy written Word of God. Read it on your knees, at least on the knees of your spirit. Read it to reassure, to feed, to regulate, to kindle, to give to your secret prayer at once body and soul. Read it that you may hold faster your certainty of being heard. Read it that you may know with blessed definiteness whom you have believed, and what you have in Him, and how He is able to keep your deposit safe. Read it in the attitude of mind in which the apostles read it, in which the Lord read it. Read it, not seldom, to turn it at once into prayer.
H. C. G. Moule

I think it's important to teach our children- as the Bible says- line upon line, precept upon precept, here a little, there a little. If you try to teach a child too rapidly, much will be lost. But the time for teaching and training is preteen. When they reach the teenage years, it's time to shut up and start listening.
Ruth Bell Graham

The Bible is my church. It is always open, and there is my High Priest ever waiting to receive me. There I have my confessional, my thanksgiving, my psalm of praise…and a congregation of whom the world is not worthy- prophets and apostles, and martyrs and confessors- in short, all I can want, there I find.
Charlotte Elliott

When you have read the Bible, you will know it is the word of God, because you will have found it the key to our own heart, your own happiness and your own duty.
Woodrow Wilson

If you believe in the Gospel what you like, and reject what you don't like, it is not the Gospel you believe, but yourself.
Augustine of Hippo

All human discoveries seem to be made only for the purpose of confirming more and more strongly the truths contained in the Holy Scriptures.
John Herschel

The Bible is the second best gift God has ever given us.
L. James Harvey

Be much with the solid teachings of God's word, and you will become solid and substantial men and women: drink them in, and feed upon them, and they shall produce in you a Christ-likeness, at which the world shall stand astonished.
C. H. Spurgeon

One of the reasons that Christians read Scripture repeatedly and carefully is to find out just how God works in Jesus Christ so that we can work in the name of Jesus Christ.
Eugene Peterson

We have missed the full impact of the Gospel if we have not discovered what it is to be ourselves, loved by God, irreplaceable in His sight, unique among our fellow men.
Bruce Larson

Anger

Forgiveness is a stunning principle, your ticket out of hate and fear and chaos.
Barbara Johnson

Patience is the virtue that transforms an angry tongue. Patience takes time to hesitate and evaluate. It rejects anger sins. True patience finds its strength in an unflinching focus on God and an unconditional love toward those who have hurt us.
Joseph Stowell

There is nothing that can be done with anger that cannot be done better without it.
Dallas Willard

Anybody can become angry – that is easy; but to be angry with the right person, to the right degree, at the right time, for the right purpose, and in the right way – that is not easy.
Aristotle

How great is the contrast between that forgiveness to which we lay claim from God towards us, and our temper towards others! God, we expect, will forgive us great offences, offences many times repeated; and will forgive them freely, liberally, and from the heart. But we are offended at our neighbor, perhaps, for the merest trifles, and for an injury only once offered; and we are but half reconciled when we deem to forgive. Even an uncertain humor, an ambiguous word, or a suspected look, will inflame our anger; and hardly any persuasion will induce us for a long time to relent.
Henry W. Thornton

Resentment is like taking poison and hoping the other person will die.
Unknown

A man that does not know how to be angry does not know how to be good.
Henry Ward Beecher

An enemy is a danger, but the danger is not what he can do to you. It is what he makes you do. If he fills you with envy, malice, hatred and all uncharitableness, he has done you real harm. But you can prevent that. Pray for him. If you say you cannot trust him, then watch and pray. But you cannot hate a man you pray for.
E. S. Waterhouse

Of the seven deadly sins, anger is possibly the most fun. To lick your wounds, to smack your lips over grievances long past, to roll over your tongue the prospect of bitter confrontations still to come, to savor to the last toothsome morsel both the pain you are given and the pain you are giving back- in many ways it is a feast fit for a king. The chief drawback is that what you are wolfing down is yourself. The skeleton at the feast is you.
Frederick Buechner

You who are letting miserable misunderstandings run on from year to year, meaning to clear them up some day; you who are keeping wretched quarrels alive because you cannot quite make up your minds that now is the day to sacrifice your pride and kill them; you who are letting your neighbor starve until you hear that he is dying of starvation or letting your friend's heart ache for a word of appreciation or sympathy, which you mean to give him some day; if you could only know and see and feel all of a sudden that time is short, how it would break the "spell." How you would go instantly and do the thing which you might never have another chance to do.
Phillips Brooks

Christmas

The holy child is waiting to be born in every instant, not just once a year.
Marianne Williamson

God grant you the light in Christmas, which is faith; the warmth of Christmas, which is love; the radiance of Christmas, which is purity.
God grant you the righteousness of Christmas, which is justice; the belief in Christmas, which is truth; the all of Christmas, which is Christ.
Wilda English

The time draws near the birth of Christ:
The moon is hid; the night is still;
The Christmas bells from hill to hill
Answer each other in the mist.
Alfred Tennyson

The blessedness of Christmas is all wrapped up in the person of Jesus. Our relationship determines the measure of the blessing.
Unknown

The most vivid memories of Christmases past are usually not of gifts given or received, but of the spirit of love; the cherished little habits of the home.
Lois Rand

At Bethlehem God became what He was not before, but did not cease being what He always was.
Paul Lowenberg

When we recall Christmas past, we usually find that the simplest things, not the great occasions, give off the greatest glow of happiness.
Bob Hope

If Jesus were born one thousand times in Bethlehem and not in me, then I would still be lost.
Corrie ten Boom

At Christmas, man is almost what God sent him here to be.
Edgar Guest

Let Christmas be a bright and happy day; but let its brightness come from the radiance of the star of Bethlehem, and its happiness be found in Christ, the sinner's loving Saviour.
H. G. Den

There's nothing sadder in this world than to awake Christmas morning and not be a child.
Erma Bombeck

There were two poor lovers who wanted to give each other Christmas presents. The man sold his most prized possession, his watch, in order to buy a handsome comb for his sweetheart's beautiful hair. Meanwhile the girl cut off and sold her hair in order to buy a chain for her lover's cherished watch.
O. Henry

Jesus…
He came not to a throne,
but to a manger.
He lived not as a king,
but as a servant.
He chose not an earthly kingdom,
but a cross.
He gave not just a little,
but everything.
Holley Gerth

Then let every heart keep Christmas within:
Christ's pity for sorrow,
Christ's hatred for sin,
Christ's care for the weakest,
Christ's courage for right.
Everywhere, everywhere,
Christmas tonight!
Phillips Brooks

Love was born at Christmas.
Christina G. Rossetti

Christmas is when God came down the stairs of heaven with a baby in His arms.
R. Eugene Sterner

I salute you. I am your friend, and my love for you goes deep. There is nothing I can give you which you have not already; but there is much, very much, which though I cannot give it, you can take. No heaven can come to us unless our hearts find rest in today. Take heaven. No peace lies in the future which is not hidden in this precious little instant. Take peace. The gloom of the world is but a shadow. Behind it, yet within our reach, is joy. There is radiance and courage in the darkness could we but see it; and to see, we have only to look. Life is so generous a giver, but we, judging its gifts by their coverings, cast them away as ugly or heavy or hard. Remove the covering, and you will find beneath it a living splendor, woven of love, and wisdom, and power. Welcome it, greet it, and you touch the angel's hand that brings it. Everything we call a trial, a sorrow, a duty, believe me, that angel's hand is there, the gift is there, and the wonder of an overshadowing Presence. Our joys, too, be not content with them as joys. They, too, conceal diviner gifts. Life is so full of meaning and purpose, so full of beauty beneath its covering, that you will find earth but cloaks your heaven. Courage, then, to claim it, that is all! But courage you have, and the knowledge that we are pilgrims wending through unknown country our way home. And so, at this Christmas time, I greet you, not quite as the world sends greeting, but with profound esteem now and forever. The day breaks and the shadows flee away.
This old Christmas greeting from a letter written between 1387-1455 by Giovanni da Fiesole (Fra Angelico)

Are you willing to stoop down and consider the needs and desires of little children;
To remember the weakness, the loneliness of people who are growing old;
To stop asking how much your friends love you and ask yourself whether you love them enough;
To bear in mind the things that other people have to bear in their hearts;
To try to understand what those who live in the same house with you really want, without waiting for them to tell you?
Then you can keep Christmas.
And if you can keep it for a day, why not always?
But you can never keep it alone.
Henry Van Dyke

Christmas is the season for kindling the fire of hospitality in the hall, the genial flame of charity in the heart.
Washington Irving

An attorney I very much admired once said that the greatest gift he ever received in his life was a note his dad gave him on Christmas. It read, "Son, this year I will give you 365 hours. An hour every day after dinner. We'll talk about whatever you want to talk about. We'll go wherever you want to go, play whatever you want to play. It will be your hour." That dad kept his promise and renewed it every year.
Ann Landers

There was a gift for each of us left under the tree of life 2000 years ago by Him whose birthday we celebrate today. The gift was withheld from no man. Some have left the packages unclaimed. Some have accepted the gift and carried it around, but have failed to remove the wrappings and look inside to discover the hidden splendor. The packages are all alike: In each is a scroll on which is written, "All that the Father hath is thine." Take and live!
Unknown

Christmas is the harvest time of love. Souls are drawn to other souls. All that we have read and thought and hoped comes to fruition at this happy time. Our spirits are astir. We feel within us a strong desire to serve. A strange, subtle force, a new kindness, animates man and child. A new spirit is growing in us. No longer are we content to relieve pain, to sweeten sorrow, to give the crust of charity. We dare to give friendship, service, the equal loaf of bread and love.
Helen Keller

You can never truly enjoy Christmas until you can look up into the Father's face and tell him you have received his Christmas gift.
John R. Rice

When Christmas doesn't fit your expectations of what the perfect holiday should be, think about how Joseph and Mary probably didn't think that manger was the perfect place for their child be born. But look at what a perfect Christmas that turned out to be.
Joel Osteen

If there is love in your heart Christmas can last forever.
Marion Schoeberlein

In the midst of the shopping and the wrapping and the arranging of presents under your tree this Christmas, may you not forget the gifts you cannot yet hold in your hands.
T. D. Jakes

The whole life of Christ was a continual Passion; others die martyrs but Christ was born a martyr. He found a Golgotha even in Bethlehem, where he was born; for to his tenderness then the straws were almost as sharp as the thorns after, and the manger as uneasy at first as his cross at last. His birth and his death were but one continual act, and his Christmas day and his Good Friday are but the evening and morning of one and the same day. And as even his birth is his death, so every action and passage that manifests Christ to us is his birth, for Epiphany is manifestation.
John Donne

Christmas is the day that holds all time together.
Alexander Smith

The best of all gifts around any Christmas tree: the presence of a happy family all wrapped up in each other.
Burton Hillis

Lost Christmas
Why wait till Christmas time again is here?
Why spend those precious hours in hectic ways
Doing the things that you could do all year
And let the noise of whirl of festival days
Drown out the angel's song? Why not take time
To lift the eyes to candles in the sky;
To walk some silent night, while carols chime
And hear the hush of wings brush softly by?
Take time to mediate: to catch the spell
Of childish trust, that simple faith you knew
When love was everywhere, and all was well…
The gift you lost may now come back to you.
Seek not for Christmas in the busy mart
But cradled somewhere in a trusting heart.
Rachel Van Crème

The joy of brightening other lives, bearing each others' burdens, easing other's loads and supplanting empty hearts and lives with generous gifts becomes for us the magic of Christmas.
W. C. Jones

I will honor Christmas in my heart and try to keep it all the year.
Charles Dickens

There's a story that's always meant a lot to Ruth and me. The story was about an African boy who gave his missionary teacher an unusually beautiful seashell as a Christmas gift. The boy had walked a great distance, over rough terrain, to the only place on the coast where these particular shells could be found. The teacher was touched. "You've traveled so far to bring me such a wonderful present," she said. The boy looked puzzled, then his eyes widened with excitement: "Oh, teacher," he explained, "long walk part of gift." Sure, there have been plenty of times over the years when all the pre-holiday shopping and sermon writing and schedule arranging seemed to be too much, and my wife, Ruth, and I have been tempted to throw up our hands and say, "It's just not worth the effort!" But then we've looked at each other and said, "Long walk part of gift." And we've laughed and gotten back to work.
Norman Vincent Peale

A good conscience is a continual Christmas.
Benjamin Franklin

Easter & Resurrection

If ever you are tempted to say, "I wish someone were to die and leave me something in his will," allow me to tell you, "Someone has!"
David Shepherd

On the third day the friends of Christ coming at daybreak to the place found the grave empty and the stone rolled away. In varying ways they realized the new wonder; but even they hardly realized that the world had died in the night. What they were looking at was the first day of a new creation, with a new heaven and a new earth; and in a semblance of the gardener God walked again in the garden, in the cool not of the evening but the dawn.
G. K. Chesterton

And he departed from our sight that we might return to our heart, and there find Him. For He departed, and behold, He is here.
Augustine

When at Easter Sunday, so fair to see, Time bowed before Eternity.
Fiona MacLeod

The resurrection is an exploding flare announcing to all sincere seekers that it is safe to believe. Safe to believe in ultimate justice. Safe to believe in eternal bodies. Safe to believe in heaven as our estate and the earth as its porch. Safe to believe in a time where questions won't keep us awake and pain won't keep us down. Safe to believe in open graves and endless days and genuine praise.
Max Lucado

How different is the epitaph on the tomb of Jesus! It is neither written in gold nor cut in stone. It is spoken by the mouth of an angel and is the exact reverse of what is put on all other tombs: "He is not here; for he is risen, as he said." (Matthew 28:6)
Billy Graham

A very learned man once said to a little child who believed in the Lord Jesus, "My poor little girl, you don't know whom you believe in. There have been many christs. In which of them do you believe?" "I know which one I believe in," replied the child. "I believe in the Christ who rose from the dead."
Unknown

The benefits [of the resurrection] are innumerable. To list a few: Our illnesses don't seem nearly so final; Our fears fade and lose their grip; Our grief over those who have gone on is diminished; Our desires to press on in spite of the obstacles is rejuvenated… Our identity as Christians is strengthened as we stand in the lengthening shadows of saints down through the centuries, who have always answered back in antiphonal voice: "He is risen, indeed!"
Charles Swindoll

Dost thou understand me, sinful soul? He wrestled with justice, that thou mightest have rest; He wept and mourned, that thou mightest laugh and rejoice; He was betrayed, that thou mightest go free; was apprehended, that thou mightest escape; He was condemned, that thou mightest be justified; and was killed, that thou mightest live; He wore a crown of thorns, that thou mightest wear a crown of glory; and was nailed to the cross, with His arms wide open, to show with what freeness all His merits shall be bestowed on the coming soul; and how heartily He will receive it into His bosom?
John Bunyan

Christianity begins where religion ends- with the resurrection of Christ.
Unknown

Just think: Every promise God has ever made finds its fulfillment in Jesus. God doesn't just give us grace; he gives us Jesus, the Lord of grace. If it's peace, it's only found in Jesus, the Prince of Peace. Even life itself is found in the Resurrection and the Life. Christianity isn't all that complicated…it's Jesus.
Joni Eareckson Tada

The Cross is a picture of violence, yet the key to peace, a picture of suffering, yet the key to healing, a picture of death, yet the key to life.
David Watson

To give you an idea of the depth of Jesus' suffering, being abandoned by God is the definition of hell.
Tony Evans

Christ has made of death a narrow starlit strip between the companionships of yesterday and the reunions of tomorrow.
William Jennings Bryan

If Christ is risen, nothing else matters. And if Christ is not risen- nothing else matters.
Jaroslav Pelikan

The only shadow on the cloudless Easter day of God's victory is the poverty of my own devotion, the memory of ineffective hours of unbelief, and my own stingy response to God's generosity.
A. E. Whitman

Easter is to our faith what water is to the ocean, what stone is to the mountain, what blood is to the body.
Raymond Linquist

Vital Christian experience comes from knowing Jesus as the living Saviour. Two irreligious young men were discussing the resurrection, telling each other why it was impossible for them to accept the doctrine. Then a deacon of a near-by church walked by, and in a joking way one of the young fellows called to him, "Say, Deacon, tell us why you believe that Jesus rose again." "Well," he answered, "one reason is that I was talking with Him for half an hour this very morning." We may all experience proof of the resurrection of Christ in the acknowledging of His living presence in our lives. No one who knows Jesus personally questions the resurrection.
Watchman-Examiner

Christ has turned all our sunsets into dawns.
Clement of Alexandria

That the Potter should die for His clay is a stupendous miracle.
Lynn Landrum

A God on the cross! That is all my theology.
Jean Lacordaire

Jesus…
He came not to a throne,
but to a manger.
He lived not as a king,
but as a servant.
He chose not an earthly kingdom,
but a cross.
He gave not just a little,
but everything.
Holley Gerth

The ascension of Christ is his liberation from all restrictions of time and space. It does not represent his removal from the earth, but his constant presence everywhere on earth.
William Temple

Never tolerate the idea of martyrdom about the cross of Jesus Christ. The cross was a superb triumph in which the foundations of hell were shaken. There is nothing more certain in time or eternity than what Jesus Christ did on the cross: He switched the whole of the human race back into a right relationship with God.
Oswald Chambers

The Easter message tells us that our enemies, sin, the curse, and death, are beaten. Ultimately they can no longer start mischief. They still behave as though the game were not decided, the battle not fought; we must still reckon with them, but fundamentally we must cease to fear them any more.
Karl Barth

When Jesus cried, "It is finished," He did not take away the conflict, the contest, the fight. No! He took away only your defeat.
Ira Taylor

I simply argue that the cross be raised again at the center of the marketplace as well as on the steeple of the church. I am recovering the claim that Jesus was not crucified in a cathedral between two candles, but on a cross between two thieves; on the town garbage heap; at a crossroad so cosmopolitan that they had to write His title in Hebrew and in Latin and in Greek; at the kind of place where cynics talk smut, and thieves curse, and soldiers gamble. Because that is where He died. And that is what He died about.
George MacLeod

The resurrection never becomes a fact of experience until the risen Lord lives in the heart of the believer.
Peter Marshall

The battle- our battle- against every temptation that can ever try to take us on has already been won on that first Easter morning. All we're involved in is a mopping up operation.
Dale Evans Rogers

The resurrection that awaits us beyond physical death will be but the glorious consummation of the risen life which already we have in Christ.
D. T. Niles

The angel rolled away the stone from Jesus' tomb, not to let the living Lord out, but to let unconvinced outsiders in.
Donald Grey Barnhouse

Death died when Christ rose.
Unknown

This is our destiny in heaven- to be like Christ: not Christ limited, as he was on earth, to the confines of time and flesh, but Christ risen, the great, free, timeless Christ of the Easter morning.
David Winter

It has never at any time been possible to fit the resurrection of Jesus into any world view except a world view of which it is the basis.
Lesslie Newbigin

The message of Easter cannot be written in the past tense. It is a message for today and the days to come. It is God's message which must reecho through your lives.
Frank Getty

We want gain without pain; we want the resurrection without going through the grave; we want life without experiencing death; we want a crown without going by way of the Cross. But in God's economy, the way up is down.
Nancy Leigh De Moss

The whole life of Christ was a continual Passion; others die martyrs but Christ was born a martyr. He found a Golgotha even in Bethlehem, where he was born; for to his tenderness then the straws were almost as sharp as the thorns after, and the manger as uneasy at first as his cross at last. His birth and his death were but one continual act, and his Christmas day and his Good Friday are but the evening and morning of one and the same day. And as even his birth is his death, so every action and passage that manifests Christ to us is his birth, for Epiphany is manifestation.

John Donne

Eternity & Death

The only ultimate disaster that can befall us, I have come to realize, is to feel ourselves at home here on earth.
Malcolm Muggeridge

Life begins when a person first realizes how soon it will end.
Marcelene Cox

Try to live with the part of your soul which understands eternity, which is not afraid of death. And that part of your soul is love.
Leo Tolstoy

King Philip II of Macedonia, father of Alexander the Great, was a wise man. He ordered one of his servants to come to him every morning without fail, and, no matter what the king was doing, declare loudly, "Remember, Philip, that you must die."
Unknown

There is a wealth of unexpressed love in the world. It is one of the chief causes of sorrow evoked by death: what might have been said or might have been done that never can be said or done.
Arthur Hopkins

If the Father has the kingdom ready for us, he will take care of us on the way.
Andrew Bonar

Those who put themselves in His hands will become perfect, as He is perfect-perfect in love, wisdom, joy, beauty, health, and immortality. The change will not be completed in this life, for death is an important part of the treatment. How far the change will have gone before death in any particular Christian is uncertain.
C. S. Lewis

Earthly fears are no fears at all. Answer the big question of eternity, and the little questions of life fall into perspective.
Max Lucado

There are no ordinary people. You have never talked to a mere mortal. Nations, cultures, arts, civilizations- these are mortal, and their life is to ours as the life of a gnat. But it is immortals we joke with, work with, marry, snub, and exploit-immortal horrors or everlasting splendors.
C. S. Lewis

We face death, but thanks to Jesus, we only face its shadow.
Max Lucado

This human life in God is from our point of view a particular period in the history of our world (from His birth to His crucifixion). We therefore imagine it is also a period in the history of God's own existence. But God has no history. He is too completely and utterly real to have one. For, of course, to have a history means losing part of your reality (because it has already slipped away into the past), and not yet having another part (because it is still in the future); in fact, having nothing but the tiny little present, which has gone before you can speak about it. God forbid we should think God was like that! Even we may hope not to be always rationed in that way.
C. S. Lewis

Since 3600 BC the world has known only 292 years of peace. In that period, stretching more than 55 centuries, there have been an incredible 14,531 wars in which over 3.6 billion people have been killed.
John Ankerberg

When at Easter Sunday, so fair to see,
Time bowed before Eternity.
Fiona MacLeod

Christ has made of death a narrow starlit strip between the companionships of yesterday and the reunions of tomorrow.
William Jennings Bryan

I can say that I never knew what joy was like until I gave up pursuing happiness, or cared to live until I chose to die. For these two discoveries I am beholden to Jesus.
Malcolm Muggeridge

A little girl whose baby brother had just died asked her mother where baby had gone. "To be with Jesus," replied the mother. A few days later, talking to a friend, the mother said, "I am so grieved to have lost my baby." The little girl heard her, and, remembering what her mother had told her, looked up into her face and asked, "Mother, is a thing lost when you know where it is?" "No, of course not." "Well, then, how can baby be lost when he has gone to be with Jesus?" Her mother never forgot this. It was the truth.
Junior King's Business

If you were going to die soon and had only one phone call you could make, who would you call and what would you say? And why are you waiting?
Stephen Levine

Death for the Christian is a turning off the light because the dawn has come.
Leon Jaworski

We are pilgrims, not settlers; this earth is our inn, not our home.
J. H. Vincent

If nothing in this world satisfies me, perhaps it is because I was made for another world.
C. S. Lewis

Learn to hold loosely all that is not eternal.
A. Maude Royden

It is love, not reason, that is stronger than death.
Thomas Mann

High up in the North, in the land called Svithjod, there stands a rock. It is 100 miles high and 100 miles wide. Once every 1000 years a little bird comes to this rock to sharpen its beak. When the rock has thus been worn away, then a single day of eternity will have gone by. *Hendrick Willem Van Loon*

Every tear from every eye becomes a babe in eternity.
William Blake

Hurry means that we gather impressions but have no experiences, that we collect acquaintances but make no friends, that we attend meetings but experience no encounter. We must recover eternity if we are to find time, and eternity is what Jesus came to restore. For without it, there can be no charity.
D. T. Niles

Eternity is primary. Heaven must become our first and ultimate point of reference. We are built for it, redeemed for it, and on our way to it. Success demands that we see and respond to now in the light of then. All that we have, are, and accumulate must be seen as resources by which we can influence and impact the world beyond. Even our tragedies are viewed as events that can bring eternal gain.
Joseph Stowell

It is remarkable that the Holy Spirit has given us very few deathbed scenes in the book of God. We have very few in the Old Testament, fewer still in the New. And I take it that the reason may be, because the Holy Ghost would have us to take more account of how we live than how we die, for life is the main business. He who learns to die daily while he lives will find it no difficulty to breathe out his soul for the last time into the hands of his faithful Creator.
Charles Spurgeon

Which would you prefer? To be king of the mountain for a day? Or to be a child of God for eternity?
Max Lucado

Lord, give me an open heart to find You everywhere, to glimpse the heaven enfolded in a bud, and to experience eternity in the smallest act of love.
Mother Teresa

God has set Eternity in our heart, and man's infinite capacity cannot be filled or satisfied with the things of time and sense.
F. B. Meyer

As the mother's womb holds us for ten months, making us ready, not for the womb itself, but for life, just so, through our lives, we are making ourselves ready for another birth…Therefore look forward without fear to that appointed hour- the last hour of the body, but not of the soul…That day, which you fear as being the end of all things, is the birthday of your eternity.
Seneca

At the close of every obituary of his believing children God adds the word "henceforth!"
A. W. Tozer

Is it a small thing in your eyes to be loved by God- to be the son, the spouse, the love, the delight of the King of glory? Christian, believe this, and think about it: you will be eternally embraced in the arms of the love which was from everlasting, and will extend to everlasting- of the love which brought the Son of God's love from heaven to earth, from earth to the cross, from the cross to the grave, from the grave to glory- that love which was weary, hungry, tempted, scorned, scourged, buffered, spat upon, crucified, pierced- which fasted, prayed, taught, healed, wept, sweated, bled, died. That love will eternally embrace you.
Richard Baxter

The following is a quotation from the words of Dr. W. B. Hinson, speaking from the pulpit a year after the commencement of the illness from which he ultimately died: "I remember a year ago when a man in this city said, 'You have got to go to your death.' I walked out to where I live, five miles out of this city, and I looked across at that mountain that I love, and I looked at the river in which I rejoice, and I looked at the stately trees that are always God's own poetry to my soul. Then in the evening I looked up into the great sky where God was lighting his lamps, and I said 'I may not see you many more times, but, Mountain, I shall be alive when you are gone; and, River, I shall be alive when you cease running toward the sea; and, Stars, I shall be alive when you have fallen from your sockets in the great down-pulling of the material universe!'" This is the confidence of one who knew the Saviour. Is it yours?
Advent Herald

All your life an unattainable ecstasy has hovered just beyond the grasp of your consciousness. The day is coming when you will wake to find, beyond all hope, that you have attained it, or else, that it was within your reach and you have lost it forever.
C. S. Lewis

When the devil tries to remind you of your past,
Just turn around and remind him of his future.
Anonymous

Yet to live always as though time were a bridge is precisely what the saints do. Their eyes are forever on the eternal, that Beyond which is also here and now and within, because they have cultivated the art of seeing Eternity through that narrow slit- the ever now moment.
Heirlooms

Life is a glorious opportunity, if it is used to condition us for eternity. If we fail in this, though we succeed in everything else, our life will have been a failure. There is no escape for the man who squanders his opportunity to prepare to meet God.
Billy Graham

The life of faith does not earn eternal life; it is eternal life; and Christ is its vehicle.
William Temple

If we work upon marble, it will perish,
If, on brass, time will efface it;
If we rear temples they will crumble in the dust,
But if we work upon immortal minds and endue them with principles,
With the just fear of God and the love of our fellowmen,
We engrave on those tablets something that will brighten all eternity.
Daniel Webster

Suddenly I heard the words of Christ and understood them, and life and death ceased to seem to me evil, and instead of despair I experienced happiness and the joy of life undisturbed by death.
Leo Tolstoy

Christ turned a brilliant guess into a solid certainty and endowed the hope of eternal life with grace, reason, and majesty.
Hugh Elmer Brown

Over the triple doorways of Milan Cathedral are three inscriptions spanning the magnificent arches. Above one is carved a wreath of roses, with the words, "All that pleases is but for a moment." Over the second is a cross, with the words, "All that troubles is but for a moment." Underneath the great central entrance to the main aisle is inscribed: "That only is important which is eternal."
Inscription, Milan Cathedral

Three-hundred million years from now, the only thing that will matter is whether you're in Heaven or in Hell.
Mark Cahill

Plan your life, budgeting for seventy years…and understand that if your time proves shorter that will not be unfair deprivation but rapid promotion.
J. I. Packer

All that is not eternal is eternally out of date.
C. S. Lewis

Death is never sudden to a saint; no guest comes unawares to him who keeps a constant table.
George Swinnock

There was an old Christian woman whose age began to tell on her memory. She had once known much of the Bible by heart. Eventually only one precious bit stayed with her. "I know whom I have believed, and am persuaded that he is able to keep that which I have committed unto him against that day." By and by part of that slipped its hold, and she would quietly repeat, "That which I have committed unto him." At last, as she hovered on the borderline between this and the spirit world, her loved ones noticed her lips moving. They bent down to see if she needed anything. She was repeating over and over again to herself the one word of the text, "Him, Him, Him." She had lost the whole Bible, but one word. But she had the whole Bible in that one word.
S. D. Gordon

Ninety-five percent of the people who died today had expected to live a lot longer.
Albert M. Wells, Jr.

In the dark immensity of night
I stood upon a hill and watched the light
Of a star,
Soundless and beautiful and far.
A scientist standing there with me
Said, "It is not the star you see,
But a glow
That left the star light years ago."
Men are like stars in a timeless sky:
The light of a good man's life shines high,
Golden and splendid
Long after his brief earth years are ended.
Grace. V. Watkins

God's people should plan for a voyage of a thousand years, but be prepared to abandon ship tonight.
Joseph Bayly

Hope is the struggle of the soul, breaking loose from what is perishable, and attesting her eternity.
Herman Melville

Who would complain if God allowed one hour of suffering in an entire lifetime of comfort? Why complain about a lifetime that includes suffering when that lifetime is a mere hour of eternity?
Philip Yancy

When Christ came into the world, peace was sung; and when He went out of the world, peace was bequeathed.
Francis Bacon

There are three important steps to take in preparation for a holy death. And these three principles should be practiced throughout life. (1) Expect that death will come knocking at your gates at any time; this will keep your priorities straight. (2) Value your time for it is the most precious possession you have. (3) Refrain from a soft and easy life; stress the holy life of self-discipline, labor, and alertness. Engage each day in self-examination.
Jeremy Taylor

The only way to live your last day as you would want to, is to live like that all the time.
Vaughan Garwood

I should count a life well spent, and the world well lost, if, after tasting all its experiences and facing all its problems, I had no more to show at its close, or to carry with me to another life, than the acquisition of a real, sure, humble, and grateful faith in the Eternal and Incarnate Son of God.
P. T. Forsyth

Jesus has made the life of his people as eternal as his own.
Charles H. Spurgeon

The wheels of death's chariot may rattle and make a noise, but they are to carry a believer to Christ.
Thomas Watson

He who has no vision of eternity will never get a true hold of time.
Thomas Carlyle

Live near to God and all things will appear little to you in comparison with eternal realities.
Robert M'Cheyne

If we look around us, a moment can seem a long time, but when we lift up our hearts heavenwards, a thousand years begin to be like a moment.
John Calvin

A man should look after a happiness that will last as long as his soul lasts.
Thomas Manton

The soul on earth is an immortal guest, compelled to starve at an unreal feast; a pilgrim panting for the rest to come; an exile, anxious for his native home.
Hannah More

Winter is on my head but eternal spring is in my heart. The nearer I approach the end, the plainer I hear around me the immortal symphonies of the world to come. For half a century I have been writing my thoughts in prose and verse; but I feel that I have not said one-thousandth part of what is in me. When I have gone down to the grave I shall have ended my life's work; but another day will begin the next morning. Life closes in the twilight but opens with the dawn.
Victor Hugo

Death is but a sharp corner near the beginning of life's procession down eternity.
John Ayscough

Christ would have lived, and taught, and preached, and prophesied, and wrought miracles in vain, if he had not crowned all by dying for our sins as our substitute! His death was our life. His death was the payment of our debt to God. Without his death we should have been of all creatures most miserable.
J. C. Ryle

Life has but two ends, and one end has been used. Take care of the other end.
Unknown

A story is told about two children who were talking about the death of their mother. The little girl asked her brother how their mother "went to God." "Well," said the boy, "it happened this way. First mother reached up as far as she could. Then God reached down. When their hands touched He took her."
Morton Wallack

ARE ALL THE CHILDREN IN?
I think oftimes as the night draws nigh
Of an old house on the hill,
Of a yard all wide and blossom starred
Where the children played at will.
And when the night at last came down,
Hushing the merry din,
Mother would look around and ask,
"Are all the children in?"
Tis many and many a year since then,
And the old house on the hill
No longer echoes to childish feet,
And the yard is still, so still.
But I see it all, as the shadows creep
And though many the years have been
Since then, I can hear my mother ask
"Are all the children in?"
I wonder if when the shadows fall
On the last short earthly day,
When we say good-bye to world outside,
All tired with our childish play.
When we step out into that Other Land
Where mother so long has been,
Will we hear her ask, just as of old,
"Are all the children in?"
Unknown

Realize that you must lead a dying life; the more a man dies to himself, the more he begins to live unto God.
Thomas Kempis

I presumed to fix my look on the eternal light so long that I consumed my sight thereon.
Dante Alighieri

He that lives to live forever, never fears dying.
William Penn

As the only person to come from eternity to earth, then return to eternity, Jesus knows the whole truth- past, present and future- and can give you a one-of-a-kind perspective.
Bruce Wilkerson

A story is told about a little boy with a big heart. His next-door neighbor was an older gentleman whose wife had recently died. When the youngster saw the elderly man crying, he climbed up onto his lap and simply sat there. Later, his mother asked the boy what he had said to their saddened neighbor. "Nothing," the child replied. "I just helped him cry." Sometimes that is the best thing we can do for people who are facing profound sorrow. Often, our attempts to say something wise and helpful are far less valuable than just sitting next to the bereaved ones, holding their hand, and crying with them.
Unknown

Christianity is not engrossed by this transitory world, but measures all things by the thought of eternity.
J. Gresham Machen

The thought of Jesus Christ laughing probably is not thought of too much, but it should be. Amidst the trials of this World, in Him we have ultimate joy, and peace. When He walked upon this Earth, it is written that He cried, more than once, and though scriptures do not depict the Christ laughing, it is safe to say He did, for He had all human characteristics…His strength was in what He did with them while He walked among us on this Earth. Once I was told of a little boy about 5 or 6 who was dying, I believe it was of cancer. He was put down to rest and he went to sleep. The end was not thought to be very far away, and while he was sleeping, he sort of put his arms out, and rolled a little onto one side, then drew his knees up somewhat and started laughing and tilted his head back a little…he continued to laugh for a short time, then he just went limp, and he died. His mother declares that Jesus Christ came and picked him up in His arms, and carried him to Heaven. She believes that he was being tickled on the tummy and made him laugh while he was being picked up. That could very well be true…we have no way of knowing how God handles things in the realm that we have yet to step. But we know we are safe with Him   Jesus Christ gives us His Peace,
Joyce Vaughan Byars

I know well there is no comfort for this pain of parting: the wound always remains, but one learns to bear the pain, and learns to thank God for what He gave, for the beautiful memories of the past, and the yet more beautiful hope for the future.
Max Muller

Evangelism & Preaching

If Christ were coming again tomorrow, I would plant a tree today.
Martin Luther

As the minister stepped up to the pulpit he discovered to his chagrin that he had forgotten his sermon notes. As it was too late to send someone for them, he turned to the congregation and said, by way of apology, that this morning he should have to depend upon the Lord for what he might say, but that for the evening service, he would be better prepared.
Unknown

Every Sunday the ducks waddle out of their houses and waddle down Main Street to their church. They waddle into the sanctuary and squat in their proper pews. The duck choir waddles in and takes its place, then the duck minister comes forward and opens the duck Bible. He reads to them: "Ducks! God has given you wings! With wings you can fly! With wings you can mount up and soar like eagles. No walls can confine you! No fences can hold you! You have wings. God has given you wings and you can fly like birds!" All the ducks shouted, "Amen!" And they all waddled home.
Soren Kierkegaard

Every person we ever meet is God's opportunity.
Frank Laubach

I like your Christ, I do not like your Christians. Your Christians are so unlike your Christ.
Mahatma Gandhi

We aren't only called to share the gospel. We are called to show the gospel.
James E. Biles, Sr.

I do not know of a denomination or local church in existence that has as its goal to teach its people to do everything Jesus said.
Dallas Willard

We must not be afraid to minister to one another. Even if the sheep in need is the one in the lead.
Jan Winebrenner & Debra Frazier

Every life without Christ is a mission field;
every life with Christ is a missionary.
Unknown

My life is my message.
Mahatma Gandhi

The sermon of your life in tough times ministers to people more powerfully than the most eloquent speaker.
Bill Bright

We are told to let our light shine, and if it does, we won't need to tell anybody it does. Lighthouses don't fire cannons to call attention to their shining- they just shine.
D. L. Moody

Once in seven years I burn all my sermons for it is a shame if I cannot write better sermons now than I did seven years ago.
John Wesley

There is a radiance hidden in your heart that the world desperately needs.
John and Stasi Eldredge

One day a lady criticized D. L. Moody for his methods of evangelism in attempting to win people to the Lord. Moody's reply was "I agree with you. I don't like the way I do it either. Tell me, how do you do it?" The lady replied, "I don't do it." Moody retorted, "Then I like my way of doing it better than your way of not doing it."
D. L. Moody

God could not have chosen anyone less qualified, or more of a sinner, than myself. And so, for this wonderful work He intends to perform through us, He selected me- for God always chooses the weak and the absurd, and those who count for nothing.
Francis of Assisi

Be careful how you live; you will be the only Bible some people ever read.
William Toms

Father, strip away from me whatever is blocking people's view of You in my life.
Tim Walter

Wherever the Gospel is preached, no matter how crudely, there are bound to be results.
Billy Graham

Christianity must mean everything to us before it can mean anything to others.
Donald Soper

You can never speak to the wrong person about Christ.
Unknown

It is more effective to spend time talking to Christ about a man than talking to a man about Christ, because if you are talking to Christ about a man earnestly, trustingly, in the course of time you cannot help talking to the man effectively about Christ.
Robert Munger

He preaches well who lives well. That's all the divinity I know.
Miguel de Cervantes

The best way to show that a stick is crooked is not to argue about it or to spend time denouncing it, but to lay a straight stick along side it.
D. L. Moody

No individual has any right to come into the world and go out of it without leaving behind him distinct and legitimate reasons for having passed through it.
George Washington Carver

There are two ways of spreading light – to be the candle or the mirror that reflects it.
Edith Wharton

The most important missionary journey a person can make is to walk next door.
Unknown

I'd rather see a sermon than hear one any day; I'd rather one should walk with me than merely tell the way.
Edgar Guest

Kindness has converted more sinners than zeal, eloquence or learning.
Frederick Faber

Preach the gospel everyday; if necessary, use words.
Francis of Assisi

Trust God for great things; with your five loaves and two fishes, he will show you a way to feed thousands.
Horace Bushnell

What other people think of me is becoming less and less important; what they think of Jesus because of me is critical.
Cliff Richard

Christians think they are prosecuting attorneys or judges, when, in realty, God has called all of us to be witnesses.
Warren Wiersbe

Have fun; love Jesus; and tell others about Him.
Tim Tebow

The secret of life is that all we have and are is a gift of grace to be shared.
Lloyd John Ogilvie

Father, strip away from me whatever is blocking people's view of You in my life.
Tim Walter

A lad who heard his father pray for missions, and especially for the needs of missionaries, that they might be supplied, and that their institutions might be amply sustained, said to him, "Father, I wish I had your money." "Why, my son, what would you do with it?" asked the father. "I would answer your prayers," was the reply.
Unknown

A man who lived some six miles from the house of worship, complained to his pastor of the distance he had to go to attend public worship. "Never mind," said the minister, "remember every Sabbath you have the privilege of preaching a sermon six miles long- you preach the gospel to all the residents and people you pass."
Unknown

Jesus said, "Go," but the church through selfishness and indifference has refused to obey. We try to substitute "write," "send," or "give," for "go." We try to salve our conscience by turning over the task of "going" to someone else and giving languidly for their support. Of course, we must send where we cannot go. But because we can't go across the world does not excuse us for refusing to go across the street.
R. C. Foster

We cannot possibly let ourselves get frozen into regarding everyone we do not know as an absolute stranger.
Albert Schweitzer

Perhaps those who say they didn't get a thing out of the sermon didn't bring anything in which to take it home.
N. A. Prichard

Id' rather see a sermon than hear one any day;
Id' rather one should walk with me than merely show the way.
The eye's a better pupil and more willing than the ear;
Fine counsel is confusing, but example's always clear.
And the best of all preachers are the men who live their creeds,
For to see the good in action is what everybody needs.
I can soon learn how to do it if you'll let me see it done;
I can watch your hands in action, but your tongue too fast may run.
And the lectures you deliver may be very wise and true,
But I'd rather get my lesson by observing what you do.
For I may misunderstand you and the high advice you give,
But there's no misunderstanding how you act and how you live.
The Lookout

Had an hour's conversation with a gentleman about new birth in Jesus Christ. Breakfasted with some gentlemen in the great cabin, who were very civil and let me put in a word for God. About eleven at night went and sat down among the sailors in the steerway and reasoned with them concerning the Christian life. Gained an opportunity, by walking at night on the deck, to talk closely to the chief mate and one of the sergeants of the regiment and hope my words were not altogether in vain.
George Whitefield (as he noted in his journal the contacts he made on shipboard)

The fact that I can plant a seed and it becomes a flower, share a bit of knowledge and it becomes another's, smile at someone and receive a smile in return, are to me continual spiritual exercises.
Leo Buscaglia

The more fully that the gospel is preached, in the grand old apostolic way, the more likely is it to accomplish the results which it did in the apostolic days.
Horatius Bonar

If you are a baptized Christian, you are already a minister. Whether you are ordained or not is immaterial. No matter how you react, the statement remains true. You may be surprised, alarmed, pleased, antagonized, suspicious, acquiescent, scornful, or enraged. Nevertheless, you are a minister of Christ.
Francis O. Ayres

Dr. Wilfred Grenfell, the missionary doctor of Labrador, was a cynical young medical student in London when Dwight L. Moody went there to preach. Said Grenfell of Moody: "When Mr. Moody finished his sermon, I resolved either to drop religion entirely or else make a real effort to do what Christ would do if He were in my place. With a mother like mine, that resolve could only have one outcome. So, beginning that night, I started doing what I thought Christ would do if He were a young doctor in London."
Wilfred Grenfell

The Christian life is a pilgrimage from earth to heaven, and our task is to take as many as possible with us as we make this journey.
Warren Wiersbe

There is no impact without contact. Evangelism is a contact sport.
Douglas M. Cecil

Have thy tools ready; God will find thee work.
Charles Kingsley

Christ desires nothing more of us than that we speak of him.
Martin Luther

We ourselves feel that what we are doing is just a drop in the ocean. But if that drop was not in the ocean, I think the ocean would be less because of that missing drop. I do not agree with the big way of doing things.
Mother Teresa

Don't judge each day by the harvest you reap, but by the seeds you plant.
Robert Louis Stevenson

Could a mariner sit idle if he heard the drowning cry?
Could a doctor sit in comfort and just let his patients die?
Could a fireman sit idle, let men burn and give no hand?
Can you sit at ease in Zion with the world around you damned?
Leonard Ravenhill

Witnessing is not a spare-time occupation or a once-a-week activity. It must be a quality of life. You don't go witnessing, you are a witness.
Dan Greene

You are a Christian today because somebody cared. Now it's your turn.
Warren W. Wiersbe

A story is told about Daniel Webster. During his days in the city of Washington the great statesman attended worship regularly in a little rural church outside the city. Some of his colleagues were disturbed about it. They said it lacked prestige. And they asked him why he attended a little church in the sticks when he would be welcome in the more fashionable churches in Washington. Webster answered that when he attended church in Washington they preached to Daniel Webster, the statesman, but in the little church, they preached to Daniel Webster, the sinner.
Unknown

Example is more forceful than precept. People look at me six days a week to see what I mean on the seventh day.
Pastor Richard Cecil

They tell me I rub the fur the wrong way. I don't. Let the cat turn around!
Billy Sunday

Let Christ stay throughout the meal. Don't dismiss Him with the blessing.
Unknown

The world wants to see demonstrators of the faith rather than defenders of the faith.
Unknown

As a Christian, I hope I can lead the kind of life that makes others look at me and say, "What's missing in my life that she has?" That's a greater testimony than anything I can say.
Marilyn Quayle

Nobody worries about Christ as long as he can be kept shut up in churches. He is quite safe inside. But there is always trouble if you try and let him out.
G. A. Studdert Kennedy

The greatest element in life is not what occupies most of its time, else sleep would stand high in the scale. Nor is it what engrosses most of its thought, else money would be very high. The two or three hours of worship and preaching weekly has perhaps been the greatest signal influence on English life. Half an hour of prayer, morning or evening, every day, may be a greater element in shaping our course than all our conduct and all our thought.
P. T. Forsyth

God does not comfort us to make us comfortable, but to make us comforters.
J. H. Jowett

Example is not the main thing in influencing others. It is the only thing.
Albert Schweitzer

A layman visited a great city church during a business trip. After the service, he congratulated the minister on his service and sermon. "But," said the manufacturer, "if you were my salesman, I'd discharge you. You got my attention by your appearance, voice and manner; your prayer, reading and logical discourse aroused my interest; you warmed my heart with a desire for what you preached; and then- and then you stopped without asking me to do something about it. In business the important thing is to get them to sign on the dotted line."
James Duff

The church as a whole must be concerned with both evangelism and social action. It is not a case of either-or; it is both-and. Anything less is only a partial Gospel, not the whole counsel of God.
Robert De Haan

I choose gentleness... Nothing is won by force. I choose to be gentle. If I raise my voice may it be only in praise. If I clench my fist, may it be only in prayer. If I make a demand, may it be only of myself.
Max Lucado

A rabbi whose congregation does not want to drive him out of town isn't a rabbi.
Talmudic saying

Too many clergymen have become keepers of an aquarium instead of fishers of men- and often they are just swiping each other's fish.
Myron Augsburger

Never make a principle out of your experience; let God be as original with other people as he is with you.
Oswald Chambers

I have never heard anything about the resolutions of the apostles, but a great deal about their acts.
Horace Mann

A group of clergymen were discussing whether or not they ought to invite Dwight L. Moody to their city. The success of the famed evangelist was brought to the attention of the men. One unimpressed minister commented, "Does Mr. Moody have a monopoly on the holy Ghost?" Another man quietly replied, "No, but the Holy Ghost seems to have a monopoly on Mr. Moody."
Unknown

Faith, Trust & Belief

As the minister stepped up to the pulpit he discovered to his chagrin that he had forgotten his sermon notes. As it was too late to send someone for them, he turned to the congregation and said, by way of apology, that this morning he should have to depend upon the Lord for what he might say, but that for the evening service, he would be better prepared.
Unknown

It may be that for a long time you have had upon your mind some strong impression of duty; but you have held back, because you could not see what the next step would be. Hesitate no longer. Step out upon what seems to be the impalpable mist: you will find a solid rock beneath your feet; and every time you put your foot forward, you will find that God has prepared a stepping-stone, and the next, and the next- each as you come to it. The bread is by the day. The manna is new every morning. He does not give us all the directions at once lest we should get confused.
F. B. Meyer

Beware of despairing about yourself; you are commanded to put your trust in God, and not in yourself.
Augustine of Hippo

I am always content with what happens, for I know that what God chooses is better than what I choose.
Epictetus

Every tomorrow has two handles. We can take hold of it with the handle of anxiety or the handle of faith.
Henry Ward Beecher

Do not lose your inward peace for anything whatsoever, even if your whole world seems upset. Commend all to God, and then lie still and be at rest in His bosom. Whatever happens, abide steadfast in a determination to cling simply to God, trusting to His eternal love for you.
Francis de Sales

Bread for today is bread enough.
E. M. Bounds

Blind as we are, we hinder God, and stop the current of His graces. But when He finds a soul penetrated with a lively faith, He pours into it His graces and favors plentifully.
Brother Lawrence

When we read of the great Biblical leaders, we see that it was not uncommon for God to ask them to wait, not just a day or two, but for years, until God was ready for them to act.
Gloria Gaither

If all things are possible with God, then all things are possible to him who believes in Him.
Corrie ten Boom

Don't be a half-Christian. There are too many of them in the world already. The world has a profound respect for a person who is sincere in his faith.
Billy Graham

The main thing is this: we should never blame anyone or anything for our defeats. No matter how evil their intentions may be, they are altogether unable to harm us until we begin to blame them and use them as excuses for our own unbelief.
A. W. Tozer

An atheist cannot find God for the same reason a thief cannot find a policeman.
Unknown

If we demonstrate unconditional love, daily prayer, persistent faith, and adherence to God's laws, we give our children a gift. If we teach them that good deeds and kind words are expressions of the Spirit, we are on track toward living more like Jesus.
Jane Jarrell

I remember a friend of mine telling a story about one of his first paying jobs. When he was in seminary, he and his wife pastored a small church in a rough part of Houston. They lived in the parsonage and received a salary of one hundred dollars a week. One day a college friend of his passed through town and stopped by for a visit. The friend's career was in sales, and at the time, 1972, he was doing quite well, with a six-figure salary. He said to the young pastor, "You were pretty sharp in school. You know, you could be doing a lot better financially if you had chosen a different profession. For instance, if you were with my company, you could be making a hundred thousand dollars a year." My friend eyed his buddy and said, " Well, I don't know if I could live on that." "What do you mean, you don't know if you could live on that? You don't look like you're making half that much now." My friend said, "Well, I don't right now, but I work for someone who promised to pay me whatever I need. This last year I didn't need much, but what if next year I needed more? I sure would be in a mess if all I had was a hundred thousand dollars."
Amy Grant

If you go to Him to be guided, He will guide you, but He will not comfort your distrust or half-trust of Him by showing you the chart of all His purposes concerning you. He will show you only into a way where, if you go cheerfully and trustfully forward, He will show you on still farther.
Horace Bushnell

My Lord, God, I have no idea where I am going. I do not see the road ahead of me. I cannot know for certain where it will end. Nor do I really know myself, and the fact that I think I am following Your will does not mean that I am actually doing so. But I believe that the desire to please You does in fact please you. And I hope that I have that desire in all that I am doing. And I know that if I do this, You will lead me by the right road though I may know nothing about it. Therefore will I trust you always though I may seem to be lost and in the shadow of death, I will not fear, for You are ever with me and You will never leave me to face my perils alone.
Thomas Merton

The lives of some professing Christians are a series of stumbles; they are never quite down and yet they are seldom on their feet. This is not a fit thing for a believer. He is invited to walk with God; by faith he can attain steady perseverance in holiness, and he should do so.
Charles H. Spurgeon

Life without faith in something is too narrow a space to live.
George Lancaster Spalding

Faith does not eliminate questions. But faith knows where to take them.
Elisabeth Elliot

We are often hindered from giving up our treasures to the Lord out of fear for their safety; this is especially true when those treasures are loved relatives and friends. But we need have no such fears. Our Lord came not to destroy but to save. Everything is safe which we commit to Him, and nothing is really safe which is not so committed.
A. W. Tozer

A Prayer Upon A Threshold
Here on my threshold, eager to start
Out through a New Year, Lord, I stand,
Waiting a moment, a prayer in my heart:
Go with me, Lord, and hold my hand.
There are such beautiful days ahead,
Blinding my eyes, Lord, may there be
Springs by the wayside, manna for bread,
And You, a companion, to walk with me.
Through any dark day, talk with me,
I am a small child, often afraid,
Lead through the darkness, let me see
Light ahead that Your lamp has made.
Here on the threshold, ready to start
Out through a year, untrod, unknown-
Now with a small child's trusting heart
I go, but I do not go alone.
Grace Noll Crowell

If the Father has the kingdom ready for us, he will take care of us on the way.
Andrew Bonar

Set goals so big that unless God helps you, you will be a miserable failure.
Bill Bright

41

My children, the three acts of faith, hope, and charity contain all the happiness of man upon the earth.
John Vianney

Faith is a gaze of a soul upon a saving God.
A. W. Tozer

God is not a deceiver, that He should offer to support us, and then, when we lean upon Him, should slip away from us.
Augustine

Sometimes your only available transportation is a leap of faith.
Margaret Shepard

One of the most powerful concepts, one which is a sure cure for lack of confidence, is the thought that God is with you and helping you. This is one of the simplest teachings in religion, namely, that Almighty God will be your companion, will stand by you, help you, and see you through. No other idea is so powerful in developing self-confidence as this simple belief when practiced. To practice it simply affirm "God is with me; God is helping me; God is guiding me." Spend several minutes each day visualizing his presence. Then practice believing that affirmation.
Norman Vincent Peale

There is no place for faith if we expect God to fulfill immediately what he promises.
John Calvin

Worship God in the difficult circumstances, and when He chooses, He will alter them in two seconds.
Oswald Chambers

It is not difficult for me to remember that the little ones need breakfast in the morning, dinner at midday, and something before they go to bed at night. Indeed I could not forget it. And I find it impossible to suppose that our heavenly Father is less tender or mindful than I…I do not believe that our heavenly Father will ever forget His children. I am a very poor father, but it is not my habit to forget my children. God is a very, very good Father. It is not His habit to forget His children.
J. Hudson Taylor

The more we know of God the more unreservedly we will trust him; the greater our progress in theology, the simpler and more childlike will be our faith.
John Gresham Machen

It is easy to say we believe in God as long as we remain in the little world we choose to live in; but get out into the great world of facts, the noisy world where people are absolutely indifferent to you, where your message is nothing more than a crazy tale belonging to a bygone age, can you believe God there?
Oswald Chambers

We can all humbly say in the sincerity of faith, "I am loved; I am called; I am secure."
Franklin Graham

An atheist can't find God for the same reason a thief can't find a policeman.
Adrian Rogers

To love means loving the unlovable. To forgive means pardoning the unpardonable. Faith means believing the unbelievable. Hope means hoping when everything seems hopeless.
Gilbert Keith Chesterton

To fear and not be afraid- that is the paradox of faith.
A. W. Tozer

How often do we attempt work for God to the limit of our incompetency, rather than the limit of God's omnipotence?
J. Hudson Taylor

God always gives His best to those who leave the choice with Him.
Warren Wiersbe

Many people are willing to believe regarding those things that seem probable to them. Faith has nothing to do with probabilities. The province of faith begins where probabilities cease and sight and sense fail. Appearances are not to be taken into account. The question is- whether God has spoken it in His Word.
George Muller

I know God will not give me anything I can't handle. I just wish that He didn't trust me so much.
Mother Teresa

I don't know what tomorrow holds, but I know who holds tomorrow.
Unknown

We may not know the way God leads… but we know God leads! We do not know the way…but we know the Guide!
Richard Halverson

Faith is knowing that God is who He says He is, has what He says He has and will do what He says He will do and then putting ourselves in a position where our lives depend on it.
Graham Steele

Faith is to believe what you do not yet see, the reward for this faith is to see what you believe.
Augustine

Faith in God – life can never take you by surprise again.
James Dobson

To take all that we are and have and hand it over to God may not be easy; but it can be done; and when it is done, the world has in it one less candidate for misery.
Paul Scherer

Faith is simply taking God at his word.
Unknown

"Come to the edge!" God said. "It's dangerous there," I answer. "Come to the edge!" God said. "But I might fall!" "Come to the edge!" God said. So I did. And He pushed me! And I flew!
Guillaume Apollinaire

One does not discover new lands without consenting to lose sight of the shore for a very long time.
Andre Gide

The Christian life is one of faith, where we find ourselves routinely overdriving our headlights but knowing it's okay because God is in control and has a purpose behind it.
Bill Hybels

What's true of biology is also true of faith: If it isn't growing, it's probably dead.
Unknown

Faith is putting all your eggs in God's basket, then counting your blessings before they hatch.
Ramona Carroll

We lie to God in prayer if we do not rely on him afterwards.
Robert Leighton

The army of Israel looked at Goliath through the eyes of man and said he's too big to beat. David looked at him through the eyes of God and said he's too big to miss.
Wally Carter

Trust God for great things; with your five loaves and two fishes, he will show you a way to feed thousands.
Horace Bushnell

All I have seen teaches me to trust the Creator for all I have not seen.
Ralph Waldo Emerson

I prayed for faith and thought it would strike me like lightning. But faith did not come. One day I read, "Now faith comes by hearing, and hearing by the Word of God." I had closed my Bible and prayed for faith. I now began to study my Bible and faith has been growing ever since.
Dwight L. Moody

I believe in Christianity as I believe that the sun has risen: not only because I see it, but because by it I see everything else.
C. S. Lewis

A ship in harbor is safe, but that is not what ships are built for.
John Shedd

Living a life of faith means never knowing where you are being led. But it does mean loving and knowing the One who is leading. It is literally a life of faith…a life of knowing Him who calls us to go.
Oswald Chambers

Imagine watching all that God might have done with your life if you had let him.
John Ortberg

Faith and works should travel side by side, step answering to step, like the legs of men walking. First faith, and then works; and then faith again, and then works again- until you can scarcely distinguish which is one and which is the other.
William Booth

Trust in your Redeemer's strength… exercise what faith you have, and by and by He shall rise upon you with healing beneath His wings. Go from faith to faith and you shall receive blessing upon blessing.
Charles H. Spurgeon

Lord…give me the gift of faith to be renewed and shared with others each day. Teach me to live this moment only, looking neither to the past with regret, nor the future with apprehension. Let love be my aim and my life a prayer.
Roseann Alexander-Isham

Faith does not operate in the realm of the possible. There is no glory for God in that which is humanly possible. Faith begins where man's power ends.
George Muller

Faith gathers strength by waiting and praying.
E. M. Bounds

Infidelity and Faith look both through the same perspective-glass, but at contrary ends. Infidelity looks through the wrong end of the glass; and therefore, sees those objects near which are afar off, and makes great things little, diminishing the greatest spiritual blessings, and removing far from us threatened evils. Faith looks at the right end, and brings the blessings that are far off close to our eye, and multiplies God's mercies, which, in the distance, lost their greatness.
Joseph Hall

Surrender the thing you fear into the hands of God. Turn it right over to God and ask Him to solve it with you. Fear is keeping things in your own hands; faith is turning them over into the hands of God.
E. Stanley Jones

Faith, like light, should always be simple and unbending; while love, like warmth, should beam forth on every side, and bend to every necessity of our brethren.
Martin Luther

Never be afraid to trust an unknown future to a known God.
Corrie Ten Boom

The steps of faith fall on the seeming void but find the rock beneath.
John Greenleaf Whittier

True faith, real and pure faith, cannot be practiced in moderation.
Stephen Arterburn

It is an unhappy division that has been made between faith and works, though in my intellect I may divide them, just as in a candle I know there is both light and heat; but yet, put out the candle and they are both gone; one remains not without the other. So it is betwixt faith and works.
John Selden

Faith is the root of all blessings. Believe and you shall be saved; believe, and you must be satisfied; believe, and you cannot but be comforted and happy.
Jeremy Taylor

Faith is obscure. By faith a man moves through darkness; but he moves securely, his hand in the hand of God. He is literally seeing through the eyes of God.
Walter Farrell

Always remember that, every time you step out of your comfort zone, you step into God's comfort zone.
Mark Cahill

Faith has been reduced to a comfortable system of beliefs about God instead of an uncomfortable encounter with God.
Michael Yaconelli

The life of faith does not earn eternal life; it is eternal life; and Christ is its vehicle.
William Temple

All created things are living in the Hand of God. The senses see only the action of the creatures; but faith sees in everything the action of God.
Jean-Pierre de Caussade

There is a story about trust in God's promises that comes from F. W. Boreham. Boreham tells about an episode during the early days of his ministry in Australia. He went to call on one of his elderly parishioners. Entering the room where the old man lay, he noticed a chair pulled up beside the man's bed. "I see that I am not your first visitor today," said Boreham. The old man then began to explain the presence of the empty chair. He said that when he was a small boy, he had difficulty praying. His pastor suggested that he overcome this difficulty by placing an empty chair in front of himself when he prayed, and by simply pretending that Jesus was sitting in that chair like an attentive friend. He said he had maintained that habit ever since. Boreham left the house a short while later. A few days later, however, then man's daughter came to tell him that he was dead. "I was out of the room only for a short time," said the daughter. "When I returned, he was gone. There was no change in him except I noticed that his hand was on the chair."
Unknown

It is not about never doubting, it is about coming out on the other side with twice the faith you had going into your doubt.
Beth Moore

A young man who wishes to remain a sound atheist cannot be too careful of his reading.
C. S. Lewis

Faith is not the belief that God will do what you want. Faith is the belief that God will do what is right.
Max Lucado

Faith given back to us after a night of doubt is a stronger thing, and far more valuable to us than faith that has never been tested.
Elizabeth Goudge

Ten thousand difficulties do not make one doubt.
John Henry Newman

Faith is not a hothouse plant that must be shielded from wind and rain, so delicate that it has to be protected, but is like the sturdy oak which becomes stronger with every wind that blows upon it. An easy time weakens faith, while strong trials strengthen it.
Katherine Workman

Faith isn't faith until it's all you're holding on to.
Unknown

Too often we forget that the great men of faith reached the heights they did only by going through the depths.
Os Guinness

I can only lie still in God's arms. I am so weak that I can hardly write, I cannot read my Bible, I cannot even pray. I can only lie still in God's arms like a little child, and trust.
Hudson Taylor, during his final days

Doubt isn't the opposite of faith; it is an element of faith.
Paul Tillich

I believe in the sun even when it isn't shining. I believe in love even when I am alone. I believe in God even when He is silent.
Jewish refugee, World War II, Poland

True faith drops its letter in the post office box and lets it go. Distrust holds on to a corner of it and wonders that the answer never comes.
A. B. Simpson

Find out how seriously a believer takes his doubts, and you have the index of how seriously he takes his faith.
Os Guinness

It is not darkness you are going to, for God is Light. It is not lonely, for Christ is with you. It is not unknown country, for Christ is there.
Charles Kingsley

If we desire our faith to be strengthened, we should not shrink from opportunities where our faith may be tried, and therefore, through trial, be strengthened.
George Mueller

Faith is the avenue to salvation. Not intellectual understanding. Not money. Not your works. Just simple faith. How much faith? The faith of a mustard seed, so small you can hardly see it. But if you will put that little faith in the person of Jesus, your life will be changed. He will come with supernatural power into your heart. It can happen to you.
Billy Graham

Christ chargeth me to believe His daylight at midnight.
Samuel Rutherford

Anxiety in human life is what squeaking and grinding are in machinery that is not oiled. In life, trust is the oil.
Henry Ward Beecher

The story is told of a poor man who plodded along toward home in an Irish town carrying a huge bag of potatoes. A horse and wagon carrying a stranger came along, and the stranger stopped the wagon and invited the man on foot to climb inside. This the poor man did, but when he sat down in the wagon he held the bag of potatoes in his arms. And when it was suggested that he should set it down, he said very warmly: "Sure, I don't like to trouble you too much. You're giving me a ride. I'll carry the potatoes!" Sometimes we think we are doing the Lord a favor when we carry the burden. But the work is His, and the burden is His, and He asks us only to be faithful.
Isaac Page

Lack of faith is such a waste of time when there is God.
Larry Burner

The past is never completely lost, however extensive the devastation. Your sorrows are the bricks and mortar of a magnificent temple. What you are today and what you will be tomorrow are because of what you have been. Your faith of yesterday is built into your faith today.
Gordon Wright

To live by faith is a far surer and happier thing than to live by feelings or by works.
C. H. Spurgeon

The central fact in the lives of the great believers is that they went from faith to doubt. Then they began to doubt their doubts.
Philip Lipis

While faith makes all things possible, it is love that makes all things easy.
Evan Hopkins

The attributes of God, though intelligible to us on their surface yet, for the very reason that they are infinite, transcend our comprehension, when they are dwelt upon, when they are followed out, and can only be received by faith.
John Henry Newman

Faith is knowing there is an ocean because you have seen a brook.
William Ward

There is not a single believer who from time to time has not had some hesitations about the existence of God. But these moments of hesitation are not harmful. On the contrary, they lead us to a better understanding of God.
Leo Tolstoy

Faith is self-surrender to the great Physician, a leaving of our case in his hands. But it is also the taking of his prescriptions and the active following of his directions.
Augustus Strong

God has charged Himself with full responsibility for our eternal happiness and stands ready to take over the management of our lives the moment we turn in faith to Him.
A. W. Tozer

A little girl was taking a long journey, and in the course of the day her train crossed a number of rivers. The water seen in advance always awakened doubts and fears in the child. She did not understand how it could safely be crossed. As they drew near the river, however, a bridge appeared and furnished the way over. Several times the same thing happened, and finally the child leaned back with a long breath of relief and confidence: "Somebody has put bridges for us all the way." So God does likewise for His children all through life.
Unknown

I ask you neither for health nor for sickness, for life nor for death; but that you may dispose of my health and my sickness, my life and my death, for your glory…You alone know what is expedient for me; you are the sovereign master, do with me according to your will. Give to me, or take away from me, only conform my will to yours. I know but one thing, Lord, that it is good to follow you, and bad to offend you. Apart from that, I know not what is good or bad in anything. I know not which is most profitable to me, health or sickness, wealth or poverty, nor anything else in the world. That discernment is beyond the power of men or angels, and is hidden among the secrets of your providence, which I adore, but do not seek to fathom.
Blaise Pascal

Whether our work is a success or a failure has nothing to do with us. Our call is not to successful service, but to faithfulness.
Oswald Chambers

If the work of God could be comprehended by reason, it would no longer be wonderful, and faith would have no merit if reason provided proof.
Gregory I the Great

Faith is not a thing which one "loses," we merely cease to shape our lives by it.
George Bernanus

If you give God a thimble, perhaps He will choose to fill it. If you give God a five-gallon bucket, perhaps He will choose to fill that. If you give Him a fifty-gallon drum, perhaps He will choose to do something extraordinary and fill even that. If God chooses to do a miracle, you'd better be ready for it. Don't buy a thimbleful of land. Buy a fifty-gallon drum.
(as told to Bill Hybels when visiting Robert Schuller to obtain his advice of the planning for Willow Creek church in Chicago)
Robert Schuller

More prayer, more exercise of faith, more patient waiting, and the result will be blessing, abundant blessing. Thus I have found it many hundreds of times, and therefore I continually say to myself, "Hope thou in God."
George Mueller

Family, Marriage & Youth

The most creative job in the world involves fashion, decorating, recreation, education, transportation, psychology, romance, cuisine, literature, art, economics, government, pediatrics, geriatrics, entertainment, maintenance, purchasing, law, religion, energy, and management. Anyone who can handle all those has to be somebody special. She (or he) is. They're a homemaker.
Richard Kerr

I remember my mother's prayers and they have always followed me. They have clung to me all my life.
Abraham Lincoln

According to the values which govern my life, my most important reason for living is to get the baton- the gospel- safely in the hands of my children.
James Dobson

If we demonstrate unconditional love, daily prayer, persistent faith, and adherence to God's laws, we give our children a gift. If we teach them that good deeds and kind words are expressions of the Spirit, we are on track toward living more like Jesus.
Jane Jarrell

It matters not how much Bible reading and prayer and catechism saying and godly teaching there may be in a home, if gentleness is lacking; that is lacking which most of all the young need in the life of a home. A child must have love. Love is to its life what sunshine is to plants and flowers. No young life can ever grow to its best in a home without gentleness. The lack is one which leaves an irreparable hurt in the lives of children.
Unknown

God is not a deceiver, that He should offer to support us, and then, when we lean upon Him, should slip away from us.
Augustine

Homes that are built on anything other than love are bound to crumble.
Billy Graham

If God had the gospel of Jesus's salvation in mind when he established marriage, then marriage only "works" to the degree that it approximates the pattern of God's self-giving love in Christ.
Timothy Keller

Since marriage is designed by Providence as a life, the worst possible way of embarking upon that life is by the premature exercise of what is meant to be its final consummation.
Hubert van Zeller

There is no more lovely, friendly or charming relationship, communion or company, than a good marriage.
Martin Luther

The most vivid memories of Christmases past are usually not of gifts given or received, but of the spirit of love; the cherished little habits of the home.
Lois Rand

Family matters. Family are the only people who will tell you when you're getting off the tracks a little. Surround yourself with people who love the Lord, love themselves and love you, and you can't really fail.
A. J. Michalka

Children are not casual guests in our home. They have been loaned to us temporarily for the purpose of loving them and instilling a foundation of values on which their future lives will be built.
James Dobson

Home is any four walls that enclose the right person.
Helen Rowland

A number of years back, my six-year-old son and I had gone shopping at one of those giant discount toy stores with toys piled to the ceiling. We had just come around the corner of an aisle when I saw a young, long-haired bearded man in a wheelchair. He must have been in some terrible accident because both his legs were missing and his face was badly scarred. Just then my six-year-old saw him too and said in a loud voice, "Look at that man, Momma!" I did my normal mother thing and tried to shush my son, telling him it was not polite to point; but my son gave a hard tug, broke free from my hand, and went running down the aisle to the man in the wheelchair. He stood right in front of him and said in a loud voice, "What a cool dude earring, man! Where did you get such a neat earring?" The young man broke into a grin that lit up his face. He was so taken aback by the compliment that he just glowed with happiness, and the two of them stood there talking awhile about his earring and other "cool stuff."
It made a life-long impression on me. For I had seen only a horribly scarred man in a wheelchair, but my six-year-old saw a man with a cool dude earring.
Unknown

I long to put the experience of fifty years at once into your young lives, to give you at once the key of that treasure chamber every gem of which has cost me tears and struggles and prayers, but you must work for these inward treasures yourselves.
Harriet Beecher Stowe

Since marriage is a spiritual relationship involving husband, wife, and God, prayer together keeps communication flowing among all three.
Dennis and Barbara Rainey

There's no such thing as a successful marriage. There are marriages that give up, and marriages that keep on trying; that's the only difference.
Garrison Keillor

World poverty is a hundred million mothers weeping…because they cannot feed their children.
Ronald Sider

If we're not telling God and our family that we love them, we just wasted a day of our life.
Ted Roberts

Parents need to fill a child's bucket of self-esteem so high that the rest of the world can't poke enough holes in it to drain it dry.
Alvin Price

In every marriage more than a week old, there are grounds for divorce. The trick is to find, and continue to find, grounds for marriage.
Robert Anderson

The ordinary acts we practice every day at home are of more importance to the soul than their simplicity might suggest.
Thomas Moore

A dining room table with children's eager, hungry faces around it, ceases to be a mere dining room table, and becomes an altar.
Simeon Strunsky

Marriage, and the process of coming to it, is not heaven! It is the bonding together of two needy sinners in order to make a partnership which is substantially greater than either of them alone.
Sinclair Ferguson

The great secret of successful marriage is to treat all disasters as incidents and none of the incidents as disasters.
Harold Nicholson

The ultimate test of a relationship is to disagree but to hold hands.
Unknown

We have found that marriage should be made up of two forgivers. We need to learn to say, "I was wrong, I'm sorry." And we also need to say, "That's all right, I love you."
Billy Graham

The family is one of nature's masterpieces.
George Santayana

Loving relationships are a family's best protection against the challenges of the world.
Bernie Wiebe

A pastor once asked a group of men on a retreat, "Men, is your wife a better Christian because she is married to you, or has your marriage been a hindrance to her spiritual growth?"
Bob Barnes

A guest at a country house coming down to breakfast one morning was met by the child of the house, who running up to him and putting his hand in his, looked up into his face with a smile, saying, "I'm your friend now; I put you in my prayer last night!"
Unknown

You don't really understand human nature unless you know why a child on a merry-go-round will wave at his parents every time around- and why his parents will always wave back.
William D. Tammeus

The goal in marriage is not to think alike, but to think together.
Robert C. Dodds

Marriage, and the process of coming to it, is not heaven! It is the bonding together of two needy sinners in order to make a partnership which is substantially greater than either of them alone.
Sinclair Ferguson

A good marriage is like an incredible retirement fund. You put everything you have into it during your productive life, and over the years it turns from silver to gold to platinum.
Willard Scott

Of course a home without love is just cold real estate…it is a minuscule world. If it has 10 books, it is partly a library; if three pictures, a little museum; if six tools, a repair shop. If one big, crowded closet of bric-a-brac, a warehouse. Whenever a piano or fiddle is in serious use, it is a part-time conservatory. At mealtime grace, or in answering a child's question about God, it is a fraction of a church. In the throes of argument or the heart of discourse, it becomes a court; in sickness it is a field hospital; when you discover old forgotten letters, pictures, souvenirs in a trunk or attic, it is a wing of archaeology. When the kids climb trees, fences, high furniture, or other forbidden obstacles, it is a commando camp…
Norman Corwin (his graphic description of the components of home life)

What is home?
A world of strife shut out- a word of love shut in.
The only spot on earth where faults and failings of fallen humanity are hidden under the mantle of charity.
The father's kingdom, the children's paradise, the mother's world.
Where you are treated the best and grumble the most.
Unknown

Benjamin West tells how he actually became a successful and important painter. When he was young, his mother went out and left him in charge of his sister Sally. In the meantime, little Benjamin discovered bottles of colored ink and began to do Sally's portrait. What a mess soon developed. Finally, when Ben's mother came home and saw the tragic mess, she said nothing. She merely picked up the paper with the portrait and said, "Why it's Sally!" and she kissed Ben. Ever since that day, West has said, "My mother's kiss made me a painter."
Raymond T. Moreland

If your Christianity doesn't work at home, then it doesn't work at all. So don't export it.
Unknown

A happy marriage is a long conversation that always seems too short.
Andre Maurois

My father didn't tell me how to live; he lived, and let me watch him do it.
Clarence Budington Kelland

The value of marriage is not that adults produce children, but that children produce adults.
Peter De Vries

The proper time to influence the character of a child is about a hundred years before he is born.
Dean Inge

It is very important that children learn from their fathers and mothers how to love one another- not in the school, not from the teacher, but from you. It is very important that you share with your children the joy of that smile. There will be misunderstandings; every family has its cross, its suffering. Always be the first to forgive with a smile. Be cheerful, be happy.
Mother Teresa

If you want your children to improve, let them overhear the nice things you say about them to others.
Haim Ginott

You can do everything else right as a parent, but if you don't begin with loving God, you're going to fail.
Alvin Vander Griend

There's not much practical Christianity in the man who lives on better terms with angels and seraphs than with his children, servants and neighbours.
Henry Ward Beecher

Children are not things to be molded, but are people to be unfolded.
Jess Lair

We must teach our children that the real measure of their success in life is how much they'd be worth if they had absolutely nothing.
Walt Mueller

There were two young boys who were raised in the home of an alcoholic father. As young men, they each went their own way. Years later, a psychologist who was analyzing what drunkenness does to children in the home searched out these two men. One had turned out to be like his father, a hopeless alcoholic. The other had turned out to be a teetotaler. The counselor asked the first man, "Why did you become an alcoholic?" And the second, "Why did you become a teetotaler?" And they both gave the same identical answer in these words, "What else could you expect when you had a father like mine?" It's not what happens to you in life but how you react to it that makes the difference. Every human being in the same situation has the possibilities of choosing how he will react, either positively or negatively.
The West Side Baptist

God oft hath a great share in a little house.
George Herbert

A healthy family is sacred territory.
Unknown

A good marriage is the union of two forgivers.
Ruth Bell Graham

I love little children, and it is not a slight thing when they, who are fresh from God, love us.
Charles Dickens

Strength of character may be acquired at work, but beauty of character is learned at home. There the affections are trained. There the gentle life reaches us, the true heaven life. In one word, the family circle is the supreme conductor of Christianity.
Henry Drummond

He who helps a child helps humanity with an immediateness which no other help given to human creatures in any other stage of their life can possibly give again.
Phillips Brooks

Parenthood is a partnership with God. You are not molding iron nor chiseling marble; you are working with the Creator of the universe in shaping human character and determining destiny.
Ruth Vaughn

The best gift a father can give to his son is the gift of himself- his time. For material things mean little, if there is not someone to share them with.
C. Neil Strait

The most important thing a father can do for his children is to love their mother.
Theodore M. Hesburgh

A child's life is like a piece of paper on which every passer-by leaves a mark.
Chinese proverb

The happiest marriage is where both parties get better mates than they deserve.
Unknown

Our earnest suggestion to the person who feels that she has been hurrying through life a bit too fast and has, in the process, grown a bit indifferent to life: Take the hand of a three-year-old and walk with him two or three blocks. The child can do to a person what any amount of philosophizing cannot.
News-Herald

There's no faith like that of children. They know that God is quiet and calm and wonderful- big and interested in them, and kind. Their requests of God usually are reasonable and honest, modest. They seldom ask for more than they deserve. They know of no reason why the world, in fact, shouldn't be mostly good.
The Leader

Christ revealed to humanity those things which their best selves already knew: that people are equal because the same spirit lives in all of them...Learn from the small children, behave like children, and treat all people on an equal basis, with love and tenderness.
Leo Tolstoy

Once the realization is accepted that even between the closest human beings infinite distances continue to exist, a wonderful living side-by-side can grow up, if they succeed in loving the distance between them, which makes it possible for each to see the other whole against a wide sky.
Rainer Rilke

Your home can be a place for dying or living, for wilting or blooming, for anxiety or peace, for discouragement or affirmation, for criticism or approval, for profane disregard or reverence, for suspicion or trust, for blame or forgiveness, for alienation or closeness, for violation or respect, for carelessness or caring. By your daily choices, you will make your home what you want it to be.
Carole Sanderson Streeter

The best part of life is when your family become your friends and your friends become your family.
Robin Roberts

I think it's important to teach our children- as the Bible says- line upon line, precept upon precept, here a little, there a little. If you try to teach a child too rapidly, much will be lost. But the time for teaching and training is preteen. When they reach the teenage years, it's time to shut up and start listening.
Ruth Bell Graham

If only God would lean out of heaven and tell me [my children] are going to make it, I could relax. But God doesn't do that. He tells us to be the parents he has called us to be in his strength and promises to do his part. Driven to prayer (after discovering that manipulation didn't work), I began to realize I was only truly positive and confident when I'd been flat on my face before the Lord.
Jill Briscoe

Let Christ stay throughout the meal.
Don't dismiss Him with the blessing.
Unknown

To really know a man, observe his
behavior with a woman, a flat tire and a
child.
Unknown

ARE ALL THE CHILDREN IN?
I think oftimes as the night draws nigh
Of an old house on the hill,
Of a yard all wide and blossom starred
Where the children played at will.
And when the night at last came down,
Hushing the merry din,
Mother would look around and ask,
"Are all the children in?"
Tis many and many a year since then,
And the old house on the hill
No longer echoes to childish feet,
And the yard is still, so still.
But I see it all, as the shadows creep
And though many the years have been
Since then, I can hear my mother ask
"Are all the children in?"
I wonder if when the shadows fall
On the last short earthly day,
When we say good-bye to world outside,
All tired with our childish play.
When we step out into that Other Land
Where mother so long has been,
Will we hear her ask, just as of old,
"Are all the children in?"
Unknown

There's nothing sadder in this world than
to awake Christmas morning and not be a
child.
Erma Bombeck

Our five-year-old Jeanie took to rising at
5:30 each morning and puttering around
just long enough to wake the rest of us
before climbing back into bed. Her
reason was always the same- she had to
see if there was a surprise. Finally we told
her firmly that she must stop and that
there wouldn't be any surprises until
Christmas, which was months away. "I
wasn't talking about living-room
surprises," she said through her tears. "I
was talking about like yesterday morning
it was raining, and this morning real
summer's here, and tomorrow morning
I'll probably find some pink in the
rosebuds." Jeanie still gets up each
morning at 5:30.
Mrs. Roy F. Carter

Remember that no time spent with
children is ever wasted.
Unknown

How do you celebrate the everyday
moment? Learn from children, puppies
and other experts.
Harvey Rich

Family life is too intimate to be preserved
by the spirit of justice. It can be sustained
by a spirit of love which goes beyond
justice.
Reinhold Niebahr

The best of all gifts around any Christmas
tree: the presence of a happy family all
wrapped up in each other.
Burton Hillis

In our pursuit of righteousness, we cannot be unrighteous. Being on our way home is no justification for tramping through a flower bed.
Unknown

At a certain meeting two and a half people were converted to Christ. A friend asked if he meant two adults and a child. The facts were just the opposite two children and an adult. When a child is led to Christ, a whole life is saved!"
D .L. Moody

One day, a child of mine came home in tears. Another child had been mean to him and hurt his feelings. I want to say now, as I said then, "When a person doesn't like you, or is mean to you, it has more to do with them than it does with you. Dry your tears. You cannot be loved by everyone, because everyone cannot love themselves. You can know that I will always love you. And the greatest gift you can give to others is to love yourself. If you do that, you can love others without worrying whether they love you back. You will have enough love for both of you."
Dorothy Dupont

One Sunday I was entertained in a farm home of a member of a rural church. I was impressed by the intelligence and unusually good behavior of the only child in the home, a little four-year-old boy. Then I discovered one reason for the child's charm. The mother was at the kitchen sink, washing the intricate parts of the cream separator when the little fellow came to her with a magazine. "Mother," he asked, "what is this man in the picture doing?" To my surprise she dried her hands, sat down on a chair and taking the boy in her lap she spent ten minutes answering his questions. After the child had left I commented on her having interrupted her chores to answer the boy's questions, saying, "Most mothers wouldn't have bothered." "I expect to be washing cream separators for the rest of my life," she told me, "But never again will my son ask me that question!"
Unknown

Fear & Worry

The best remedy for those who are afraid, lonely or unhappy is to go outside, somewhere where they can be quiet, alone with the heavens, nature and God. Because only then does one feel that all is as it should be and that God wishes to see people happy, amidst the simple beauty of nature. As long as this exists, and it certainly always will, I know that then there will always be comfort for every sorrow, whatever the circumstances may be. And I firmly believe that nature brings solace in all troubles.
Anne Frank

If a care is too small to be turned into a prayer it is too small to be made into a burden.
Corrie ten Boom

Beware of despairing about yourself; you are commanded to put your trust in God, and not in yourself.
Augustine of Hippo

To fear and not be afraid- that is the paradox of faith.
A. W. Tozer

It helps to write down half a dozen things which are worrying me. Two of them, say, disappear; about two nothing can be done, so it's no use worrying; and two perhaps can be settled.
Winston Churchill

Every tomorrow has two handles. We can take hold of it with the handle of anxiety or the handle of faith.
Henry Ward Beecher

Forgiveness is a stunning principle, your ticket out of hate and fear and chaos.
Barbara Johnson

When considering the size of your problems, there are two categories that you should never worry about: the problems that are small enough for you to handle, and the ones that aren't too big for God to handle.
Marie T. Freeman

All our fret and worry is caused by calculating without God.
Oswald Chambers

If you look at the world, you'll be distressed.
If you look within, you'll be depressed.
But if you look at Christ, you'll be at rest.
Corrie Ten Boom

Care for the next minute is just as foolish as care for the morrow, or for a day in the next thousand years- in neither can we do anything, in both God is doing everything.
George Macdonald

Earthly fears are no fears at all. Answer the big question of eternity, and the little questions of life fall into perspective.
Max Lucado

It has come to pass that man's knowledge has surpassed his wisdom. He is afraid of what he knows.
Guy D. Newman

You can tell the size of your God by looking at the size of your worry list. The longer your list, the smaller your God.
Unknown

We are often hindered from giving up our treasures to the Lord out of fear for their safety; this is especially true when those treasures are loved relatives and friends. But we need have no such fears. Our Lord came not to destroy but to save. Everything is safe which we commit to Him, and nothing is really safe which is not so committed.
A. W. Tozer

Fear. His modus operandi is to manipulate you with the mysterious, to taunt you with the unknown. Fear of death, fear of failure, fear of God, fear of tomorrow- his arsenal is vast. His goal? To create cowardly, joyless Christians. He doesn't want you to make that journey to the mountain. He figures if he can rattle you enough, you will take your eyes off the peaks and settle for a dull existence in the flat lands.
Max Lucado

Don't worry about tomorrow. God is already there.
Unknown

The remarkable thing about fearing God is that when you fear God you fear nothing else, whereas if you do not fear God you fear everything else.
Oswald Chambers

One is given strength to bear what happens to one, but not the 100 and 1 different things that might happen.
C. S. Lewis

Worry does not empty tomorrow of its sorrow, it empties today of its strength. It does not enable us to escape evil. It makes us unfit to face evil when it comes. It is the interest you pay on trouble before it comes.
Corrie ten Boom

I try not to worry about life too much because I read the last page of THE book and it all turns out all right.
Billy Graham

The best answer to fear is to have a firm grasp of what it means to be accepted by God.
John Gunstone

"Come to the edge!" God said. "It's dangerous there," I answer. "Come to the edge!" God said. "But I might fall!" "Come to the edge!" God said. So I did. And He pushed me! And I flew!
Guillaume Apollinaire

The way to worry about nothing is to pray about everything.
Unknown

Never dwell on the tomorrow; remember, that it's God's and not ours.
E. B. Pusey

Remember that everyone you meet is afraid of something, loves something, and has lost something.
Unknown

Have you ever learned the beautiful art of letting God take care of you and giving all your thought and strength to pray for others and for the kingdom of God? It will relieve you of a thousand cares.
A. B. Simpson

He that takes his cares on himself loads himself in vain with an uneasy burden. I will cast my cares on God; he has bidden me; they cannot burden him.
Joseph Hall

God never built a Christian strong enough to carry today's duties and tomorrow's anxieties piled on top of them.
Theodore Ledyard Cuyler

Surrender the thing you fear into the hands of God. Turn it right over to God and ask Him to solve it with you. Fear is keeping things in your own hands; faith is turning them over into the hands of God.
E. Stanley Jones

I compare the troubles which we have to undergo to a great bundle of fagots, far too large for us to carry. But God does not require us to carry the whole at once. He mercifully unties the bundle, and gives us first one stick, which we are to carry today and then another which we are to carry tomorrow, and so on. This we might easily manage, if we would only take the burden appointed for us each day; but we choose to increase our troubles by carrying sticks over again today, and adding tomorrow's burden to our load, before we are required to carry it.
John Newton

True freedom from fear consists of totally resigning one's life into the hands of the Lord.
David Wilkerson

Will you let the fear of a false world, that has no love for you, keep you from the fear of that God, who has only created you, that he may love and bless you to all eternity?
William Law

If you feel insecure, then it must be that you are looking inward at yourself rather than upward at Jesus Christ.
Howard Kelly

All worry is atheism, because it is a want of trust in God.
Fulton Sheen

Men who fear God face life fearlessly. Men who do not fear God end up fearing everything.
Richard Halverson

Fear will always knock on your door. Just don't invite it in for dinner. And for heaven's sake, don't offer it a bed for the night.
Max Lucado

Fear not the knife that God wields, for his hand is sure.
Francois Fenelon

Anxiety in human life is what squeaking and grinding are in machinery that is not oiled. In life, trust is the oil.
Henry Ward Beecher

Don't tell me that worry doesn't do any good. I know better. The things I worry about don't happen.
Unknown

Man, like the bridge, was designed to carry the load of the moment, not the combined weight of a year at once.
William Ward

God only made each day to be 24 hours long because He knew that's about all we can handle. When we get into trouble, it is often because we are either hanging on to hours from yesterday, or borrowing them from tomorrow.
Vickie Girard

In God, the unknown is friendly.
Unknown

Every step toward Christ kills a doubt. Every thought, word, and deed for Him carries you away from discouragement.
Theodore L. Cuyler

Forgiveness

God expects more failure from us than we do from ourselves because God knows who we are. We are not the righteous person who occasionally sins, we are the sinful person who occasionally- by God's grace- gets it right. When we start from this perspective we are released from the bondage of perfectionism and are able to forgive ourselves once and for all. We are to take our cue from him. We may be disappointed with ourselves but God is not. We may feel like condemning ourselves, but God does not.
James Bryan Smith

It is only imperfection that complains of what is imperfect. The more perfect we are, the more gentle and quiet we become toward the defect of others.
Francois Fenelon

Forgiveness is the oil of relationships.
Josh McDowell

Love is an act of endless forgiveness, a tender look which becomes a habit.
Peter Ustinov

Forgiveness is a stunning principle, your ticket out of hate and fear and chaos.
Barbara Johnson

The greatest wonder that I ever heard of is that God should ever justify me. I feel myself to be a lumpy of unworthiness, a mass of corruption, and a heap of sin apart from His almighty love. I know and am fully assured that I am justified by faith which is in Christ Jesus, and I am treated as if I had been perfectly just and made an heir of God and a joint-heir with Christ. And yet, by nature I must take my place among the most sinful. I, who am altogether undeserving, am treated as if I had been deserving. I am loved with as much love as if I had always been Godly, whereas before I was ungodly. Who can help being astonished at this? Gratitude for such favor stands dressed in robes of wonder.
Charles H. Spurgeon

Patience is the virtue that transforms an angry tongue. Patience takes time to hesitate and evaluate. It rejects anger sins. True patience finds its strength in an unflinching focus on God and an unconditional love toward those who have hurt us.
Joseph Stowell

A wise man will make haste to forgive, because he knows the true value of time.
Samuel Johnson

The three hardest tasks in the world are neither physical feats nor intellectual achievements, but moral acts: to return love for hate, to include the excluded, and to say, "I was wrong."
Sydney J. Harris

It would seem, after having been a Christian for almost 80 years, that I would no longer do ugly things that need forgiving. Yet I am constantly doing things to others that cause me to have to go back and ask their forgiveness. Sometimes these are things I actually do- other times they are simply attitudes I let creep in which break the circle of God's perfect love.
Corrie ten Boom

Forgiveness is the precondition of love.
Catherine Marshall

We are all fallen creatures and all very hard to live with.
C. S. Lewis

To love means loving the unlovable. To forgive means pardoning the unpardonable. Faith means believing the unbelievable. Hope means hoping when everything seems hopeless.
Gilbert Keith Chesterton

We judge others by their actions; we judge ourselves by our intentions.
Unknown

Forgiveness is the greatest expression of love.
Unknown

Forgiveness is not an emotion, it's a decision.
Randall Worley

Know all and you will pardon all.
Thomas Kempis

To forgive is to set a prisoner free and discover the prisoner was you.
Unknown

We have found that marriage should be made up of two forgivers. We need to learn to say, "I was wrong, I'm sorry." And we also need to say, "That's all right, I love you."
Billy Graham

Let us be the first to give a friendly sign; to nod first, smile first, speak first, and- if such a thing is necessary- forgive first.
Unknown

Some people confess a sin a thousand times, I tell them to confess it once, then thank God a thousand times for forgiving them.
Maurice Horn

One of the most lasting pleasures you can experience is the feeling that comes over you when you genuinely forgive an enemy – whether he knows it or not.
O. A. Battista

To carry a grudge is like being stung to death by one bee.
William H. Walton

There is no use in talking as if forgiveness were easy. For we find that the work of forgiveness has to be done over and over again.
C. S. Lewis

The word resentment means to re-feel… to feel again. Someone wrongs or wounds you; in resenting it, you re-feel the injury. And you re-hurt yourself. The Hebrew Talmud says that a person who bears a grudge is "Like one who, having cut one hand while handling a knife, avenges himself by stabbing the other hand."
Norman Vincent Peale

Saints are men who permit God's forgiveness to come into them so fully that not only are their sins washed out, but also their very selves, their egos, and the root of their self will. And again we see, the intensity of their power really to forgive is in exact proportion to the degree that they have permitted themselves to be forgiven and so brought back to God.
Unknown

Forgiveness is God's invention for coming to terms with a world in which, despite their best intentions, people are unfair to each other and hurt each other deeply.
Sharon Jaynes

How great is the contrast between that forgiveness to which we lay claim from God towards us, and our temper towards others! God, we expect, will forgive us great offences, offences many times repeated; and will forgive them freely, liberally, and from the heart. But we are offended at our neighbor, perhaps, for the merest trifles, and for an injury only once offered; and we are but half reconciled when we deem to forgive. Even an uncertain humor, an ambiguous word, or a suspected look, will inflame our anger; and hardly any persuasion will induce us for a long time to relent.
Henry W. Thornton

You who are letting miserable misunderstandings run on from year to year, meaning to clear them up some day; you who are keeping wretched quarrels alive because you cannot quite make up your minds that now is the day to sacrifice your pride and kill them; you who are letting your neighbor starve until you hear that he is dying of starvation or letting your friend's heart ache for a word of appreciation or sympathy, which you mean to give him some day; if you could only know and see and feel all of a sudden that time is short, how it would break the "spell." How you would go instantly and do the thing which you might never have another chance to do.
Phillips Brooks

Forgiveness means the offense is gone. I may remember the offense, but I will "remember it against them no more!"
David Stoop

Love is an act of endless forgiveness, a tender look which becomes a habit.
Peter Ustinov

Forgiveness is not an elective in the curriculum of servanthood. It is a required course, and the exams are always tough to pass.
Charles Swindoll

To understand is not only to pardon, but in the end to love.
Walter Lippmann

The holy heart can be hurt. But it answers injury with love and prayer and forgiveness.
W. E. McCumber

A good marriage is the union of two forgivers.
Ruth Bell Graham

When a person forgives another, he is promising to do three things about the intended wrongdoing: not to use it against the wrongdoer in the future; not to talk about it to others; and not to dwell on it himself.
Jay Adams

I discovered that it is not on our forgiveness any more than on our goodness that the world's healing hinges, but on His. When He tells us to love our enemies, He gives, along with the command, the love itself.
Corrie ten Boom

It is a melancholy fact that there are few Christian duties so little practiced as that of forgiveness.
J. C. Ryle

There's no point in burying a hatchet if you're going to put up a marker on the site.
Sydney Harris

To be a Christian means to forgive the inexcusable, because God has forgiven the inexcusable in you.
C. S. Lewis

We evaluate our friends with a Godlike justice, but we want them to evaluate us with a Godlike compassion.
Sydney Harris

If our greatest need had been information, God would have sent an educator. If our greatest need had been technology, God would have sent us a scientist. If our greatest need had been money, God would have sent us an economist. But since our greatest need was forgiveness, God sent us a Savior.
Roy Lessin

Love is an act of endless forgiveness.
Jean Vanier

How life catches up with us and teaches us to love and forgive each other.
Judy Collins

One forgives as much as one loves.
Francois Rochefoucauld

I think that if God forgives us we must forgive ourselves. Otherwise it is almost like setting up ourselves as a higher tribunal than Him.
C. S. Lewis

It is a vital moment of truth when a man discovers that what he condemns most vehemently in others is that to which he is himself prone.
Unknown

Tolerance comes with age. I see no fault committed that I myself could not have committed at some time or other.
Johann Wolfgang von Goethe

The day the child realizes that all adults are imperfect he becomes an adolescent; the day he forgives them, he becomes an adult; the day he forgives himself he becomes wise.
Alden Nowlan

God has promised forgiveness to your repentance, but He has not promised tomorrow to your procrastination.
Augustine

Friendship

President Lincoln once said a few kind words about the Confederates. A woman retorted that she wondered how the president could speak kindly of his enemies, when he should rather wish them destroyed. "But ma'am," Lincoln replied. "Do I not destroy them when I make them my friends?"
Unknown

The closer we are to God, the closer we are to those who are close to him.
Thomas Merton

When you meet a man or woman who puts Jesus Christ first, knit that one to your soul.
Oswald Chambers

Friendship is not a reward for our discrimination and good taste in finding one another out. It is the instrument by which God reveals to each the beauties of all the others.
C. S. Lewis

If two friends ask you to judge a dispute, don't accept, because you will lose one friend; on the other hand, if two strangers come with the same request, accept because you will gain one friend.
Augustine

A good friend will sharpen your character, draw your soul into the light, and challenge your heart to love in a greater way.
Unknown

The better part of one's life consists of one's friendships.
Abraham Lincoln

A friend is a gift you give yourself.
Robert Louis Stevenson

The truth is friendship is every bit as sacred and eternal as marriage.
Katherine Mansfield

I set out to find a friend but couldn't find one; I set out to be a friend, and friends were everywhere.
Unknown

We need old friends to help us grow old and new friends to help us stay young.
Letty Cottin Pogrebin

Some people come into our lives and quickly go. Some stay for a while and leave footprints on our hearts – and we are never, ever the same.
Unknown

Each friend represents a world in us, a world possibly not born until they arrive, and it is only by this meeting that a new world is born.
Anaïs Nin

To the world you may be just one person, but to one person you may be the world.
Unknown

A friend is one who sees through you and still enjoys the view.
Wilma Askinas

We can never replace a friend. When a man is fortunate enough to have several, he finds they are all different. No one has a double in friendship.
Johann Von Schiller

A friend is long sought, hardly found, and with difficulty kept.
Jerome

Friends do not live in harmony merely, as some say, but in melody.
Henry David Thoreau

A friend is a poem.
Unknown

A loyal friend laughs at your jokes when they're not so good, and sympathizes with your problems when they're not so bad.
Arnold H. Glasow

Two great talkers will not travel far together.
George Borrow

It is very proper for friends, when they part, to part with prayer.
Matthew Henry

The mind never unbends itself so agreeably as in the conversation of a well-chosen friend. There is indeed no blessing of life that is any way comparable to the enjoyment of a discreet and virtuous friend. It eases and unloads the mind, clears and improves the understanding, engenders thought and knowledge, animates virtue and good resolutions, soothes and allays the passions, and finds employment for most of the vacant hours of life.
Joseph Addison

A guest at a country house coming down to breakfast one morning was met by the child of the house, who running up to him and putting his hand in his, looked up into his face with a smile, saying, "I'm your friend now; I put you in my prayer last night!"
Unknown

Strangers are friends that you have yet to meet.
Roberta Lieberman

Is any pleasure on earth as great as a circle of Christian friends by a fire?
C. S. Lewis

Many a friendship- long, loyal, and self-sacrificing- rested at first upon no thicker a foundation than a kind word.
Frederick W. Faber

Let me live in a house by the side of the road and be a friend to man.
Sam Walter Foss

My friends are my estate.
Emily Dickinson

God often places someone at a camp, a club, or a church as a certain intersection to build you up: Someone to say something that you'll never forget or to encourage you at a moment of need.
Gregg Matte

To have a good friend is one of the highest delights of life; to be a good friend is one of the noblest and most difficult undertakings.
Unknown

Oh, the comfort, the inexpressible comfort of feeling safe with a person, having neither to weigh thoughts, nor measure words, but pouring them all out, just as they are, chaff and grain together, certain that a faithful hand will take and sift them, keep what is worth keeping, and with a breath of kindness blow the rest away.
Dinah Maria Mulock Craik

What a pity that so many people are living with so few friends when the world is full of lonesome strangers who would give anything just to be somebody's friend.
Milo L. Arnold

Let Christ stay throughout the meal. Don't dismiss Him with the blessing.
Unknown

We can never replace a friend. When a man is fortunate enough to have several, he finds they are all different. No one has a double in friendship.
Johann Von Schiller

The ornaments of a house are the friends who visit it.
Unknown

Not many sounds in life, and I include all urban and all rural sounds, exceed in interest a knock at the door.
Charles Lamb

On my way back I met a little girl with a pitcher in her hand. We both stopped, and with the instinctive, unconventional camaraderie of childhood plunged into an intimate, confidential conversation. She was a jolly little soul, with black eyes and two long braids of black hair. We told each other how old we were, and how many dolls we had, and almost everything else there was to tell except our names which neither of us thought about. When we parted, I felt as though I were leaving a life long friend. We never met again.
Lucy Maud Montgomery

71

The best part of life is when your family become your friends and your friends become your family.
Robin Roberts

Once the realization is accepted that even between the closest human beings infinite distances continue to exist, a wonderful living side-by-side can grow up, if they succeed in loving the distance between them, which makes it possible for each to see the other whole against a wide sky.
Rainer Rilke

We evaluate our friends with a Godlike justice, but we want them to evaluate us with a Godlike compassion.
Sydney Harris

Don't wait for people to be friendly, show them how.
Unknown

General

Our problem is that we come to a point in our Christian life where we become comfortable and we stop surrendering all things to Christ. Surrender means that I have given God permission to change, mold or to rid my life of anything that hinders me from becoming all that He wants me to be. We need to surrender to God and allow Him to change us.
Jeff Simms

God sends rain and fruitful seasons, but though they come, they never come in the same way in any one year, and I find that, as a rule, when I need anything, that it comes from a quarter that I never expected, and that from the quarter where it had come before it does not now. Thus God keeps the eye on Himself and not on the donor.
J. B. Stoney

Good for the body is the work of the body, and good for the soul is the work of the soul, and good for either is the work of the other.
Henry David Thoreau

The beauty seen is partly in him who sees it.
Christian Bovee

There is no avoiding, and no substitute for, the sometimes long, arduous experience of discovering the will of God in our own lives.
Sinclair Ferguson

It is later than it has ever been before, and the smartest thing any man can do is to set his watch by God's clock.
Vance Havner

Much as we wish, not one of us can bring back yesterday or shape tomorrow. Only today is ours, and it will not be ours for long, and once it is gone it will never in all time be ours again. Thou only knowest what it holds in store for us, yet even we know something of what it will hold. The chance to speak the truth, to show mercy, to ease another's burden. The chance to resist evil, to remember all the good times and good people of our past, to be brave, to be strong, to be glad.
Frederick Buechner

Find out what your temptations are and you will find out largely what you are yourself.
Henry Ward Beecher

The will of God is the measure of things.
Unknown

The mind is like a clock that is constantly running down. It has to be wound up daily with good thoughts.
Fulton J. Sheen

God isn't a talent scout looking for someone who is "good enough" or "strong enough." He is looking for someone with a heart set on Him, and He will do the rest.
Vance Havner

Late have I loved You, Beauty so old and so new: late have I loved You. And see, You were within and I was in the external world and sought You there, and in my unlovely state I plunged into those lovely created things which You made. You were with me, and I was not with You. The lovely things kept me far from You, though if they did not have their existence in You, they had no existence at all. You called and cried out loud and shattered my deafness. You were radiant and resplendent, You put to flight my blindness. You were fragrant, and I drew in my breath and now pant after You. I tasted You, and I feel but hunger and thirst for You. You touched me, and I am set on fire to attain the peace which is Yours. For what am I to myself without You, but a guide to my own downfall?
Augustine

God is impressed, not with noise or size or wealth, but with quiet things…things done in secret- the inner motives, the true heart condition.
Charles Swindoll

I am filled with shame and confusion, when I reflect on the one hand upon the great favors which God has done, and incessantly continues to do; and on the other, upon the ill use I have made of them, and my small advancement in the way of perfection.
Brother Lawrence

Time to think: *it is the source of power.*
Time to play: *it is the secret of perpetual youth.*
Time to read: *it is the fountain of wisdom.*
Time to pray: *it is the greatest power on earth.*
Time to laugh: *it is the music of the soul.*
Time to give: *it is too short a day to be selfish.*
Unknown

God designed the human machine to run on Himself. He is the fuel our spirits were designed to burn…That is why it is no good asking God to make us happy in our own way without bothering about religion. God cannot give us a happiness apart from Himself, because there is no such thing.
C. S. Lewis

The key step between the Bible and life is apply. That's where the truths of scripture begin to move beyond statements of fact or principles…Biblical application means allowing the truth of scripture to penetrate our lives, to make a difference in how we live.
Dave Veerman

Not what we give but that we share,
For the gift without the giver is bare.
James Russell Lowell

The best thing to give your enemy is
forgiveness;
to an opponent, tolerance;
to a friend, your heart;
to your child, a good example;
to a father, deference;
to your mother, conduct that will make
her proud of you;
to yourself, respect;
to all men, charity.
John Balfour

The destined end of a man is not
happiness, nor health, but holiness. God's
one aim is the production of saints.
Oswald Chambers

Our gracious heavenly Father entrusts us
to confess our mess. And to show us that
it's okay to let down our pretenses, His
Word is full of stories about unlikely
people becoming heroes- a stuttering ex-
con who leads God's people out of
slavery; an unethical little "IRS agent"
who becomes a friend of Jesus; a sleazy
woman whose testimony triggers a revival
in her hometown. If you're embarrassed
by your past, you're in good company!
Lisa Harper

I keep the telephone of my mind open to
peace, harmony, health, love and
abundance. Then, whenever doubts,
anxiety, or fear try to call me, they keep
getting a busy signal- and soon they'll
forget my number.
Edith Armstrong

God is more interested in the workman
than in the work.
Warren Wiersbe

If your inner voice is telling you that you
can't paint, by all means, hurry up and
paint and silence the voice.
Vincent Van Gogh

God leaves us here because He has a
mission for us to fulfill. We aren't here by
accident; neither are we here simply to
enjoy the good things life has to offer. We
are here because God put us here, and He
has a sovereign purpose in keeping us
here. It's true for us as individuals, and it's
true for His body, the Church, in all of its
fullness. As Jesus prayed just before His
arrest and trial, "I am not praying that
You take them out of the world...As You
sent Me into the world, I also have sent
them into the world." (John 17:15,18)
Billy Graham

Anyone who serves God will discover
sooner or later that the great hindrance to
his work is not others but himself.
Watchman Nee

How rare it is to find a soul quiet enough
to hear God speak!
Francios Fenelon

Only God knows how many Handel's
Messiahs could have been written, but
were not.
Charles E. Blair

At a church dinner, there was a pile of apples on one end of a table with a sign that read, "Take Only One Apple, Please. God Is Watching." On the other end of the table was a pile of cookies where a youth had placed a sign saying, "Take All The Cookies You Want. God Is Watching The Apples."
Unknown

This is my "depressed stance." When you're depressed, it makes a lot of difference how you stand. The worst thing you can do is straighten up and hold your head high because then you'll start to feel better. If you're going to get any joy out of being depressed, you've got to stand like this.
Charlie Brown

In order to be utterly happy the only thing necessary is to refrain from comparing this moment with other moments in the past, which I often did not fully enjoy because I was comparing them with other moments of the future.
Andre Gide

How can you possess the miseries of envy when you possess in Christ the best of all portions?
C. H. Spurgeon

Always put off until tomorrow what you shouldn't do at all.
Morris Mandel

Treasure this day,
and treasure yourself.
Truly, neither will ever
happen again.
Ray Bradbury

The foolish person seeks happiness in the distance; the wise person grows it under his feet.
James Oppenheim

What the heart has once owned and had, it shall never lose.
H. W. Beecher

Being a Christian means accepting the terms of creation, accepting God as our maker and redeemer, and growing day by day into an increasingly glorious creature in Christ, developing joy, experiencing love, maturing in peace.
Eugene Peterson

My worth to God in public is what I am in private.
Oswald Chambers

Virtue shows quite as well in rags and patches as she does in purple and fine linen.
Charles Dickens

The brook would lose its song if the rocks were removed.
Unknown

The most important thought I ever had was that of my individual responsibility to God.
Daniel Webster

You aren't an accident. You weren't mass-produced. You aren't an assembly-line product. You were deliberately planned, specifically gifted, and lovingly positioned on this earth by the Master Craftsman.
Max Lucado

If God has made your cup sweet, drink it with grace. If he has made it bitter, drink it in communion with Him.
Oswald Chambers

My new word: "Blesson." It's when you're able to view painful lessons as blessings. A blesson is what happens when you see the blessing in the lesson that your challenge taught you.
Karen Salmansohn

Most Christians expect little from God, ask little, and therefore receive little, and are content with little.
A. W. Pink

Man is certainly stark mad; he cannot make a worm, and yet he will be making gods by the dozens.
Michel de Montaigne

The mother eagle teaches her little ones to fly by making their nest so uncomfortable that they are forced to leave it and commit themselves to the unknown world of air outside. And just so does our God to us.
Hannah Whitall Smith

He converses and delights Himself with me incessantly, in a thousand and a thousand ways, and treats me in all respects as His favourite.
Brother Lawrence

If you are a saint, God will continually upset your program, and if you are wedded to your program, you will become that most obnoxious creature under heaven- an irritable saint.
Oswald Chambers

I have a point of view. You have a point of view. God has view.
Madeleine L'Engle

There was a tedious four-day trial at which a defendant stoutly maintained his innocence. On the fourth day he suddenly decided to plead guilty. The judge angrily inquired, "Why didn't you plead guilty right at the start and save us all this time, trouble, and cost?" "Honest, Judge," whined the defendant, "I was convinced I was innocent until I heard all the evidence against me."
Unknown

To forgive is to set a prisoner free and discover the prisoner was you.
Unknown

An old man lived with his son in a fort. One day the son lost his horse. The neighbors rushed into the house to express their sympathy, but the old man said: "How do you know that this is bad luck?" A few days later, the horse came back with a number of wild horses. So the neighbors flocked indoors to congratulate him, but the old man said: "How do you know this is good luck?" Now that he had so many horses to ride, the son one day rode away on one of the wild horses. He fell off, breaking his leg. Again the neighbors knocked at the door to say: "Alas! Alas!" but the old man said: "Tut! Tut! How do you know this is bad luck?" Sure enough, before many weeks had passed, there was a great war in the Middle Flowery Kingdom, but because the old man's son was crippled, he did not have to go off to fight.
Chinese story

God writes the Gospel not in the Bible alone, but on trees, and flowers, and clouds, and stars.
Martin Luther

Emphasize reconciliation, not resolution. It is unrealistic to expect everyone to agree about everything. Reconciliation focuses on the relationship, while resolution focuses on the problem. When we focus on reconciliation, the problem loses significance and often becomes irrelevant.
Rick Warren

We drift toward compromise and call it tolerance; we drift toward disobedience and call it freedom; we drift toward superstition and call it faith. We cherish the indiscipline of lost self-control and call it relaxation; we slouch toward prayerlessness and delude ourselves into thinking we have escaped legalism; we slide toward godlessness and convince ourselves we have been liberated.
D. A. Carson

Let Jesus be in your heart, eternity in your spirit, the world under your feet, the will of God in your actions. And let the love of God shine forth from you.
Catherine of Genoa

Manners are a sensitive awareness of the feelings of others. If you have that awareness, you have good manners, no matter what fork you use.
Emily Post

He who counts the stars and calls them by their names, is in no danger of forgetting His own children. He knows your case as thoroughly as if you were the only creature He ever made, or the only saint He ever loved.
C. H. Spurgeon

People often say that motivation doesn't last. Well, neither does bathing – that's why we recommend it daily.
Zig Ziglar

Laughter removes all barriers. When people are laughing together, there are no age differences, no racial barriers, and no economic distinctions. It is just people enjoying their existence.
Bruce Bickel

Horizontal relationships- relationships between people- are crippled at the outset unless the vertical relationship- the relationship between each person and God- is in place.
Ed Young

We have not been created for the purpose of finding our ultimate satisfaction in a job. There is no spouse whom we were ever meant to take as the ultimate concern in our life. We have been made for the purpose of knowing God.
Mark Dever

Genuine, hearty laughter is one of the greatest gifts imparted to us by our Father. It has the amazing power to diminish our pain, lifting our souls in joyous good cheer, while providing bright hope for the unknown days ahead.
W. Phillip Keller

One of the best-kept secrets in Christianity is that God accepts us. True, He can't stand our sinful acts, but He loves us. He doesn't have us on performance-based acceptance; He has us on Jesus-based acceptance.
Billy Gillham

When one life is changed, the world is changed.
Thomas Johns

God has an exasperating habit of laying his hands on the wrong man.
Joseph Blinco

The Christian has to live in the world, but he must draw all his resources from outside of the world.
Donald Barnhouse

Out of the will of God there is no such thing as success; in the will of God there is no such thing as failure.
David Amstutz

To be sensible of our corruption and abhor our own transgressions is the first symptom of spiritual health.
J. C. Ryle

Contentment comes when we remember that what God chooses is far better than what we choose.
Unknown

I was frustrated out of my mind, trying to figure out the will of God. I was doing everything but letting into the presence of God and asking Him to show me.
Paul Little

Keep your lamp burning, and let God place it where He will.
Unknown

If you are holding something back from God, then God is holding something back from you.
John Blanchard

Where God guides he provides. He is responsible for our upkeep if we follow his directions. He is not responsible for expenses not on his schedule.
Vance Havner

Duty and today are ours; results and the future belong to God.
Unknown

A novice monk asked a seasoned old veteran of the abbey, "After you entered the monastery, did you still struggle with the devil?" "No." Answered the older monk. "I struggled with God." "With God?" Exclaimed his neophyte friend, "How could you hope to win?" The older monk softly replied, "When I struggle with God, I hope to lose."
Unknown

It is no advantage to be near the light if the eyes are closed.
Augustine

If God seems far away- guess who moved.
L. James Harvey

It is in the ordinary duties and labors of life that the Christian can and should develop his spiritual union with God.
Thomas Merton

God does not have to go through me to reach the people He wants to help, but I am lucky if I make it easy for Him to do so.
Ben Stein

What then is the difference between the good man and the bad? Only this: They both suffer, they both have pain, they both know tension and trouble, but there is a difference in what they suffer for, in what they have trouble from, in what takes away their peace of mind. The measure of a man is that which bothers him, that which disturbs his mind, that which annoys him and costs him pain.
Jack Riemer

Thou hast made us for Thyself, and the heart of man is restless until it finds its rest in Thee.
Augustine

A small decision now can change all your tomorrows.
Robert Schuller

A Christian is the world's Bible- and some of them need revising.
D. L. Moody

If you wish to possess finally all that is yours, give yourself entirely to God.
Hadewijch of Antwerp

You are not a reservoir with a limited amount of resources; you are a channel attached to unlimited divine resources.
Unknown

My relationship with God is the only relationship that counts, and if it's right, all other relationships in my life will be right, no matter how they turn out.
Ben Stein

Habit is a cable; we weave a thread of it every day, and at last we cannot break it.
Horace Mann

We are not our own, any more than what we possess is our own. We did not make ourselves; we cannot be supreme over ourselves. We cannot be our own masters. We are God's property by creation, by redemption, by regeneration.
John Henry Newman

If God lights the candle, none can blow it out.
C. H. Spurgeon

I was still trying to be in control, but the only thing I was really in control of was my own misery. What God wanted from me was a deeper surrender, a full and unconditional reliance on his loving will for me.
Unknown

Sainthood lies in the habit of referring the smallest actions to God.
C. S. Lewis

However holy or Christlike a Christian may become, he is still in the condition of "being changed."
John Stott

A dear old Quaker lady was asked to explain her obviously youthful appearance, her appealing vivacity, and her winning charm. She replied sweetly, "I used for the lips- truth, for the voice- prayer, for the eyes- pity, for the hands- charity, for the figure- uprightness, for the heart- love." How's that for a make-up-kit?
Abraham Besdin

I am born happy every morning.
Unknown

I am always content with what happens, for I know that what God chooses is better than what I choose.
Epictetus

You have become a mature person when keeping a secret gives you more satisfaction than passing it along.
Unknown

God has no problems, only plans.
Corrie ten Boom

We struggle with the complexities and avoid the simplicities.
Norman Vincent Peale

God loves with a great love the man whose heart is bursting with a passion for the IMPOSSIBLE.
William Booth

You have made us for yourself and our hearts are restless until they rest in you.
Augustine of Hippo

Have patience with all things, but chiefly have patience with yourself. Do not lose courage in considering your own imperfections, but instantly set about remedying them- every day begin the tasks anew.
Francis De Sales

Happiness is like a butterfly. The more you chase it, the more it will elude you. But if you turn your attention to other things, it comes softly and sits on your shoulder.
Unknown

The degree of blessing enjoyed by any man will correspond exactly with the completeness of God's victory over him.
A. W. Tozer

God is waiting for us to come to Him with our needs…God's throne room is always open…Every single believer in the whole world could walk into the throne room all at one time, and it would not even be crowded.
Charles Stanley

God didn't want me to do more for Him. He wanted me to be more with Him.
Bruce Wilkinson

In the world to come I shall not be asked, "Why were you not Moses?" I shall be asked, "Why were you not Zusya?"
Rabbi Zusya

The smallest good act today is the capture of a strategic point from which, a few months later, you may be able to go on to victories you never dreamed of.
C. S. Lewis

To have a God who is almighty, all wise, all good and merciful to go to as your constant friend, as your continual benefactor, as your safeguard and guide, it should- it must- sweeten every bitter drought of life.
Elias Boudinot

It is not darkness you are going to, for God is Light. It is not lonely, for Christ is with you. It is not unknown country, for Christ is there.
Charles Kingsley

Some of the roads most used lead nowhere.
Jewish proverb

Conscience warns us as a friend before it punishes us as a judge.
King Stanislas I

If you are in the wrong place, the right place is empty.
Unknown

The fatal metaphor of progress, which means leaving things behind us, has utterly obscured the real idea of growth, which means leaving things inside us.
G. K. Chesterton

Too many of us have a Christian vocabulary rather than a Christian experience.
Charles F. Banning

If God is here for us and not elsewhere, then in fact this place is holy and this moment is sacred.
Isabel Anders

Never say there is nothing beautiful in the world anymore. There is always something to make you wonder in the shape of a tree, the trembling of a leaf.
Albert Schweitzer

It's not the ship in the water but the water in the ship that sinks it. So it's not the Christian in the world but the world in the Christian that constitutes the danger.
John Wilbur Chapman

In God's world, for those who are in earnest, there is no failure. No work truly done, no word earnestly spoken, no sacrifice freely made, was ever made in vain.
Frederick W. Robertson

God will only mend a broken heart when He is given all the pieces.
Unknown

Lord, if I dig a pit for others
Let me fall into it;
But if I dig it for myself,
Give me sense enough to walk around it.
Sherwood Wirt

Day by day we should weigh what we have granted to the spirit of the world against what we have denied to the spirit of Jesus, in thought and especially in deed.
Albert Schweitzer

The more we let God take us over, the more truly ourselves we become- because he made us. He invented all the different people that you and I were intended to be...It is when I turn to Christ, then I give up myself to His personality, that I first begin to have a real personality of my own.
C. S. Lewis

The promises of God are certain, but they do not all mature in 90 days.
Adoniram Gordon

Religion should be our steering wheel, not our spare tire.
Charles L. Wheeler

God's plan will continue on God's schedule.
A. W. Tozer

One should gather a little nosegay of devotion. My meaning is as follows: Those who have been walking in a beautiful garden do not leave it willingly without taking away with them four or five flowers, in order to inhale their perfume and carry them about during the day: even so, when we have considered some mystery in meditation, we should choose one or two or three points in which we have found most relish, and which are specially proper to our advancement, in order to remember them throughout the day, and to inhale their perfume spiritually. Now we should do this in the place where we have made our meditation, either staying where we are, or walking about alone for a little while afterwards.
Francis de Sales

Even if you've missed God's plan entirely for years and years and years, that plan can still swing into operation the minute you're ready to step up and step in, with God at your side.
Tony Evans

God expects us to grow spiritually. The end result is His responsibility. Our job is to cooperate with the process.
Rory Noland

God washes the eyes by tears until they can behold the invisible land where tears shall come no more.
Henry Ward Beecher

(Written about AD 130, this is one of the earliest descriptions of Christians.)
They dwell in their own countries but simply as sojourners. As citizens, they share in all things with others, and yet endure all things as if foreigners. Every foreign land is to them as their native country, and every land of their birth as a land of strangers. They marry, as do others; they beget children; but they do not destroy their offspring. They have a common table but not a common bed. They are in the flesh, but they do not live after the flesh. They pass their days on the earth, but are citizens of heaven. They obey the prescribed laws, and at the same time surpass the laws in their lives. They love all, and are persecuted by all. They are poor, yet they make many rich; they are completely destitute, and yet they enjoy complete abundance. They are reviled, and yet they bless. When they do good they are punished as evildoers; undergoing punishment, they rejoice because they are brought to life.
Epistle to Diognetus

I thought when I became a Christian I had nothing to do but just to lay my oars in the bottom of the boat and float along. But I soon found that I would have to go against the current.
Dwight L. Moody

People who wrestle with their consciences usually go for two falls out of three.
Los Angeles Times Syndicate

A traveler, as he passed through a forest, saw a part of a huge oak, which appeared misshapen, and almost seemed to spoil the scenery. "If," sad he, "I was the owner of this forest, I would cut down that tree." But when he had ascended the hill, and taken a full view of the forest, this same tree appeared the most beautiful part of the landscape. "How erroneously," said he, "I judged when I saw only a part!" The full view, the harmony and proportion of things, are all necessary to clear up our judgment.
Unknown

Our dependence upon God ought to be so entire and absolute that we should never think it necessary, in any kind of distress, to have recourse to human consolations.
Thomas a Kempis

If you believe in a God who controls the big things, you have to believe in a God who controls the little things. It is we, of course, to whom things look "little" or "big."
Elisabeth Elliot

A child on a farm sees a plane fly overhead and dreams of a faraway place. A traveler on the plane sees the farmhouse…and dreams of home.
Carl Burns

Don't let yesterday use up too much of today.
Will Rogers

Failure is often God's own tool for carving some of the finest outlines in the character of His children; and even in this life, bitter and crushing failures have often in them the germs of new and quite unimagined happiness.
Thomas Hodgkin

We are apt to mistake our vocation by looking out of the way for occasions to exercise great and rare virtues, and by stepping over the ordinary ones that lie directly in the road before us.
Hannah More

Ask the astronomer if God is a haphazard God. He will tell you that every star moves with precision in its celestial path. Ask the scientist if God is a haphazard God. He will tell you that his formulas and equations are fixed, and that to ignore the laws of science would be a fool's folly. If the laws in the material realm are so fixed and exact, is it reasonable that God could afford to be haphazard in the spiritual realm where eternal destinies of souls are at stake? Just as God has equations and rules in the material realm, God has equations and rules in the spiritual.
Billy Graham

Our future is not about what we have or don't have, or about what might happen or what might not happen. Our future is all about Who we know and how well we know Him.
Cindi McMenamin

Isn't it strange how a 20 dollar bill seems like such a large amount when you donate it to church, but such a small amount when you go shopping?

Isn't it strange how 2 hours seem so long when you're at church, and how short they seem when you're watching a good movie?

Isn't it strange that you can't find a word to say when you're praying but you have no trouble thinking what to talk about with a friend?

Isn't it strange how difficult and boring it is to read one chapter of the Bible but how easy it is to read 100 pages of a popular novel?

Isn't it strange how everyone wants front-row-tickets to concerts or games but they do whatever is possible to sit at the last row in Church?

Isn't it strange how we need to know about an event for Church 2-3 weeks before the day so we can include it in our agenda, but we can adjust it for other events in the last minute?

Isn't it strange how difficult it is to learn a fact about God to share it with others; but how easy it is to learn, understand, extend and repeat gossip?

Isn't it strange how we believe everything that magazines and newspapers say but we question the words in the Bible?

Isn't it strange how everyone wants a place in heaven but they don't want to believe, do, or say anything to get there?

Isn't it strange how we send jokes in e-mails and they are forwarded right away but when we are going to send messages about God, we think about it twice before we share it with others?
Unknown

In men whom men condemn as ill
I find so much of goodness still,
In men whom men pronounce divine
I find so much of sin and blot,
I do not dare to draw a line
Between the two, where God has not.
Joaquin Miller

I once visited a weaver's school where the students were making beautiful patterns. I asked, "When you make a mistake must you cut it out and start from the beginning?" A student said, "No, our teacher is such a great artist that when we make a mistake, he uses it to improve the beauty of the pattern." That is what the Lord does with our mistakes.
Corrie ten Boom

You have been created by God and for God, and someday you will stand amazed at the simple yet profound ways He has used you even when you weren't aware of it.
Kay Arthur

Christians are not called to win battles, but to find ways of being in battles.
David Jenkins

We live charmed lives if we are living in the center of God's will. All the attacks that Satan can hurl against us are not only powerless to harm us, but are turned into blessing on the way.
Charles H. Spurgeon

God heals, and the doctor takes the fee.
Benjamin Franklin

No one can help another very much in these crises of life; but love and sympathy count for something.
Thomas Henry Huxley

There is no safer place for your hopes and dreams than in the loving hands of your faithful Father.
Leslie Ludy

Let me find thy light in my darkness, thy life in my death, thy joy in my sorrow, thy grace in my sin, thy riches in my poverty, thy glory in my valley.
Arthur Bennett

A holy life is not an ascetic, or gloomy or solitary life, but a life regulated by divine truth and faithful in Christian duty. It is living above the world while we are still in it.
Tryon Edwards

Have your heart right with Christ, and He will visit you often, and so turn weekdays into Sundays, meals into sacraments, homes into temples and earth into heaven.
Charles Haddon Spurgeon

There are three stages in the work of God: Impossible; Difficult; Done.
Hudson Taylor

The Christian who is truly spiritual revels as much in his ignorance of God as in his knowledge of him.
John Blanchard

The Christian man must aim at that complete obedience to God in which life finds its highest happiness, its greatest good, its perfect consummation, its peace.
William Barclay

Many Christians estimate difficulties in the light of their own resources, and thus attempt little and often fail in the little they attempt. All Godís giants have been weak men who did great things for God because they reckoned on His power and presence being with them.
James Hudson Taylor

Nothing else but seeing God in everything can make us loving and patient with those who annoy us. When we realize that they are only the instruments for accomplishing His purpose in our lives, we will actually be able to thank them [inwardly] for the blessings they bring us.
Hannah Whitall Smith

Fulfillment doesn't automatically happen as a result of linking up with the "right" person, job, or even ministry. Fulfillment happens as a result of being in God's will.
Marilyn Olson

Never lose an opportunity of seeing anything beautiful. Beauty is God's handwriting.
Charles Kingsley

You are one of a kind, designed to glorify God as only you can.
Unknown

Basis for happiness: something to do; something to love; something to look forward to.
Kanawha Reporter

If a man cannot be a Christian in the place where he is, he cannot be a Christian anywhere.
Henry Ward Beecher

Beware of no man more than of yourself; we carry our worst enemies within us.
Charles Spurgeon

Change your thoughts and you change your world.
Norman Vincent Peale

Do not free a camel of the burden of his hump; you may be freeing him from being a camel.
G. K. Chesterton

The truly happy person is the one who can enjoy the scenery even when he must take a detour.
Unknown

You can't tell what a man is like or what he is thinking when you are looking at him. You must get around behind him and see what he has been looking at.
Will Rogers

I neglect God and his angels for the noise of a fly, for the rattling of a coach, for the whining of a door.
John Donne

There is so much good in the worst of us, and so much bad in the best of us, that it behooves all of us not to talk about the rest of us.
Robert Louis Stevenson

God cares about details. If you comb out some hairs in the morning, the record in Heaven is changed.
John Rice

God doesn't call people who are qualified. He calls people who are willing, and then He qualifies them.
Richard Parker

I have held many things in my hands, and I have lost them all, but whatever I have placed in God's hands, that I still possess.
Martin Luther

There is no pillow so soft as a clear conscience.
French proverb

God always answers in the deeps, never in the shallows of our soul.
Unknown

The Christian ideal has not been tried and found wanting; it has been found difficult and left untried.
G. K. Chesterton

It does not take great men to do great things; it only takes consecrated men.
Phillips Brooks

We know that people we love are both good and bad, but we expect strangers to be one or the other.
Russell Banks

There is not enough darkness in all the world to put out the light of even one small candle.
Robert Alden

I have more trouble with D. L. Moody than with any other man I ever met.
D. L. Moody

Make me a captive Lord, then I shall be truly free.
Augustine

God

We all long for heaven where God is, but we have it in our power to be in heaven with Him right now- to be happy with Him at this very moment. But being happy with Him now means loving like He loves, helping like He helps, giving as He gives, serving as He serves, rescuing as He rescues, being with Him twenty-four hours a day- touching Him in His distressing disguise.
Mother Teresa

The spirituality of my childhood is the one I would most like to have restored. It was pure and fresh and honest. I read God everywhere!
Macrina Wiederkehr

Every single creature is full of God and is a book about God.
Meister Eckhart

You can never prove God; you can only find Him.
Kate Douglas Wiggin

Inside the will of God there is no failure. Outside the will of God there is no success.
Bernard Edinger

We are doing God next year. Please send all details and pamphlets.
Letter from a British schoolgirl to the Anglican Church Information Office

A missionary told how she was once describing the loving character of God to a gathering of Chinese women. As she told of the Father's love, compassion, and mercy with great enthusiasm, one of the Chinese women turned to her neighbor and said, "Haven't I often told you that there ought to be a God like that?"
Unknown

Unless you have found God in your own soul, the whole world will seem meaningless to you.
Rabindranath Tagore

Life passes, riches fly away, popularity is fickle, the senses decay, the world changes. One alone is true to us; One alone can be all things to us; One alone can supply our need.
John Henry Newman

The best reason to pray is that God is really there. In praying our unbelief starts to melt. God moves smack into the middle of even an ordinary day.
Emily Griffin

The closer we are to God, the closer we are to those who are close to him.
Thomas Merton

Somehow, somewhere, I know that God loves me, even though I do not feel that love as I can feel a human embrace, even though I do not hear a voice as I hear human words…God is greater than my senses, greater than my thoughts, greater than my heart. I do believe that He touches me in places that are unknown even to myself.
Henri J. M. Nouwen

How hard is it for God to get your attention? Do you regularly practice turning aside in your day? That is, taking a moment to listen to God- because God, through the Holy Spirit, really is speaking, because we know, every place is filled with the presence of God. There is not an inch of space, not a moment of time, that God does not inhabit.
John Ortberg

God is bigger than all of us, beyond all of us. When I pray, I don't really pray for anything, I just try to understand God's will and do the best I can.
Harry Connick, Jr.

A deep and sober daily concern to please God is the rarest of rarities.
Vance Havner

An atheist cannot find God for the same reason a thief cannot find a policeman.
Unknown

People often say, "I do not understand love of God; what is love of God?" It would be more exact to say, "cannot understand love in this world without love of God."
Leo Tolstoy

I can understand the greatness of God but I cannot understand his humility. It becomes so clear in him being in love with each one of us separately and completely. It is as if there is no one but me in the world. He loves me so much. Each one of us can say this with great conviction.
Mother Teresa

I wake up early in the morning to do my dreaming- at four o'clock, 'cause I'm not a big sleeper. I think of God as a farmer throwing out nuggets of wisdom and inspiration first thing. I get out there and pick 'em up before everyone else. In the wee hours, the world is quiet and I can really listen to God.
Dolly Parton

If God's justice could be recognized as just by human comprehension, it would not be divine.
Martin Luther

God's thoughts, His will, His love, His judgements are all man's home. To think His thoughts, to choose His will, to love His loves, to judge His judgements, and thus to know that He is in us, is to be at home.
George MacDonald

Pray remember what I have recommended to you, which is, to think often on God, by day, by night, and even in diversions. He is always near you and with you; leave Him not alone. You would think it rude to leave a friend alone who came to visit you; why then must God be neglected? Do not then forget Him; this is the glorious employment of a Christian; in a word, this is our profession. If we do not know it we must learn it.
Brother Lawrence

Often, in the midst of great problems, we stop short of the real blessing God has for us, which is a fresh vision of who He is.
Anne Graham Lotz

Our dependence upon God ought to be so entire and absolute that we should never think it necessary, in any kind of distress, to have recourse to human consolations.
Thomas a Kempis

The springs of love are in God, not in us.
Oswald Chambers

Every single act of love bears the imprint of God.
Unknown

Care for the next minute is just as foolish as care for the morrow, or for a day in the next thousand years- in neither can we do anything, in both God is doing everything.
George Macdonald

Four stages of growth in Christian maturity...
Love of self for self's sake
Love of God for self's sake
Love of God for God's sake
Love of self for God's sake.
Bernard of Clairvaux

In the soul-searching of our lives, we are to stay quiet so we can hear Him say all that He wants to say to us in our hearts.
Charles Swindoll

There is only one basis for really enjoying life, and that is, to walk in the way in which God leads you. Then you are prepared to find delight in all sorts of wayward incidents....When a man is drifting through life, seeking nothing outside of self-gratification, the world must become increasingly a barren and forbidding wilderness. But it is wonderful how many delights fall to the lot of him who is led by God. For such a one the clasp of a friend's hand, a cool drink in the heat of noon, a merry salutation from a passing traveler, a glimpse of beauty by the road, a quiet resting place at night, are all full of unspeakable pleasure.
Leaves of Gold

If the Father has the kingdom ready for us, he will take care of us on the way.
Andrew Bonar

Whoever does not see God in every place does not see God in any place.
Menachem Mendel

I believe now that God is kind enough not only to work in our present and future, but He's also able to reach into the past and cut out the wasted years and stitch up our lives in such a way that even the scars eventually are removed.
Jeannie C. Riley

Many do not advance in Christian progress because they stick in penances and particular exercises, while they neglect the love of God, which is the end.
Brother Lawrence

Let me entreat you to give up all your efforts after growing, and simply to let yourselves grow. Leave it all to the Husbandman whose care it is, and who alone is able to manage it. No difficulties in your case can baffle Him. If you will only put yourselves absolutely into His hands, and let Him have His own way with you, no dwarfing of your growth in the years that are past, no apparent dryness of your inward springs of life, no crookedness or deformity in your development can in the least mar the perfect work that He will accomplish.
Hannah W. Smith

Set goals so big that unless God helps you, you will be a miserable failure.
Bill Bright

Of all the dispositions and habits which lead to political prosperity, religion and morality are indispensable supports. It is impossible to rightly govern the world without God and the Bible.
George Washington

It was when I was happiest that I longed most. The sweetest thing in all my life has been the longing to find the place where all the beauty came from.
C. S. Lewis

God Almighty would in no way permit evil in His works were He not so omnipotent and good that even out of evil He could work good.
Augustine

This human life in God is from our point of view a particular period in the history of our world (from His birth to His crucifixion). We therefore imagine it is also a period in the history of God's own existence. But God has no history. He is too completely and utterly real to have one. For, of course, to have a history means losing part of your reality (because it has already slipped away into the past), and not yet having another part (because it is still in the future); in fact, having nothing but the tiny little present, which has gone before you can speak about it. God forbid we should think God was like that! Even we may hope not to be always rationed in that way.
C. S. Lewis

May you grow to be as beautiful as God meant you to be when He thought of you first.
George MacDonald

You can tell the size of your God by looking at the size of your worry list. The longer your list, the smaller your God.
Unknown

One of the most powerful concepts, one which is a sure cure for lack of confidence, is the thought that God is with you and helping you. This is one of the simplest teachings in religion, namely, that Almighty God will be your companion, will stand by you, help you, and see you through. No other idea is so powerful in developing self-confidence as this simple belief when practiced. To practice it simply affirm "God is with me; God is helping me; God is guiding me." Spend several minutes each day visualizing his presence. Then practice believing that affirmation.
Norman Vincent Peale

Nothing can separate you from His love, absolutely nothing. God is enough for time, and God is enough for eternity. God is enough!
Hannah Whitall Smith

It is not difficult for me to remember that the little ones need breakfast in the morning, dinner at midday, and something before they go to bed at night. Indeed I could not forget it. And I find it impossible to suppose that our heavenly Father is less tender or mindful than I…I do not believe that our heavenly Father will ever forget His children. I am a very poor father, but it is not my habit to forget my children. God is a very, very good Father. It is not His habit to forget His children.
J. Hudson Taylor

The more we know of God the more unreservedly we will trust him; the greater our progress in theology, the simpler and more childlike will be our faith.
John Gresham Machen

Fire. God of Abraham, God of Isaac, God of Jacob, not of the philosophers and scholars. Certainty. Certainty. Feeling. Joy. Peace.
Blaise Pascal, written on a sheet of paper and sewed into his jacket.

Nature is too thin a screen; the glory of the omnipresent God bursts through everywhere.
Ralph Waldo Emerson

We need to find God, and he can't be found in noise and restlessness. God is the friend of silence. See how nature- trees, flowers, grass- grows in silence; see the stars, the moon, and the sun, see how they move in silence. We need silence to be able to touch souls.
Mother Teresa

He knows God rightly who knows Him everywhere.
Meister Eckhart

Mark it down. God never turns away the honest seeker. Go to God with your questions. You may not find all the answers, but in finding God, you known the One who does.
Max Lucado

Our God, our help in ages past,
Our hope for years to come,
Our shelter from the stormy blast,
And our eternal home.
Isaac Watts

There is a silence in the beauty of the universe which is like a noise when compared with the silence of God.
Simone Weil

Live near to God, and all things will appear little to you in comparison with eternal realities.
Robert Murray M'Cheyne

The Hebrew evening/morning sequence conditions us to the rhythms of grace. We go to sleep, and God begins his work…We wake into a world we didn't make, into a salvation we didn't earn.
Eugene Peterson

The first command in Ephesians 5 tells us to be imitators of God by reflecting the way he loves us. Our love for others flows out of our sense of being deeply loved. Instead of constantly looking for the right person, God tells us to become the right person. Instead of looking for love, God tells us to realize that love has already found us! God loves as no one else ever can.
Chip Ingram

God didn't want me to do more for Him. He wanted me to be more with Him.
Bruce Wilkinson

If God does not enter your kitchen, there is something wrong with your kitchen. If you can't take God into your recreation, there is something wrong with your play. We all believe in the God of the heroic. What we need most these days is the God of the humdrum, the commonplace, the everyday.
Peter Marshall

There are strange ways of serving God;
You sweep a room or turn a sod,
And suddenly, to your surprise,
You hear the whirr of seraphim,
And find you're under God's own eyes
And building palaces for him.
Hermann Hagedorn

Trust God's love. His perfect love. Don't fear he will discover your past. He already has. Don't fear disappointing him in the future. He can show you the chapter in which you will. With perfect knowledge of the past and perfect vision of the future, he loves you perfectly in spite of both.
Max Lucado

Have you ever thought what a wonderful privilege it is that every one each day and each hour of the day has the liberty of asking God to meet him in the inner chamber and to hear what He has to say?
Andrew Murray

If we're not telling God and our family that we love them, we just wasted a day of our life.
Ted Roberts

The phone rang. It was my friend Annette. She had been going through a rough time. "I feel so alone," she said. "I've even lost God and don't know how to find him." I'd felt the same way once, and told Annette how making a gratitude list had helped. "Write down the numbers one through fifty down the side of a piece of paper," I explained. "Then go back and count the things you're thankful for. And remember, it's not the things you're supposed to be thankful for, but the things you really are thankful for." "Okay then, I'll give it a try," Annette said, hanging up. Not long after, the phone rang again. It was Annette. "I found him!" she exclaimed joyfully.
Lora Clark

As well might a gnat seek to drink in the ocean, as a finite creature to comprehend the Eternal God.
Charles Spurgeon

What comes into our minds when we think about God is the most important thing about us.
A. W. Tozer

There's a difference between knowing God and knowing about God. When you truly know God, you have energy to serve him, boldness to share him, and contentment in him.
J. I. Packer

Your God is too small.
J. B. Phillips

A lot of people want to serve God, but only in an advisory capacity.
Unknown

Anyone can count the seeds in an apple, but only God can count the number of apples in a seed.
Robert Schuller

For every step you take toward God, God takes two steps toward you; and if you come to God walking, God comes to you running.
James Martin

We may not know the way God leads… but we know God leads! We do not know the way…but we know the Guide!
Richard Halverson

One with God is a majority.
Billy Graham

With God, even when nothing is happening – something is happening.
Reubin Welch

The remarkable thing about fearing God is that when you fear God you fear nothing else, whereas if you do not fear God you fear everything else.
Oswald Chambers

God is here. Wherever we are, God is here. There is no place, there can be no place, where He is not.
A. W. Tozer

COMPILED BY GREG POTZER

God's in His Heaven – All's right with the world.
Robert Browning

We need never shout across the spaces to an absent God. He is nearer than our own soul, closer than our most secret thoughts.
A. W. Tozer

The universe is one of God's thoughts.
Johann Schiller

The face of Christ does not indeed show us everything, but it shows us the one thing we need to know – the character of God. God is the God who sent Jesus.
P. Carnegie Simpson

A God you understood would be less than yourself.
Flannery O'Connor

The God of the infinite is the God of the infinitesimal.
Blaise Pascal

An infinite God can give all of Himself to each of His children. He does not distribute Himself that each may have a part, but to each one He gives all of Himself as fully as if there were no others.
A. W. Tozer

Only when we are brought to the end of ourselves are we in a position to see more of God than we have seen.
Unknown

Most commit the same mistake with God that they do with their friends: they do all the talking.
Fulton J. Sheen

I looked at God and He looked at me, and we were one forever.
C. H. Spurgeon

At Bethlehem God became what He was not before, but did not cease being what He always was.
Paul Lowenberg

The one use of the Bible is to make us look at Jesus, that through Him we might know His Father and our Father, His God and our God.
George MacDonald

It is God to whom and with whom we travel, and while He is the End of our journey, He is also at every stopping place.
Elisabeth Elliot

Get yourself into the presence of the loving Father. Just place yourself before Him, and look up into His face; think of His love, His wonderful, tender, pitying love.
Andrew Murray

The light of God surrounds me;
The love of God enfolds me;
The power of God protects me;
The presence of God watches over me.
Wherever I am, God is.
James Freeman

God's center is everywhere. His circumference is nowhere.
Thomas Watson

Lord, give me an open heart to find You everywhere, to glimpse the heaven enfolded in a bud, and to experience eternity in the smallest act of love.
Mother Teresa

Whenever the insistence is on the point that God answers prayer, we are off the track. The meaning of prayer is that we get hold of God, not of the answer.
Oswald Chambers

A unit joined to infinity adds nothing to it any more than one foot added to infinite length. The finite is swallowed up by the infinite and becomes pure zero. So are our minds before God.
Blaise Pascal

The Lord has taught us that nobody can know God unless God teaches him.
Irenaeus

One phrase summarizes the horror of hell. "God isn't there."
Max Lucado

The first of all beautiful things is the continual possession of God.
Gregory of Nazianzus

God often visits us, but most of the time we are not at home.
French proverb

The enjoyment of God is the only happiness with which our souls can be satisfied. To go to heaven, fully to enjoy God, is infinitely better than the most pleasant accommodations here. Fathers and mothers, husbands, wives, or children, or the company of earthly friends, are but shadows; but God is the substance. These are but scattered beams, but God is the sun. These are but streams. But God is the ocean.
Jonathan Edwards

Silence is the first language of God; all else is a poor translation.
Thomas Merton

The imagery of the heavens as being two thousand million light-years in diameter is awesome when compared to the tiny earth, but trivial when compared to the imagery of the "hand that measured the heavens."
Fulton J. Sheen

I came from God, and I'm going back to God, and I won't have any gaps of death in the middle of my life.
George Macdonald

In every place where you find the imprint of men's feet there am I.
The Talmud

Live your human task in the liberating certainty that nothing in the world can separate you from God's love for you.
Brakkenstein Community of Blessed Sacrament Fathers

Grant me God and miracles take care of
themselves!
A. W. Tozer

God is as great in minuteness as He is in
magnitude.
Charles Caleb Colton

That which is infinite is as much above
what is great as it is above what is small.
Thus God, being infinitely great, He is as
much above kings as He is above beggars;
He is as much above the highest angel as
He is above the meanest worm.
Jonathan Edwards

God is the most obligated being that there
is. He is obligated by his own nature. He
is infinite in his wisdom; therefore he can
never do anything that is unwise. He is
infinite in his justice; therefore he can
never do anything that is unjust. He is
infinite in his goodness; therefore he can
never do anything that is not good. He is
infinite in his truth; therefore it is
impossible that he should lie.
J. Gresham Machen

What we believe about God is the most
important thing about us.
A. W. Tozer

It is impossible to be too preoccupied
with God, and it is only as we fill our
hearts and minds with him that we
become melted out of our likeness and
moulded into his.
John Blanchard

He is not a God far off, but one who may
be witnessed and possessed.
Margaret Fell Fox

I wish you could convince yourself that
God is often nearer to us, and more
effectually present with us, in sickness
than in health.
Brother Lawrence

May the strength of God pilot us.
May the power of God preserve us.
May the wisdom of God instruct us.
May the hand of God protect us.
May the way of God direct us.
May the shield of God defend us.
May the host of God guard us against the
snares of evil and the temptations of the
world.
May Christ be with us.
Christ before us.
Christ in us.
Christ over us.
May Thy salvation, O Lord, be always
ours this day and forever more.
St. Patrick Breastplate

To see God in everything makes life the
greatest adventure there is.
Unknown

The attributes of God, though intelligible
to us on their surface yet, for the very
reason that they are infinite, transcend our
comprehension, when they are dwelt
upon, when they are followed out, and
can only be received by faith.
John Henry Newman

God is perfect love and perfect wisdom. We do not pray in order to change His Will, but to bring our wills into harmony with His.
William Temple

God can never be outmaneuvered, taken by surprise, or caught at a disadvantage. He is a God who knows no crisis… Before an emergency arises, God in his providence has made adequately and perfectly timed provision to meet it.
J. Oswald Sanders

A God who let us prove his existence would be an idol.
Dietrich Bonhoeffer

Say to yourself, "I am loved by God more than I can either conceive or understand." Let this fill all your soul and all your prayers and never leave you. You will soon see that this is the way to find God.
Henri De Tourville

We are called to an everlasting preoccupation with God.
A. W. Tozer

The eye with which I see God is the same with which God sees me.
Meister Eckhart

God does not answer our desperate questionings; he simply gives us himself.
Francois Mauriac

When you feel unlovable, unworthy and unclean, when you think that no one can heal you:
Remember, Friend,
God Can.
When you think that you are unforgivable for your guilt and your shame:
Remember, Friend,
God Can.
When you think that all is hidden and no one can see within:
Remember, Friend,
God Can.
And when you have reached the bottom and you think that no one can hear:
Remember, my dear Friend,
God Can.
And when you think that no one can love the real person deep inside of you:
Remember, my dear Friend,
God Does.
Unknown

We do not segment our lives, giving some time to God, some to our business or schooling, while keeping parts to ourselves. The idea is to live all of our lives in the presence of God, under the authority of God, and for the honor and glory of God. That is what the Christian life is all about.
R. C. Sproul

Often, in the midst of great problems, we stop short of the real blessing God has for us, which is a fresh vision of who He is.
Anne Graham Lotz

Peace is not the absence of conflict, but the presence of God no matter what the conflict.
Unknown

We have to pray with our eyes on God, not on the difficulties.
Oswald Chambers

If you really want to know God, go to his people. Go to your barber and talk about God. Tell the carpenter about what you're experiencing. Take time to read the lives of the saints. They always knock you off your feet because they tell you the preoccupations you have aren't the ones you should have. Get in touch with those women and men who did crazy things like falling in love with God.
Henri Nouwen

I was regretting the past and fearing the future. Suddenly my Lord was speaking: "My name is I am." He paused. I waited. He continued, "When you live in the past with its mistakes and regrets, it is hard. I am not there. My name is not I WAS. When you live in the future, with its problems and fears, it is hard. I am not there. My name is not I WILL BE. When you live in this moment, it is not hard. I am here. My name is I AM.
Helen Mallicoat

Our desires must not only be offered up to God, but they must all terminate in him, desiring nothing more than God, but still more and more of him.
Matthew Henry

Something of God flows into us from the blue of the sky, the taste of honey, the delicious embrace of water whether cold or hot, and even from sleep itself.
C. S. Lewis

In God, the unknown is friendly.
Unknown

There is a God shaped vacuum in the heart of every man which cannot be filled by any created thing, but only by God, the Creator, made known through Jesus.
Blaise Pascal

A very strange and solemn feeling came over me as I stood there, with no sound but the rustle of the pines, no one near me, and the sun so glorious, as for me alone. It seemed as if I felt God as I never did before, and I prayed in my heart that I might keep that happy sense of nearness in my life.
Louisa May Alcott

There are very few who in their hearts do not believe in God, but what they will not do is give him exclusive right of way.
Dwight L. Moody

With the goodness of God to desire our highest welfare, the wisdom of God to plan it, and the power of God to achieve it, what do we lack?
A. W. Tozer

We should never tire of the thought of God's power.
Donald Grey Barnhouse

Do not ask "what can I do?" but "what can He not do?"
Corrie ten Boom

He is to be seen in the light of a cottage window as well as in the sun or the stars.
Arthur G. Clutton-Brock

The first of all beautiful things is the continual possession of God.
Gregory of Nazianzus

Grace & Mercy

The breathing I did yesterday will not keep me alive today- I must continue to breathe afresh every moment, or my life will cease. In like manner, yesterday's grace and spiritual strength must be renewed, and the Holy Spirit must continue to breathe on my soul from moment to moment in order that I may continue to enjoy Him and to work the works He has assigned me.
Augustus Toplady

The grace of God means something like: Here is your life. You might never have been, but you are because the party wouldn't have been complete without you. Here is the world. Beautiful and terrible things will happen. Don't be afraid. I am with you.
Frederick Buechner

Nothing marks so much the solid advancement of a soul, as the view of one's wretchedness without anxiety and without discouragement.
Francois Fenelon

God's mercies come day by day. They come when we need them- not earlier and not later. God gives us what we need today. If we needed more, He would give us more. When we need something else, He will give that as well. Nothing we truly need will ever be withheld from us. Search your problems, and within them you will discover the well-disguised mercies of God.
Ray Pritchard

Because of God's grace, there is nothing we can do that will make Him love us more than He already does. And there is nothing we can do or have done that will cause Him to love us any less.
Steven Curtis Chapman

There is nothing but God's grace. We walk upon it; we breathe it; we live and die by it; it makes the nails and axles of the universe.
Robert Louis Stevenson

Ah! the bridge of grace will bear your weight, brother. Thousands of big sinners have gone across that bridge, yea, tens of thousands have gone over it. I can hear their trampings now as they traverse the great arches of the bridge of salvation. They come by their thousands, by their myriads; e'er since the day when Christ first entered into His glory, they come, and yet never a stone has sprung in that mighty bridge. Some have been the chief of sinners, and some have come at the very last of their days, but the arch has never yielded beneath their weight. I will go with them trusting to the same support; it will bear me over as it has borne them.
C. H. Spurgeon

Grace is not simply leniency when we have sinned. Grace is the enabling gift of God not to sin. Grace is power, not just pardon. Therefore the effort we make to obey God is not an effort done in our own strength, but in the strength which God supplies.
John Piper

The Hebrew evening/morning sequence conditions us to the rhythms of grace. We go to sleep, and God begins his work…We wake into a world we didn't make, into a salvation we didn't earn.
Eugene Peterson

God appoints our graces to be nurses to other men's weakness.
Henry Ward Beecher

When I speak of a person growing in grace, I mean simply this- that his sense of sin is becoming deeper, his faith stronger, his hope brighter, his love more extensive, and his spiritual mindedness more marked.
J. C. Ryle

Just think: Every promise God has ever made finds its fulfillment in Jesus. God doesn't just give us grace; he gives us Jesus, the Lord of grace. If it's peace, it's only found in Jesus, the Prince of Peace. Even life itself is found in the Resurrection and the Life. Christianity isn't all that complicated…it's Jesus.
Joni Eareckson Tada

Grace means that God already loves us as much as an infinite God can possibly love.
Philip Yancey

God has not promised skies always blue, flower-strewn pathways all our lives through;
God has not promised sun without rain, joy without sorrow, peace without pain.
But God has promised strength for the day,
rest for the labor, light for the way, grace for the trials, help from above, unfailing sympathy, undying love.
Annie Johnson Flint

Have confidence in God's mercy, for when you think He is a long way from you, He is often quite near.
Thomas Kempis

The secret of life is that all we have and are is a gift of grace to be shared.
Lloyd John Ogilvie

I am not what I ought to be,
I am not what I wish to be,
I am not what I hope to be;
but, by the grace of God,
I am not what I was.
John Newton

To accept grace is to admit failure, a step we are hesitant to take. We opt to impress God with how good we are rather than confessing how great he is.
Max Lucado

Grace comes not to take away a man's affections, but to take them up.
William Fenner

What I have today I have because of His mercy. I did not earn it. I do not deserve it. I did not pay for it. I have no rights to it. I cannot keep it except for one thing- God's mercy.
David Crosby

God's mercy is so great that you may sooner drain the sea of its water, or deprive the sun of its light, or make space too narrow, than diminish the great mercy of God.
Charles Spurgeon

The God of Christianity never claims to be fair. He goes beyond fair. The Bible teaches that he decided not to give us what we deserve- that's mercy. In addition, God decided to give us exactly what we didn't deserve- we call that grace.
Andy Stanley

God appoints our graces to be nurses to other men's weaknesses.
Henry Ward Beecher

The word grace emphasizes at one and the same time the helpless poverty of man and the limitless kindness of God.
William Barclay

Grace means primarily the free, forgiving love of God in Christ to sinners and the operation of that love in the lives of Christians.
A. M. Hunter

Grace is love that cares and stoops and rescues.
John R. W. Stott

Beauty and grace are performed whether or not we will or sense them. The least we can do is try to be there.
Annie Dillard

All men who live with any degree of serenity live by some assurance of grace.
Reinhold Niebuhr

A man can no more take in a supply of grace for the future than he can eat enough for the next six months or take sufficient air into his lungs at one time to sustain life for a week. We must draw upon God's boundless store of grace from day to day as we need it.
Dwight L. Moody

Between here and heaven, every minute that the Christian lives will be a minute of grace.
C. H. Spurgeon

None so empty of grace as he that thinks he is full.
Thomas Watson

Guidance

As the minister stepped up to the pulpit he discovered to his chagrin that he had forgotten his sermon notes. As it was too late to send someone for them, he turned to the congregation and said, by way of apology, that this morning he should have to depend upon the Lord for what he might say, but that for the evening service, he would be better prepared.
Unknown

It is easy to follow a person's footprints if we walk close behind him, but if we walk some distance back, we might fail to see them as clearly. Similarly, if we follow close after the Lord, we would easily see the footsteps along the way, but if we try to follow afar off, we would find it difficult to know the path of His will.
Andrew Bonar

No one has any more time than you have. It is the discipline and stewardship of your time that is important. The management of time is the management of self; therefore if you manage time with God, He will be begin to manage you.
Jill Briscoe

A priest ought to be in no place where his Master would not go, nor employed in anything which his Master would not do.
Henry Edward Manning

People who make decisions based merely on what seems most advisable to them will inevitably choose something inferior to God's best. Jesus, the ultimate model for the Christian life, did not rely on His own best thinking, but depended completely on His heavenly Father for wisdom in everything.
Henry Blackaby

The Will of God will never take you to where the Grace of God will not protect you.
Unknown

Be thou a bright flame before me,
Be thou a guiding star above me,
Be thou a smooth path below me,
And be a kindly Shepherd behind me,
Today, tonight and for ever.
Alexander Carmichael

My Lord, God, I have no idea where I am going. I do not see the road ahead of me. I cannot know for certain where it will end. Nor do I really know myself, and the fact that I think I am following Your will does not mean that I am actually doing so. But I believe that the desire to please You does in fact please you. And I hope that I have that desire in all that I am doing. And I know that if I do this, You will lead me by the right road though I may know nothing about it. Therefore will I trust you always though I may seem to be lost and in the shadow of death, I will not fear, for You are ever with me and You will never leave me to face my perils alone.
Thomas Merton

We regret losing a purse full of money, but a good thought which has come to us, which we've heard or read, a thought which we should have remembered and applied to our life, which could have improved the world- we lose this thought and promptly forget about it, and we do not regret it, though it is more precious than millions.
Leo Tolstoy

I am eighty-five years old and I am so thankful that I am able to continue the work I love. God has a plan for every life. All of us are called to be the light of the world wherever He places us. We are within His perfect guidance when we trust and obey Him. A tool does not decide where to work. It is the Master who decides where it is to be used.
Corrie ten Boom

When you meet a man or woman who puts Jesus Christ first, knit that one to your soul.
Oswald Chambers

When we allow the Holy Spirit to guide us, He will concern Himself with how we use our time and spend our money; with honesty and moral integrity and Christlike quality of character; with what is happening to our children; with the health of our relationship with other people and with our God. If our need is severe enough, the Holy Spirit will turn our lives upside down.
Catherine Marshall

If you go to Him to be guided, He will guide you, but He will not comfort your distrust or half-trust of Him by showing you the chart of all His purposes concerning you. He will show you only into a way where, if you go cheerfully and trustfully forward, He will show you on still farther.
Horace Bushnell

In the soul-searching of our lives, we are to stay quiet so we can hear Him say all that He wants to say to us in our hearts.
Charles Swindoll

Our salvation includes more than pardon from sin, deliverance from hell and a ticket to heaven. It includes all that we shall need on our journey.
Vance Havner

God does not have to come and tell me what I must do for Him, He brings me into a relationship with Himself where I hear His call and understand what He wants me to do, and I do it out of sheer love to Him… When people say they have had a call to foreign service, or to any particular sphere of work, they mean that their relationship to God has enabled them to realize what they can do for God.
Oswald Chambers

There is only one basis for really enjoying life, and that is, to walk in the way in which God leads you. Then you are prepared to find delight in all sorts of wayward incidents….When a man is drifting through life, seeking nothing outside of self-gratification, the world must become increasingly a barren and forbidding wilderness. But it is wonderful how many delights fall to the lot of him who is led by God. For such a one the clasp of a friend's hand, a cool drink in the heat of noon, a merry salutation from a passing traveler, a glimpse of beauty by the road, a quiet resting place at night, are all full of unspeakable pleasure.
Leaves of Gold

But whatever you do, find the God-centered, Christ-exalting, Bible-saturated passion of your life, and find your way to say it and live for it and die for it. And you will make a difference that lasts. You will not waste your life.
John Piper

Those who put themselves in His hands will become perfect, as He is perfect-perfect in love, wisdom, joy, beauty, health, and immortality. The change will not be completed in this life, for death is an important part of the treatment. How far the change will have gone before death in any particular Christian is uncertain.
C. S. Lewis

Let me entreat you to give up all your efforts after growing, and simply to let yourselves grow. Leave it all to the Husbandman whose care it is, and who alone is able to manage it. No difficulties in your case can baffle Him. If you will only put yourselves absolutely into His hands, and let Him have His own way with you, no dwarfing of your growth in the years that are past, no apparent dryness of your inward springs of life, no crookedness or deformity in your development can in the least mar the perfect work that He will accomplish.
Hannah W. Smith

Of all the dispositions and habits which lead to political prosperity, religion and morality are indispensable supports. It is impossible to rightly govern the world without God and the Bible.
George Washington

The place God calls you to is the place where your deep gladness and the world's deep hunger meet.
Frederick Buechner

One of the most powerful concepts, one which is a sure cure for lack of confidence, is the thought that God is with you and helping you. This is one of the simplest teachings in religion, namely, that Almighty God will be your companion, will stand by you, help you, and see you through. No other idea is so powerful in developing self-confidence as this simple belief when practiced. To practice it simply affirm "God is with me; God is helping me; God is guiding me." Spend several minutes each day visualizing his presence. Then practice believing that affirmation.
Norman Vincent Peale

I can say from experience that 95% of knowing the will of God consists in being prepared to do it before you know what it is.
Donald Grey Barnhouse

"Be yourself" is about the worst advice you could give some people.
Unknown

Mark it down. God never turns away the honest seeker. Go to God with your questions. You may not find all the answers, but in finding God, you known the One who does.
Max Lucado

The moment you wake up each morning, all your wishes and hopes for the day rush at you like wild animals. And the first job each morning consists in shoving it all back; in listening to that other voice, taking that other point of view, letting that other, larger, stronger, quieter life coming flowing in.
C. S. Lewis

How do you celebrate the everyday moment? Learn from children, puppies and other experts.
Harvey Rich

Always ask, "What would Jesus do?"
Unknown

Each day just ask Jesus to go with you and listen to his counsel. Ask for discernment and wisdom and The God of all will grant you these things for he has promised to answer whatever you ask if you ask for something which is in his will for you. The only time it won't go well with you, if the Lord wants you somewhere else.
Unknown

In some ways I find guidance, if anything, gets harder rather than easier the longer I am a Christian. Perhaps God allows this so that we have to go on relying on him and not on ourselves.
Dennis Watson

110

Faith is self-surrender to the great Physician, a leaving of our case in his hands. But it is also the taking of his prescriptions and the active following of his directions.
Augustus Strong

The essential truth is that discernment is a function of a loving, personal relationship to the Lord. It can normally be only as deep and as solid as that relationship itself. The true discerner must be a praying, loving person.
Unknown

When Jesus is truly our Lord, he directs our lives and we gladly obey him. Indeed, we bring every part of our lives under his lordship- our home and family, our sexuality and marriage, our job or unemployment, our money and possessions, our ambitions and recreations.
John Stott

Heaven

We all long for heaven where God is, but we have it in our power to be in heaven with Him right now- to be happy with Him at this very moment. But being happy with Him now means loving like He loves, helping like He helps, giving as He gives, serving as He serves, rescuing as He rescues, being with Him twenty-four hours a day- touching Him in His distressing disguise.
Mother Teresa

The world rings changes, it is never constant but in its disappointments. The world is but a great inn, where we are to stay a night or two, and be gone; what madness is it so to set our heart upon our inn, as to forget our home?
Thomas Watson

To pretend to describe the excellence, the greatness of duration of the happiness of heaven by the most artful composition of words would be but to darken and cloud it; to talk of raptures and ecstasies, joy and singing, is but to set forth very low shadows of the reality.
Jonathan Edwards

How far away is heaven? It is not so far as some imagine. It wasn't very far for Daniel. It was not so far off that Elijah's prayer, and those of others could not be heard there. Men full of the Spirit can look right into heaven.
Dwight L. Moody

What kind of place is heaven? First, heaven is home. The Bible takes the word "home," with all its tender associations and with all of its sacred memories and tells us that heaven is home. Second, heaven is a home which is permanent. We have the promise of a home where Christ's followers will remain forever. Third, the Bible teaches that heaven is a home which is beautiful beyond every imagination. Heaven could not help but be so, because God is a God of beauty. Fourth, the Bible teaches that heaven will be a home which is happy, because there will be nothing to make it sad. In heaven, families and friends will be reunited. God's house will be a happy home because Christ will be there. He will be the center of heaven. To Him all hearts will turn, and upon Him as eyes will rest.
Billy Graham

If you read history you will find that the Christians who did most for the present world were just those who thought most of the next. The Apostles themselves, who set on foot the conversion of the Roman Empire, the great men who built up the Middle Ages, the English Evangelicals who abolished the slave trade, all left their mark on earth, precisely because their minds were occupied with heaven. It is since Christians have largely ceased to think of the other world that they have become so ineffective in this. Aim at heaven and you will get earth thrown in; aim at earth and you will get neither.
C. S. Lewis

God is at home. We are in the far country.
Meister Eckhart

Between us and heaven or hell there is only life, which is the frailest thing in the world.
Blaise Pascal

If nothing in this world satisfies me, perhaps it is because I was made for another world.
C. S. Lewis

In Christ Jesus heaven meets earth and earth ascends to heaven.
Henry Law

God's in His Heaven – All's right with the world.
Robert Browning

Build your nest in no tree here…for the Lord of the forest has condemned the whole woods to be demolished.
Samuel Rutherford

Afflictions are the steps to heaven.
Elizabeth Seton

If you are a Christian, you are not a citizen of this world trying to get to heaven; you are a citizen of heaven making your way through this world.
Vance Havner

All this and heaven too.
Matthew Henry

I think earth, if chosen instead of Heaven, will turn out to have been, all along, only a region in Hell; and earth, if put second to Heaven, to have been from the beginning a part of Heaven itself.
C. S. Lewis

Heaven is full of answers to prayers for which no one ever bothered to ask.
Billy Graham

Our little time of suffering is not worthy of our first night's welcome home to Heaven.
Samuel Rutherford

The Christian life is a pilgrimage from earth to heaven, and our task is to take as many as possible with us as we make this journey.
Warren Wiersbe

Think-
Of stepping on shore and finding it
Heaven;
Of taking hold of a hand and finding it
God's hand;
Of breathing a new air and finding it
celestial air;
Of feeling invigorated and finding it
immortality;
Of passing from storm and tempest to an
unbroken calm;
Of waking up, and finding it Home!
Robert E. Selle

Some read the Bible to learn, and some
read the Bible to hear from heaven.
Andrew Murray

Lord, give me an open heart to find You
everywhere, to glimpse the heaven
enfolded in a bud, and to experience
eternity in the smallest act of love.
Mother Teresa

The imagery of the heavens as being two
thousand million light-years in diameter is
awesome when compared to the tiny
earth, but trivial when compared to the
imagery of the "hand that measured the
heavens."
Fulton J. Sheen

We cannot resist the conviction that this
world is for us only the porch of another
and more magnificent temple of the
Creator's majesty.
Frederick William Faber

Three-hundred million years from now,
the only thing that will matter is whether
you're in Heaven or in Hell.
Mark Cahill

Home interprets heaven;
Home is heaven for beginners.
Charles Henry Parkhurst

From heaven even the most miserable life
will look like one bad night at an
inconvenient hotel.
Teresa of Avila

Our Father refreshes us on the journey
with some pleasant inns, but will not
encourage us to mistake them for home.
C. S. Lewis

If we look around us, a moment can seem
a long time, but when we lift up our
hearts heavenwards, a thousand years
begin to be like a moment.
John Calvin

We talk about heaven being so far away. It
is within speaking distance to those who
belong there. Heaven is a prepared place
for a prepared people.
Dwight Moody

Every Christian is born great because he
is born for heaven.
Jean Baptiste Massillon

The hope of heaven under troubles is like
wind and sails to the soul.
Samuel Rutherford

Aim at heaven and you will get earth thrown in. Aim at earth and you will get neither.
C. S. Lewis

We are as near to heaven as we are far from self, and far from the love of a sinful world.
Samuel Rutherford

Some days, it is enough encouragement just to watch the clouds break up and disappear, leaving behind a blue patch of sky and bright sunshine that is so warm upon my face. It's a glimpse of divinity; a kiss from heaven.
Unknown

Holy Spirit

As the minister stepped up to the pulpit he discovered to his chagrin that he had forgotten his sermon notes. As it was too late to send someone for them, he turned to the congregation and said, by way of apology, that this morning he should have to depend upon the Lord for what he might say, but that for the evening service, he would be better prepared.
Unknown

The breathing I did yesterday will not keep me alive today- I must continue to breathe afresh every moment, or my life will cease. In like manner, yesterday's grace and spiritual strength must be renewed, and the Holy Spirit must continue to breathe on my soul from moment to moment in order that I may continue to enjoy Him and to work the works He has assigned me.
Augustus Toplady

How hard is it for God to get your attention? Do you regularly practice turning aside in your day? That is, taking a moment to listen to God- because God, through the Holy Spirit, really is speaking, because we know, every place is filled with the presence of God. There is not an inch of space, not a moment of time, that God does not inhabit.
John Ortberg

Where the soul is full of peace and joy, outward surroundings and circumstances are of comparatively little account.
Hannah Witall Smith

Will God ever ask you to do something you are not able to do? The answer is yes- all the time! It must be that way, for God's glory and kingdom. If we function according to our ability alone, we get the glory; if we function according to the power of the Spirit within us, God gets the glory. He wants to reveal Himself to a watching world.
Henry Blackaby

He who has the Holy Spirit in his heart and the Scripture in his hands has all he needs.
Alexander MacLaren

The Holy Spirit is the One who is poured out upon you like a healing balm- to sooth, to calm, and to comfort. He is the One who renews your strength, revives your spirit, refills your cup, restores your strength, and refreshes your spirit.
Roy Lessin

When we allow the Holy Spirit to guide us, He will concern Himself with how we use our time and spend our money; with honesty and moral integrity and Christlike quality of character; with what is happening to our children; with the health of our relationship with other people and with our God. If our need is severe enough, the Holy Spirit will turn our lives upside down.
Catherine Marshall

How far away is heaven? It is not so far as some imagine. It wasn't very far for Daniel. It was not so far off that Elijah's prayer, and those of others could not be heard there. Men full of the Spirit can look right into heaven.
Dwight L. Moody

Confusion and impotence are the inevitable results when the wisdom and resources of the world are substituted for the presence and power of the Spirit.
Samuel Chadwick

It is remarkable that the Holy Spirit has given us very few deathbed scenes in the book of God. We have very few in the Old Testament, fewer still in the New. And I take it that the reason may be, because the Holy Ghost would have us to take more account of how we live than how we die, for life is the main business. He who learns to die daily while he lives will find it no difficulty to breathe out his soul for the last time into the hands of his faithful Creator.
Charles Spurgeon

I can usually sense that a leading is from the Holy Spirit when it calls me to humble myself, serve somebody, encourage somebody or give something away. Very rarely will the evil one lead us to do those kinds of things.
Bill Hybels

God permits troubles to beset His children, but He also refreshes them. He grants them respite when the heart is still and the soul joyous, and you will agree with me that such moments of the secret joy of the Spirit are far more precious than the highest pleasures this world can offer.
The Lutheran Witness

You may have no family, no food, no clothes, no future, no spouse, no health, or no children, yet be rich beyond your wildest dreams because you have the Holy Spirit in your life.
Jill Briscoe

The gift of the Holy Spirit closes the gap between the life of God and ours. When we allow the love of God to move in us we can no longer distinguish ours and his; he becomes us, he lives us. It is the first fruits of the Spirit, the beginning of our being made divine.
Austin Farrer

Pulling weeds and planting seeds. That's the story of life. We are individual lots on which either weeds of selfishness or fruit of the Holy Spirit grows and flourishes.
Dennis and Barbara Rainey

Speak to Him, thou, for He hears, and
Spirit with Spirit can meet-
Closer is He than breathing, and nearer
than hands and feet.
Alfred Tennyson

Do not pray for more of the Holy Spirit.
The Holy Spirit is the Third Person of the
Trinity and is not in pieces. Every child of
God has all of Him, but does He have all
of us?
Julia Kellersberger

The gift of the Holy Ghost closes the last
gap between the life of God and ours.
When we allow the love of God to move
in us, we can no longer distinguish ours
and his; he becomes us, he lives us. It is
the first fruits of the spirit, the beginning
of our being made divine.
Austin Farrer

The service of the Holy Spirit is that He
helps us to distinguish pleasure from
happiness and develop real joy. There are
many experiences which give us
temporary pleasure but do not add up to
abiding satisfaction. Their thrills pass
quickly, and sometimes leave a trail of
regret and remorse. Some of our sense
pleasures are like lightning flashes, while
true joy is like the sunlight.
Ralph Sockman

Trying to do the Lord's work in your own
strength is the most confusing,
exhausting, and tedious of all work. But
when you are filled with the Holy Spirit,
then the ministry of Jesus just flows out
of you.
Corrie Ten Boom

We can be assured that each step deeper
into the Lord's Presence will reveal areas
in our hearts which need to be cleansed.
Do not be afraid. When the Spirit shows
you areas of sin, it is not to condemn you,
but to cleanse you.
Francis Frangipane

Lord, the Scripture says: "There is a time
for silence and a time for speech."
Saviour, teach me the silence of humility,
the silence of wisdom, the silence of love,
the silence of perfection, the silence that
speaks without words, the silence of faith.
Lord, teach me to silence my own heart
that I may listen to the gentle movement
of the Holy Spirit within me and sense
the depths which are of God.
Frankfurt prayer (Sixteenth century)

A very strange and solemn feeling came
over me as I stood there, with no sound
but the rustle of the pines, no one near
me, and the sun so glorious, as for me
alone. It seemed as if I felt God as I never
did before, and I prayed in my heart that I
might keep that happy sense of nearness
in my life.
Louisa May Alcott

A group of clergymen were discussing whether or not they ought to invite Dwight L. Moody to their city. The success of the famed evangelist was brought to the attention of the men. One unimpressed minister commented, "Does Mr. Moody have a monopoly on the holy Ghost?" Another man quietly replied, "No, but the Holy Ghost seems to have a monopoly on Mr. Moody."
Unknown

Honesty

We are the most appealing to others, and happiest within, when we are completely ourselves.
Luci Swindoll

Today I'm giving two examinations. One in trigonometry and the other in honesty. I hope you will pass them both. If you must fail one, fail trigonometry. There are many good people in the world who can't pass trig, but there are no good people in the world who cannot pass a test of honesty.
What Dr. Madison Sarratt used to tell his class at Vanderbilt University each year.

Love and trust, in the space between what's said and what's heard in our life, can make all the difference in the world.
Fred Rogers

Each of us leads a secret thought life, an invisible life known only to us- it is not known to others. This secret life is usually very different from the visible you- the you that is known by others. Yet it is the real you, the you that is known by our God.
Patrick Morley

An honest man with an open Bible and a pad and pencil is sure to find out what is wrong with him very quickly.
A. W. Tozer

To be really truthful, we have to do more than stop lying. Really, most of the work is positively learning how to speak the whole truth in love.
Tim Stafford

Honesty is like a flu shot. It may give you a short, sharp pain, but it keeps you healthier in the long run.
Willard Harley Jr.

Truthfulness is much more than the absence of lies. It is genuine communication of minds and hearts. Real truthfulness reflects the character of God, who is always exactly what He says he is, and who speaks painful but joyful truth, never any small talk to our hearts. Think of Jesus: ever kind, but relentlessly truthful.
Tim Stafford

Honesty, or dishonesty, is shown in every little act of life.
Mabel Hale

Hope

My children, the three acts of faith, hope, and charity contain all the happiness of man upon the earth.
John Vianney

Each dawn holds a new hope for a new plan, making the start of each day the start of a new life.
Gina Blair

To love means loving the unlovable. To forgive means pardoning the unpardonable. Faith means believing the unbelievable. Hope means hoping when everything seems hopeless.
Gilbert Keith Chesterton

The hope we have in Christ is an absolute certainty. We can be sure that the place Christ is preparing for us will be ready when we arrive, because with Him nothing is left to chance. Everything He promised He will deliver.
Billy Graham

When God is about to do something great, he starts with a difficulty. When he is about to do something truly magnificent, he starts with an impossibility.
Armin Gesswein

If you are a stranger to prayer, you are a stranger to the greatest source of power known to human beings.
Billy Sunday

Jesus Christ came into my prison cell last night, and every stone flashed like a ruby.
Samuel Rutherford

If you do not hope, you will not find what is beyond your hopes.
Clement of Alexandria

The future is as bright as the promises of God.
Adoniram Judson

Man can live about forty days without food, about three days without water, about eight minutes without air…but only for one second without hope.
Hal Lindsey

Hope is the struggle of the soul, breaking loose from what is perishable, and attesting her eternity.
Herman Melville

The hope of heaven under troubles is like wind and sails to the soul.
Samuel Rutherford

Hope is not wishful thinking, nor fanciful imagination. Hope is the realism of the man of faith who knows that there is a line of meaningful development from the past, through the present, into the future. Hopelessness is the true condition of hell.
Joshua Haberman

Humor & Laughter

Laugh, if you are wise.
Latin proverb

Laughter is an instant vacation. Giving is a two-week cruise- with pay.
Bob Hope

A keen sense of humor helps us to overlook the unbecoming, understand the unconventional, tolerate the unpleasant, overcome the unexpected, and outlast the unbearable.
Billy Graham

As you're rushing through life, take time to stop a moment, look into people's eyes, say something kind, and try to make them laugh!
Barbara Johnson

True humor springs not more from the head than from the heart; it is not contempt, its essence is love; it issues not in laughter, but in still smiles, which lie far deeper. It is a sort of inverse sublimity, exalting, as it were, into our affections what is below us, while sublimity draws down into our affections what is above us.
Thomas Carlyle

The thought of Jesus Christ laughing probably is not thought of too much, but it should be. Amidst the trials of this World, in Him we have ultimate joy, and peace. When He walked upon this Earth, it is written that He cried, more than once, and though scriptures do not depict the Christ laughing, it is safe to say He did, for He had all human characteristics…His strength was in what He did with them while He walked among us on this Earth. Once I was told of a little boy about 5 or 6 who was dying, I believe it was of cancer. He was put down to rest and he went to sleep. The end was not thought to be very far away, and while he was sleeping, he sort of put his arms out, and rolled a little onto one side, then drew his knees up somewhat and started laughing and tilted his head back a little…he continued to laugh for a short time, then he just went limp, and he died. His mother declares that Jesus Christ came and picked him up in His arms, and carried him to Heaven. She believes that he was being tickled on the tummy and made him laugh while he was being picked up. That could very well be true…we have no way of knowing how God handles things in the realm that we have yet to step. But we know we are safe with Him   Jesus Christ gives us His Peace,
Joyce Vaughan Byars

Laughter has no foreign accent.
Paul Lowney

Those who do not know how to weep
with their whole heart don't know how to
laugh either.
Golda Meir

On the average, children laugh 300 times
a day, adults..only 15!
Joann Bruso

Laughter is the shortest distance between
two people.
Victor Borge

Jesus Christ

If Christ were coming again tomorrow, I would plant a tree today.
Martin Luther

Jesus Christ is the center of everything,
And he that does not know Him
Knows nothing of nature,
And nothing of himself.
Blaise Pascal

The love of Christ becomes the mightiest force in the world to the man who is yielded to it.
E. W. Kenyon

And he departed from our sight that we might return to our heart, and there find Him. For He departed, and behold, He is here.
Augustine

How different is the epitaph on the tomb of Jesus! It is neither written in gold nor cut in stone. It is spoken by the mouth of an angel and is the exact reverse of what is put on all other tombs: "He is not here; for he is risen, as he said." (Matthew 28:6)
Billy Graham

Dost thou understand me, sinful soul? He wrestled with justice, that thou mightest have rest; He wept and mourned, that thou mightest laugh and rejoice; He was betrayed, that thou mightest go free; was apprehended, that thou mightest escape; He was condemned, that thou mightest be justified; and was killed, that thou mightest live; He wore a crown of thorns, that thou mightest wear a crown of glory; and was nailed to the cross, with His arms wide open, to show with what freeness all His merits shall be bestowed on the coming soul; and how heartily He will receive it into His bosom?
John Bunyan

A very learned man once said to a little child who believed in the Lord Jesus, "My poor little girl, you don't know whom you believe in. There have been many christs. In which of them do you believe?" "I know which one I believe in," replied the child. "I believe in the Christ who rose from the dead."
Unknown

I like your Christ, I do not like your Christians. Your Christians are so unlike your Christ.
Mahatma Gandhi

If we demonstrate unconditional love, daily prayer, persistent faith, and adherence to God's laws, we give our children a gift. If we teach them that good deeds and kind words are expressions of the Spirit, we are on track toward living more like Jesus.
Jane Jarrell

When you meet a man or woman who puts Jesus Christ first, knit that one to your soul.
Oswald Chambers

Jesus is the yes to every promise of God.
William Barclay

Spread abroad the name of Jesus in humility and with a meek heart; show him your feebleness, and he will become your strength.
Thomas Merton

The destiny of every human being depends on his relationship to Jesus Christ. It is not on his relationship to life, or on his service or his usefulness, but simply and a solely on his relationship to Jesus Christ.
Oswald Chambers

I do not know of a denomination or local church in existence that has as its goal to teach its people to do everything Jesus said.
Dallas Willard

If you look at the world, you'll be distressed.
If you look within, you'll be depressed.
But if you look at Christ, you'll be at rest.
Corrie Ten Boom

Happiness depends on happenings, but joy depends on Jesus.
Unknown

What kind of place is heaven? First, heaven is home. The Bible takes the word "home," with all its tender associations and with all of its sacred memories and tells us that heaven is home. Second, heaven is a home which is permanent. We have the promise of a home where Christ's followers will remain forever. Third, the Bible teaches that heaven is a home which is beautiful beyond every imagination. Heaven could not help but be so, because God is a God of beauty. Fourth, the Bible teaches that heaven will be a home which is happy, because there will be nothing to make it sad. In heaven, families and friends will be reunited. God's house will be a happy home because Christ will be there. He will be the center of heaven. To Him all hearts will turn, and upon Him as eyes will rest.
Billy Graham

The holy child is waiting to be born in every instant, not just once a year.
Marianne Williamson

God grant you the light in Christmas, which is faith; the warmth of Christmas, which is love; the radiance of Christmas, which is purity.
God grant you the righteousness of Christmas, which is justice; the belief in Christmas, which is truth; the all of Christmas, which is Christ.
Wilda English

The time draws near the birth of Christ:
The moon is hid; the night is still;
The Christmas bells from hill to hill
Answer each other in the mist.
Alfred Tennyson

The blessedness of Christmas is all wrapped up in the person of Jesus. Our relationship determines the measure of the blessing.
Unknown

For Jesus, prayer was a vital element in making God's power available to people in need.
Jim Reapsome

To follow Jesus doesn't remove us from the stuff of life. It is not resolution. It is tension and journey.
David Crowder

The problem with spending your life climbing up the ladder is that you will go right past Jesus, for he's coming down.
John Ortberg

To become Christ-like is the only thing in the whole world worth caring for, the thing before which every ambition of man is folly and all lower achievement vain.
Henry Drummond

To ascertain where you really are with the Lord, recall what saddened you the past month. Was it the realization that you do not love Jesus enough? That you did not seek his face in prayer often enough? That you did not care for his people enough? Or did you get depressed over a lack of respect, criticism from an authority figure, your finances, a lack of friends, fears about the future, or your bulging waistline?
Brennan Manning

Much of the history of Christianity has been devoted to domesticating Jesus- to reducing that elusive, enigmatic, paradoxical person to dimensions we can comprehend, understand, and convert to our own purposes. So far it hasn't worked.
Andrew Greeley

When Christ reveals himself there is satisfaction in the slenderest portion, and without Christ there is emptiness in the greatest fullness.
Alexander Grosse

The best way to prepare for the coming of Christ is never to forget the presence of Christ.
William Barclay

Just think: Every promise God has ever made finds its fulfillment in Jesus. God doesn't just give us grace; he gives us Jesus, the Lord of grace. If it's peace, it's only found in Jesus, the Prince of Peace. Even life itself is found in the Resurrection and the Life. Christianity isn't all that complicated…it's Jesus.
Joni Eareckson Tada

Christ has made of death a narrow starlit strip between the companionships of yesterday and the reunions of tomorrow.
William Jennings Bryan

I can say that I never knew what joy was like until I gave up pursuing happiness, or cared to live until I chose to die. For these two discoveries I am beholden to Jesus.
Malcolm Muggeridge

Vital Christian experience comes from knowing Jesus as the living Saviour. Two irreligious young men were discussing the resurrection, telling each other why it was impossible for them to accept the doctrine. Then a deacon of a near-by church walked by, and in a joking way one of the young fellows called to him, "Say, Deacon, tell us why you believe that Jesus rose again." "Well," he answered, "one reason is that I was talking with Him for half an hour this very morning." We may all experience proof of the resurrection of Christ in the acknowledging of His living presence in our lives. No one who knows Jesus personally questions the resurrection.
Watchman-Examiner

God will answer all our questions in one way and one way only- namely, by showing us more of his Son.
Watchman Nee

I need Christ, not something that resembles Him.
C. S. Lewis

The older we get in the Lord, the simpler life becomes as we realize it's all about Jesus.
Jon Courson

When Christ came into my life, I came about like a well-handled ship.
Robert Louis Stevenson

Christ has turned all our sunsets into dawns.
Clement of Alexandria

One drop of Christ's blood is worth more than heaven and earth.
Martin Luther

In Christ Jesus heaven meets earth and earth ascends to heaven.
Henry Law

If Christ lives in us, controlling our personalities, we will leave glorious marks on the lives we touch. Not because of our lovely characters, but because of his.
Eugenia Price

We need Jesus every moment of every day. To say anything else is ludicrous.
Tommy Tenney

Apart from Christ we know neither what our life nor our death is; we do not know what God is nor what we ourselves are.
Blaise Pascal

Jesus Christ came into my prison cell last night, and every stone flashed like a ruby.
Samuel Rutherford

The face of Christ does not indeed show us everything, but it shows us the one thing we need to know – the character of God. God is the God who sent Jesus.
P. Carnegie Simpson

God's loving initiative to step into time and space to restore us to Himself is still a cause for wonder and praise.
Gloria Gaither

He so loved us that, for our sake,
He was made man in time,
although through him all times were made.
He was made man, who made man.
He was created of a mother whom he created.
He was carried by hands that he formed.
He cried in the manger in wordless infancy, he the Word,
without whom all human eloquence is mute.
Augustine

At Bethlehem God became what He was not before, but did not cease being what He always was.
Paul Lowenberg

Jesus…
He came not to a throne,
but to a manger.
He lived not as a king,
but as a servant.
He chose not an earthly kingdom,
but a cross.
He gave not just a little,
but everything.
Holley Gerth

Many will say that Jesus was a good moral teacher. Let's be realistic. How could he be a great moral teacher and knowingly mislead people at the most important point of his teaching- his own identity?
Josh McDowell

Being a Christian is more than just an instantaneous conversion; it is like a daily process whereby you grow to be more and more like Christ.
Billy Graham

The one use of the Bible is to make us look at Jesus, that through Him we might know His Father and our Father, His God and our God.
George MacDonald

When I met Christ, I felt that I had swallowed sunshine.
E. Stanley Jones

Have fun; love Jesus; and tell others about Him.
Tim Tebow

There is not a single thing that Jesus cannot change, control, and conquer because He is the living Lord.
Franklin Graham

Is it a small thing in your eyes to be loved by God- to be the son, the spouse, the love, the delight of the King of glory? Christian, believe this, and think about it: you will be eternally embraced in the arms of the love which was from everlasting, and will extend to everlasting- of the love which brought the Son of God's love from heaven to earth, from earth to the cross, from the cross to the grave, from the grave to glory- that love which was weary, hungry, tempted, scorned, scourged, buffered, spat upon, crucified, pierced- which fasted, prayed, taught, healed, wept, sweated, bled, died. That love will eternally embrace you.
Richard Baxter

The friendship of Jesus is lasting. Other friends may grow old and cold. It is not so with the friendship of our Savior. Other friends may possibly misunderstand us, Jesus never. His love is the same in youth as in old age. The friendship will rather grow stronger in old age. When you have lost what to you seemed everything, and you find yourself friendless and alone, despised and forsaken, Jesus will be your dear and precious friend.
Leaves of Gold

The life of faith does not earn eternal life; it is eternal life; and Christ is its vehicle.
William Temple

Suddenly I heard the words of Christ and understood them, and life and death ceased to seem to me evil, and instead of despair I experienced happiness and the joy of life undisturbed by death.
Leo Tolstoy

Christ turned a brilliant guess into a solid certainty and endowed the hope of eternal life with grace, reason, and majesty.
Hugh Elmer Brown

In a British army discussion period on the religions of the world, men began to voice their opinions concerning Jesus. To one He was "a good enough man"; to another, "an impossible idealist"; to another, "a revolutionary"; and to another, "a fanatic." At last a lad got to his feet and, with flushed face and stammering tongue, said: "Excuse me, but you're all wrong. He is more than that." The he paused, and a wit who knew the lad interposed with: "He's got inside information!" "So I have!" flashed back the young Christian. "You see, I know Him!" The men did not laugh. They recognized the fact that the lad had got hold of something beyond their surface appraisals.
The War Cry

There is a story about trust in God's promises that comes from F. W. Boreham. Boreham tells about an episode during the early days of his ministry in Australia. He went to call on one of his elderly parishioners. Entering the room where the old man lay, he noticed a chair pulled up beside the man's bed. "I see that I am not your first visitor today," said Boreham. The old man then began to explain the presence of the empty chair. He said that when he was a small boy, he had difficulty praying. His pastor suggested that he overcome this difficulty by placing an empty chair in front of himself when he prayed, and by simply pretending that Jesus was sitting in that chair like an attentive friend. He said he had maintained that habit ever since. Boreham left the house a short while later. A few days later, however, then man's daughter came to tell him that he was dead. "I was out of the room only for a short time," said the daughter. "When I returned, he was gone. There was no change in him except I noticed that his hand was on the chair."
Unknown

The wheels of death's chariot may rattle and make a noise, but they are to carry a believer to Christ.
Thomas Watson

A man was carrying a heavy basket. His son asked to help him. The father cut a stick and placed it through the handle of the basket so that the end toward himself was very short; while the end toward the boy was three or four times as long. Each took hold of his end of the stick, and the basket was lifted and easily carried. The son was bearing the burden with the father, but he found his work easy and light because his father assumed the heavy end of the stick. Just so it is when we bear the yoke with Christ; He sees to it that the burden laid on us is light; He carries the heavy end.
John T. Faris

Blessed be God for his unspeakable gift. We need Him. Souls desire Him as the heart panteth after the waterbrooks. He came to the world in the fullness of time. He comes at this advent season to us. Today may be for some soul here the fullness of time. Let us open the gates and admit Him, that this Christ may be our Christ forever; that living with Him and dying with Him, we may also be glorified together with Him.
David J. Burrell

Many are willing that Christ should be something, but few will consent that Christ should be everything.
Alexander Moody Stuart

All that I had, He took; all that He has, He has given me in Jesus Christ!
Subodh Sahu

Shut out suffering, and you see only one side of this strange and fearful thing, the life of man. Brightness and happiness and rest- that is not life. It is only one side of life. Christ saw both sides.
F. W. Robertson

IN CHRIST WE HAVE
A love that can never be fathomed;
A life that can never die;
A righteousness that can never be tarnished;
A peace that can never be understood;
A rest that can never be disturbed;
A joy that can never be diminished;
A hope that can never be disappointed;
A glory that can never be clouded;
A light that can never be darkened;
A happiness that can never be interrupted;
A strength that can never be enfeebled;
A purity that can never be defiled;
A beauty that can never be marred;
A wisdom that can never be baffled;
A resource that can never be exhausted.
Unknown

Without Christ I was like a fish out of water. With Christ I am in the ocean of love.
Sadhu Singh

A Christian should be a striking likeness of Jesus Christ. You have read lives of Christ, beautifully written; but the best life of Christ is His living biography, written out in the words and action of His people.
Charles H. Spurgeon

What the sunshine is to the flower, the Lord Jesus Christ is to my soul.
Alfred Tennyson

May the strength of God pilot us.
May the power of God preserve us.
May the wisdom of God instruct us.
May the hand of God protect us.
May the way of God direct us.
May the shield of God defend us.
May the host of God guard us against the snares of evil and the temptations of the world.
May Christ be with us.
Christ before us.
Christ in us.
Christ over us.
May Thy salvation, O Lord, be always ours this day and forever more.
St. Patrick Breastplate

Christ would have lived, and taught, and preached, and prophesied, and wrought miracles in vain, if he had not crowned all by dying for our sins as our substitute! His death was our life. His death was the payment of our debt to God. Without his death we should have been of all creatures most miserable.
J. C. Ryle

Being a Christian is more than just an instantaneous conversion- it is a daily process whereby you grow to be more and more like Christ.
Billy Graham

This is our destiny in heaven- to be like Christ: not Christ limited, as he was on earth, to the confines of time and flesh, but Christ risen, the great, free, timeless Christ of the Easter morning.
David Winter

This is the unique element in the gospel, which tells us that what we could never do, God has done. We cannot climb up to heaven to discover God, but God has come down to earth, in the person of his Son, to reveal himself to us in the only way we could really understand: in terms of a human life.
J. N. D. Anderson

His words are the essence of truth...Jesus never uttered opinions. He never guessed; He knew, and He knows.
A. W. Tozer

Like Buddha under the Bo tree, Jesus, on his tree, has his eyes closed too. The difference is this. The pain and sadness of the world that Buddha's eyes close out is the pain and sadness of the world that the eyes of Jesus close in.
Frederick Buechner

The Bible is the second best gift God has ever given us.
L. James Harvey

As the only person to come from eternity to earth, then return to eternity, Jesus knows the whole truth- past, present and future- and can give you a one-of-a-kind perspective.
Bruce Wilkerson

One of the reasons that Christians read Scripture repeatedly and carefully is to find out just how God works in Jesus Christ so that we can work in the name of Jesus Christ.
Eugene Peterson

If our greatest need had been information, God would have sent an educator. If our greatest need had been technology, God would have sent us a scientist. If our greatest need had been money, God would have sent us an economist. But since our greatest need was forgiveness, God sent us a Savior.
Roy Lessin

There is a God shaped vacuum in the heart of every man which cannot be filled by any created thing, but only by God, the Creator, made known through Jesus.
Blaise Pascal

Whatever you may possess, and however fruitful your activities, regard them all as worthless without the inward certainty and experience of Jesus' love.
The Cloud of Unknowing

The thought of Jesus Christ laughing probably is not thought of too much, but it should be. Amidst the trials of this World, in Him we have ultimate joy, and peace. When He walked upon this Earth, it is written that He cried, more than once, and though scriptures do not depict the Christ laughing, it is safe to say He did, for He had all human characteristics…His strength was in what He did with them while He walked among us on this Earth. Once I was told of a little boy about 5 or 6 who was dying, I believe it was of cancer. He was put down to rest and he went to sleep. The end was not thought to be very far away, and while he was sleeping, he sort of put his arms out, and rolled a little onto one side, then drew his knees up somewhat and started laughing and tilted his head back a little…he continued to laugh for a short time, then he just went limp, and he died. His mother declares that Jesus Christ came and picked him up in His arms, and carried him to Heaven. She believes that he was being tickled on the tummy and made him laugh while he was being picked up. That could very well be true…we have no way of knowing how God handles things in the realm that we have yet to step. But we know we are safe with Him Jesus Christ gives us His Peace,
Joyce Vaughan Byars

Always ask, "What would Jesus do?"
Unknown

The argument for the risen Christ is the living Christian.
Winifred Kirkland

Every step toward Christ kills a doubt. Every thought, word, and deed for Him carries you away from discouragement.
Theodore L. Cuyler

Joy

If you're a believer- if you're "in Christ" – then kick up your heels! Celebrate the Lord! Celebrate yourself! Discover a life of pleasure you never dreamed possible.
Anne Ortlund

No man truly has joy unless he lives in love.
Thomas Aquinas

Joy is the echo of God's life within us.
Joseph Marmion

We need to remind each other that the cup of sorrow is also the cup of joy, that precisely what causes us sadness can become the fertile ground for gladness.
Henri Nouwen

Happiness depends on happenings, but joy depends on Jesus.
Unknown

There is absolutely no evidence that complexity and materialism lead to happiness. On the contrary, there is plenty of evidence that simplicity and spirituality lead to joy, a blessedness that is better than happiness.
Dennis Swanberg

I can seldom read scripture now without tears of joy and gratitude.
Hudson Taylor

Joy cannot be pursued. It comes from within. It is a state of being. It does not depend on circumstances, but triumphs over circumstances. It produces a gentleness of spirit and a magnetic personality.
Billy Graham

The place God calls you to is the place where your deep gladness and the world's deep hunger meet.
Frederick Buechner

Joy untouched by thankfulness is always suspect.
Theodor Haecker

I can say that I never knew what joy was like until I gave up pursuing happiness, or cared to live until I chose to die. For these two discoveries I am beholden to Jesus.
Malcolm Muggeridge

God's peace is joy resting.
His joy is peace dancing.
F. F. Bruce

Joy is the echo of God's life within us.
Joseph Marmion

The surest mark of a Christian is not faith, or even love, but joy.
Samuel Shoemaker

Joy is the serious business of heaven.
C. S. Lewis

The most fruitful and the most joy-filled Christians are the most pruned Christians.
Bruce Wilkinson

God give me joy in the common things:
In the dawn that lures, the eve that sings.
In the new grass sparkling after rain,
In the late wind's wild and weird refrain;
In the springtime's spacious field of gold,
In the precious light by winter doled…
God give me joy in the tasks that press,
In the memories that burn and bless;
In the thought that life has love to spend,
In the faith that God's at journey's end.
Thomas Curtis Clark

Joy is distinctly a Christian word and a Christian thing. It is the reverse of happiness. Happiness is the result of what happens of an agreeable sort. Joy has its springs deep down inside. And that spring never runs dry, no matter what happens. Only Jesus gives that joy. He had joy, singing its music within, even under the shadow of the cross. It is an unknown word and thing except as He has sway within.
Samuel Dickey Gordon

God permits troubles to beset His children, but He also refreshes them. He grants them respite when the heart is still and the soul joyous, and you will agree with me that such moments of the secret joy of the Spirit are far more precious than the highest pleasures this world can offer.
The Lutheran Witness

Joy is not gush; joy is not jolliness. Joy is just perfect acquiescence in God's will because the soul delights itself in God Himself.
Hammer William Webb-Peploe

This is the secret of joy. We shall no longer strive for our own way; but commit ourselves, easily and simply, to God's way, acquiesce in his will and in so doing find our peace.
Evelyn Underhill

The service of the Holy Spirit is that He helps us to distinguish pleasure from happiness and develop real joy. There are many experiences which give us temporary pleasure but do not add up to abiding satisfaction. Their thrills pass quickly, and sometimes leave a trail of regret and remorse. Some of our sense pleasures are like lightning flashes, while true joy is like the sunlight.
Ralph Sockman

There is only one way to bring peace to the heart, joy to the mind, and beauty to the life; it is to accept and do the will of God.
William Barclay

Joy is a deep spiritual union with the unchanging God. A man's life, said Jesus Christ, is not fulfilled, nor is it filled full of, nor by, the abundance of things which he possesses. Here is one of the most important statements ever given to a bewildered, heart-hungry world. Joy, then, is a living spring hidden deep in the inner life that is no more dependent upon things than the sunrise is dependent upon a cock's crowing.
A. P. Gouthey

The only real life is one lived close to God. This does not happen by itself; you must make an effort to make this happen, and this effort will bring you joy.
Leo Tolstoy

I thank thee more that all our joy is
touched with pain;
That shadows fall on brightest hours, that
thorns remain;
So that earth's bliss may be our guide, and
not our chain.
For thou, who knowest, Lord, how soon
our weak heart clings,
Hast given us joys, tender and true, yet all
with wings;
So that we see, gleaming on high, diviner
things.
Adelaide Anne Proctor

Too many Christians envy the sinners their pleasure and the saints their joy, because they don't have either one.
Martin Luther

The most certain sign of wisdom is a continual cheerfulness.
Michel De Montaigne

Kindness, Compassion & Service

We all long for heaven where God is, but we have it in our power to be in heaven with Him right now- to be happy with Him at this very moment. But being happy with Him now means loving like He loves, helping like He helps, giving as He gives, serving as He serves, rescuing as He rescues, being with Him twenty-four hours a day- touching Him in His distressing disguise.
Mother Teresa

It is only imperfection that complains of what is imperfect. The more perfect we are, the more gentle and quiet we become toward the defect of others.
Francois Fenelon

Every person we ever meet is God's opportunity.
Frank Laubach

Kind words are the music of the world.
Frederick W. Faber

We are all healers who can reach out and offer health, and we are all patients in constant need of help.
Henri Nouwen

The life I touch for good or ill will touch another life, and in turn another, until who knows where the trembling stops or in what far place my touch will be felt.
Frederick Buechner

There are many people who can do big things, but there are very few people who will do the small things.
Mother Teresa

The story is told of a church that secured a new preacher, and the word spread around town about how well he preached. The church members were abuzz about what an improvement he was over their former preacher, and how much more attention they gave to his sermons. When the town cynic asked what made this new preacher so much better than his predecessor, he was told, "The old preacher told us that we're all sinners, and that if we didn't repent, we'd burn in hell forever!" This cynic then asked, "And what does this new one say?" The answer was, "That we're all sinners, and that if we don't repent, we'll burn in hell forever!" When the cynic responded that he didn't see any difference between the two of them, he was told, "This new preacher says it with tears in his eyes."
Tony Campolo

I choose gentleness. Nothing is won by force. I choose to be gentle. If I raise my voice may it be only in praise. If I clench my fist, may it be only in prayer. If I make a demand, may it be only of myself.
Max Lucado

Life is short and we have not too much time for gladdening the hearts of those who are traveling the dark way with us. Oh, be swift to love! Make haste to be kind.
Henry Frederick Amiel

Give rest to the weary, visit the sick, support the poor; for this also is prayer.
Aphrahat

Constant kindness can accomplish much. As the sun makes ice melt, kindness causes misunderstanding, mistrust, and hostility to evaporate.
Albert Schweitzer

An American tourist in India stood by in awe as he watched Mother Teresa lovingly clean the infected wounds of a horribly disfigured leper, "Sister," he commented, "I wouldn't do that for a million dollars!" Her response, "Neither would I, brother. Neither would I."
Mother Teresa

I like your Christ, I do not like your Christians. Your Christians are so unlike your Christ.
Mahatma Gandhi

There is nothing stronger in the world than gentleness.
Han Suyin

The more vigor you need, the more gentleness and kindness you must combine with it. All stiff, harsh goodness is contrary to Jesus.
Francois de Fenelon

"Sometimes I would like to ask God why He allows poverty, suffering, and injustice when He could do something about it."
"Well, why don't you ask Him?"
"Because I'm afraid He would ask me the same question."
Unknown

Every time you smile at someone, it is an action of love, a gift to that person, a beautiful thing.
Mother Teresa

Prayer is striking the winning blow at the concealed enemy. Service is gathering up the results of that blow among the men we see and touch.
Samuel Gordon

If you eat food every day, you should care about the people who don't.
Eva Longoria

What a wonderful miracle, if only we could look through each other's eyes for an instant.
Henry David Thoreau

We shall never know all the good that a simple smile can do.
Mother Teresa

I believe now that God is kind enough not only to work in our present and future, but He's also able to reach into the past and cut out the wasted years and stitch up our lives in such a way that even the scars eventually are removed.
Jeannie C. Riley

What the heart gives away is never gone. It is kept in the hearts of others.
Robin St. John

The three hardest tasks in the world are neither physical feats nor intellectual achievements, but moral acts: to return love for hate, to include the excluded, and to say, "I was wrong."
Sydney J. Harris

Beautiful faces are they that wear
The light of a pleasant spirit there;
Beautiful hands are they that do
Deeds that are noble, good and true;
Beautiful feet are they that go
Swiftly to lighten another's woe.
McGuffey's Second Reader

That best portion of a good man's life,
His little nameless, unremembered acts
Of kindness and of love.
William Wordsworth

The three essential rules when speaking of others are: Is it true? Is it kind? Is it necessary?
Unknown

A friend who was working in the Dominican Republic with Habitat for Humanity had befriended a small boy named Etin. He noticed that when Etin wore a shirt at all it was always the same dirty, tattered one. A box of used clothes had been left at the camp, and my friend found two shirts in it that were in reasonably good shape and about Etin's size, so he gave them to the grateful boy. A few days later he saw another boy wearing one of the shirts. When he next met up with Etin he explained that the shirts were meant for him. Etin just looked at him and said, "But you gave me two!"
Unknown

My children, the three acts of faith, hope, and charity contain all the happiness of man upon the earth.
John Vianney

The measure of a life is not its duration but its donation.
Corrie Ten Boom

A few years ago I had managed to screw up my life so badly that I found myself without a home and without hope. I'm ashamed to admit it, but even then I was so absorbed by my own self-pity that all I could think of was begging enough money to buy the cheapest drink I could find. One day I was sitting in front of a store panhandling when a woman walked by with a small boy in tow. She ignored my pitch and hurried away. As I watched them go down the sidewalk the small boy broke free and came running back. He stood in front of me, fumbling in his coat pocket; he pulled out a five-dollar bill that was almost certainly more money than he had ever held before, and handed it to me. I was completely dumbstruck and just sat there staring at him with the money in my hand. By then his mother had returned and with tears in her eyes gently led the boy away. He turned back once to wave and they were gone. I don't know how long I sat there, but I have not had another drink since then.
Unknown

When I was young, I admired clever people. Now that I am old, I admire kind people.
Abraham Joshua Heschel

Language can easily be a barrier rather than a bridge, whereas in every language the smile, the gentle touch, the embrace are the same- and in every century, too.
Philip Pare

Today I bent the truth to be kind, and I have no regret, for I am far surer of what is kind than I am of what is true.
Robert Brault

World poverty is a hundred million mothers weeping…because they cannot feed their children.
Ronald Sider

The place God calls you to is the place where your deep gladness and the world's deep hunger meet.
Frederick Buechner

As you're rushing through life, take time to stop a moment, look into people's eyes, say something kind, and try to make them laugh!
Barbara Johnson

Nobody is kind to only one person at once, but to many persons in one.
Frederick W. Faber

In the diary of an elderly woman who lived alone, she often penned: "No one called today."
Unknown

There is a radiance hidden in your heart that the world desperately needs.
John and Stasi Eldredge

I used to think I was poor. Then they told me I wasn't poor, I was needy. Then they told me it was self-defeating to think of myself as needy, that I was culturally deprived. Then they told me deprived was a bad image, that I was underprivileged. Then they told me underprivileged was overused, that I was disadvantaged. I still don't have a dime, but I do have a great vocabulary.
Jules Feiffer

Nothing is more dangerous than to live out the will of God in today's contemporary world. It changes your whole monetary lifestyle…Let me put it quite simply: If Jesus had $40,000 and knew about the kids who are suffering and dying in Haiti, what kind of car would he buy?
Tony Campolo

It is in the shelter of each other that the people live.
Irish proverb

Our life of poverty is as necessary as the work itself. Only in heaven will we see how much we owe to the poor for helping us to love God better because of them.
Mother Teresa

A lot of people want to serve God, but only in an advisory capacity.
Unknown

Be kind, for everyone you meet is fighting a great battle.
Philo of Alexandria

It is one of the most beautiful compensations of this life that no man can sincerely try to help another without helping himself.
Ralph Waldo Emerson

We do not exist for ourselves.
Thomas Merton

There is a wonderful law of nature that the three things we crave most – happiness, freedom, and peace of mind – are always attained by giving them to someone else.
Unknown

A smile takes but a moment, but its effects sometimes last forever.
J. E. Smith

Lord, make me an instrument of Your peace. Where there is hatred let me sow love; where there is injury, pardon; where there is despair, hope; where there is darkness, light; and where there is sadness, joy.
Francis of Assisi

What makes loneliness an anguish is not that I have no one to share my burden, but this: I have only my own burden to bear.
Dag Hammarskjold

We are all pencils in the hand of a writing God, who is sending love letters to the world.
Mother Teresa

No individual has any right to come into the world and go out of it without leaving behind him distinct and legitimate reasons for having passed through it.
George Washington Carver

One kind word can warm three winter months.
Japanese proverb

Blessed is the influence of one true, loving human soul on another.
George Eliot

There are two ways of spreading light – to be the candle or the mirror that reflects it.
Edith Wharton

Tell me how much you know of the sufferings of your fellow men and I will tell how much you have loved them.
Unknown

Every person I have known who has been truly happy, has learned how to serve others.
Albert Schweitzer

The bread that you store up belongs to the hungry; the cloak that lies on your chest belongs to the naked; and the gold that you have hidden in the ground belongs to the poor.
Basil of Caesarea

Don't forget, a person's greatest emotional need is to feel appreciated.
Unknown

Remember that everyone you meet is afraid of something, loves something, and has lost something.
Unknown

Let us be the first to give a friendly sign; to nod first, smile first, speak first, and- if such a thing is necessary- forgive first.
Unknown

If you want happiness for an hour, take a nap. If you want happiness for a day, go fishing. If you want happiness for a year, inherit a fortune. If you want happiness for a lifetime, help somebody.
Chinese proverb

Kindness has converted more sinners than zeal, eloquence or learning.
Frederick Faber

Never lose sight of the fact that old age needs so little but needs that little so much.
Margaret Willour

Sometimes someone says something really small, and it just fits right into this empty place in your heart.
My So-Called Life

Lord, give me an open heart to find You everywhere, to glimpse the heaven enfolded in a bud, and to experience eternity in the smallest act of love.
Mother Teresa

You have it easily in your power to increase the sum total of this world's happiness now. How? By giving a few words of sincere appreciation to someone who is lonely or discouraged. Perhaps you will forget tomorrow the kind words you say today, but the recipient may cherish them over a lifetime.
Dale Carnegie

Feelings are everywhere – be gentle.
J. Masai

To the world you may be just one person, but to one person you may be the world.
Unknown

God is pleased with no music below so much as with the thanksgiving songs of relieved widows and supported orphans; of rejoicing, comforted, and thankful persons.
Jeremy Taylor

The hungry need bread and the homeless need a roof; the dispossessed need justice and the lonely need fellowship; the undisciplined need order and the slaves need freedom. To allow the hungry to remain hungry would be blasphemy against God and one's neighbor, for what is nearest to God is precisely the need of one's neighbor.
Dietrich Bonhoeffer

Faith and works should travel side by side, step answering to step, like the legs of men walking. First faith, and then works; and then faith again, and then works again- until you can scarcely distinguish which is one and which is the other.
William Booth

Come along inside, we'll see if tea and buns can make the world a better place.
Kenneth Grahame

A smile creates happiness in the home, fosters good will in business and is the countersign of friends. It is rest to the weary, daylight to the discouraged, sunshine to the sad, and nature's best antidote for trouble. Yet it cannot be bought, begged, borrowed, or stolen, for it is something that is no earthly good to anybody until it is given away. Keep smiling- and let your smile be one of sincerity. Don't just force it out to make a sale, to keep out of a fight, or for similar reasons. But smile from the heart out, making those who see you smile do likewise in a feeling of good fellowship.
James M. Tulloch

To worship rightly is to love each other, Each smile a hymn, each kindly deed a prayer.
John Greenleaf Whittier

Dan Clark recalls that when he was a teenager, he and his father once stood in line to buy tickets for the circus. As they waited, they noticed the family immediately in front of them. The parents were holding hands, and they had eight children in tow, all behaved well and all probably under the age of twelve. Based on their clean but simple clothing, he suspected they didn't have a lot of money. The kids jabbered about the exciting things they expected to see, and he could tell that the circus was going to be a new adventure for them. As the couple approached the counter, the attendant asked how many tickets they wanted. The man proudly responded, "Please let me buy eight children's tickets and two adult tickets so I can take my family to the circus." When the attendant quoted the price, the man's wife let go of his hand, and her head drooped. The man leaned a little closer and asked, "How much did you say?" The attendant again quoted the price. The man obviously didn't have enough money. He looked crushed. Clark says his father watched all of this, put his hand in his pocket, pulled out a twenty-dollar bill, and dropped it on the ground. His father then reached down, picked up the bill, tapped the man on the shoulder, and said, "Excuse me, sir, this fell out of your pocket."

The man knew exactly what was going on. He looked straight into Clark's father's eyes, took his hand, shook it, and with a tear streaming down his cheek, replied, "Thank you, thank you, sir. This really means a lot to me and my family."

Clark and his father went back to their car and drove home. They didn't have enough money to go to the circus that night, but it didn't matter. They had encouraged a whole family. And it was something neither family would ever forget.
John C. Maxwell

We hurt people by being too busy. Too busy to notice their needs. Too busy to drop that note of comfort or encouragement or assurance of love. Too busy to listen when someone needs to talk. Too busy to care.
Billy Graham

The greatest good you can do for another is not just to share your riches but to reveal to him his own.
Benjamin Disraeli

Goodness is love in action, love with its hands to the plow, love with the burden on its back, love following His footsteps who went about continually doing good.
James H. Hamilton

Strangers are friends that you have yet to meet.
Roberta Lieberman

Charity begins today. Today somebody is suffering, today somebody is in the street, today somebody is hungry. Our work is for today, yesterday has gone, tomorrow has not yet come. We have only today.
Mother Teresa

You who are letting miserable misunderstandings run on from year to year, meaning to clear them up some day; you who are keeping wretched quarrels alive because you cannot quite make up your minds that now is the day to sacrifice your pride and kill them; you who are letting your neighbor starve until you hear that he is dying of starvation or letting your friend's heart ache for a word of appreciation or sympathy, which you mean to give him some day; if you could only know and see and feel all of a sudden that time is short, how it would break the "spell." How you would go instantly and do the thing which you might never have another chance to do.
Phillips Brooks

Many a friendship- long, loyal, and self-sacrificing- rested at first upon no thicker a foundation than a kind word.
Frederick W. Faber

A simple gesture can make an enormous difference. Without even knowing it, you could change the life of another person.
Laura Schroff

There is a treasury of blessing to be found in sharing with shut-ins; they have much to give and often no one to give it to.
William J. Johnston

Few kindnesses are as warmly welcomed as sincere, objective interest.
Norman G. Shidle

It is an unhappy division that has been made between faith and works, though in my intellect I may divide them, just as in a candle I know there is both light and heat; but yet, put out the candle and they are both gone; one remains not without the other. So it is betwixt faith and works.
John Selden

A young man who saw all the sin, selfishness, and injustice in the world complained to his pastor that God had made a mess of things. "Why," the boy said, "I could make a better world myself." "Good," said the pastor, "go to it; that is just why you're here!"
Unknown

We need to arrange a servanthood conference, with workshops in love, forgiveness, feet-washing, cross bearing- in short, workshops in Christlikeness. God is not waiting for people to get big enough to use, but to get small enough in their own eyes for Him to entrust with His mission and Spirit. Christ cannot be represented by swaggering leaders who "lord it over" the flock of God. He cannot be represented by puffed-up laymen who nominate themselves as church bosses. He can be honestly manifested only in the lives of those who feel, as did Paul, that they are "less than the least of all the saints."
W. E. McCumber

Let me live in a house by the side of the road and be a friend to man.
Sam Walter Foss

The Day's Result
Is anybody happier because you passed
his way? Does anyone remember that you
spoke to him today? The day is almost
over and its toiling time is through; Is
there anyone to utter now a kindly word
of you? Did you give a cheerful greeting
to the friend who came along, Or a
churlish sort of "Howdy"; then vanish in
the throng? Were you selfish, pure and
simple, as you rushed along your way, Or
is someone mighty grateful for a deed you
did today? Can you say tonight, in parting
with the day that's slipping fast, That you
helped a single brother of the many that
you passed? Is a single heart rejoicing over
what you did or said? Does the man
whose hopes were fading now with
courage look ahead? Did you waste the
day or lose it, was it well or poorly spent?
Did you leave a trail of kindness, or a scar
of discontent? As you close your eyes in
slumber, do you think that God would
say, "You have earned one more
tomorrow by the work you did today?"
Unknown

The fact that I can plant a seed and it
becomes a flower, share a bit of
knowledge and it becomes another's,
smile at someone and receive a smile in
return, are to me continual spiritual
exercises.
Leo Buscaglia

O Lord, baptize our hearts into a sense of
the conditions and needs of all men.
George Fox, founder of the Quaker Society

Christ has no body on earth now but
yours, no hands but yours, no feet but
yours. Yours are the eyes through which
to look out Christ's compassion to the
world. Yours are the feet with which He
is to go about doing good, and yours are
the hands with which he is to bless us
now.
Teresa of Avila

Dr. Wilfred Grenfell, the missionary
doctor of Labrador, was a cynical young
medical student in London when Dwight
L. Moody went there to preach. Said
Grenfell of Moody: "When Mr. Moody
finished his sermon, I resolved either to
drop religion entirely or else make a real
effort to do what Christ would do if He
were in my place. With a mother like
mine, that resolve could only have one
outcome. So, beginning that night, I
started doing what I thought Christ would
do if He were a young doctor in
London."
Wilfred Grenfell

O, heavenly Father: we thank thee for
food and remember the hungry.
We thank thee for health and remember
the sick.
We thank thee for friends and remember
the friendless.
We thank thee for freedom and remember
the enslaved.
May these remembrances stir us to
service,
That thy gifts to us may be used for
others.
Amen.
Pauline Phillips

We cannot possibly let ourselves get frozen into regarding everyone we do not know as an absolute stranger.
Albert Schweitzer

Have thy tools ready; God will find thee work.
Charles Kingsley

Kindness is just the word for [certain] small acts. Kindness is love flowing out in little gentlenesses. We ought to carry our lives so that they will be perpetual benedictions wherever we go. All we need for such a ministry is a heart full of love for Christ; for if we truly love Christ we shall also love our fellow men, and love will always find ways of helping. A heart filled with gentleness cannot be miserly of its benedictions.
James R. Miller

Kind words make good echoes.
Unknown

God often places someone at a camp, a club, or a church as a certain intersection to build you up: Someone to say something that you'll never forget or to encourage you at a moment of need.
Gregg Matte

We ourselves feel that what we are doing is just a drop in the ocean. But if that drop was not in the ocean, I think the ocean would be less because of that missing drop. I do not agree with the big way of doing things.
Mother Teresa

Love has hands to help others. It has feet to hasten to the poor and needy. It has eyes to see misery and want. It has ears to hear the sighs and sorrows of men. This is what love looks like.
Augustine

Life becomes harder for us when we live for others, but it also becomes richer and happier.
Albert Schweitzer

What a pity that so many people are living with so few friends when the world is full of lonesome strangers who would give anything just to be somebody's friend.
Milo L. Arnold

Remember that man's name is to him the sweetest and most important sound in the English language.
Dale Carnegie

A Christian should be a striking likeness of Jesus Christ. You have read lives of Christ, beautifully written; but the best life of Christ is His living biography, written out in the words and action of His people.
Charles H. Spurgeon

Christ revealed to humanity those things which their best selves already knew: that people are equal because the same spirit lives in all of them...Learn from the small children, behave like children, and treat all people on an equal basis, with love and tenderness.
Leo Tolstoy

Peace of mind should not be an objective of life. More often than not, peace of mind leads to a state of peace without mind. There are causes that should call us; there are cries of help that should move us; there are people who need us; there are conditions that demand us. Floating around in one's own tub of butter should not be a goal for an intelligent life. Let us find tranquility in the doing, not in the being.
Saul Teplitz

We may wonder whom can I love and serve? Where is the face of God to whom I can pray? The answer is simple. That naked one. That lonely one. That unwanted one is my brother and my sister. If we have no peace, it is because we have forgotten that we belong to each other.
Mother Teresa

Not many sounds in life, and I include all urban and all rural sounds, exceed in interest a knock at the door.
Charles Lamb

In Jesus the service of God and the service of the least of the brethren were one.
Dietrich Bonhoeffer

The question of bread for myself is a material question; but the question of bread for my neighbour, for everybody, is a spiritual and a religious question.
Nikolai Berdyaev

Perhaps with charity one shouldn't think. Charity like love should be blind.
Graham Greene

There is a story about an old woman who was in distress because she had lost her sense of God. A friend who was with her one day said, "Pray to God. Ask Him to touch you. He will put His hand on you." The old woman began to pray and suddenly felt a hand touching her. She cried out in joy, "He has touched me!" Then she added, "But do you know, it felt just like your hand!" Her friend said, "Sure, what do you think God would be doing? Did you think He'd reach a long arm out of heaven to touch you? He just took the hand that was nearest and used that."
Unknown

A deep plunge into the waters of sorrow is the hopefullest way of getting through them on one's daily road of life again. No one can help another very much in these crises of life; but love and sympathy count for something.
Thomas Henry Huxley

God does not comfort us to make us comfortable, but to make us comforters.
J. H. Jowett

The least pain in our little finger gives us more concern and uneasiness than the destruction of millions of our fellow beings.
William Hazlitt

Being happy with God now means:
Loving as he loves,
Helping as he helps,
Giving as he gives,
Serving as he serves,
Rescuing as he rescues,
Being with him twenty-four hours,
Touching him in his distressing disguise.
Mother Teresa

Like Buddha under the Bo tree, Jesus, on his tree, has his eyes closed too. The difference is this. The pain and sadness of the world that Buddha's eyes close out is the pain and sadness of the world that the eyes of Jesus close in.
Frederick Buechner

To feel sorry for the needy is not the mark of a Christian- to help them is.
Fred Clark

The joy of brightening other lives, bearing each others' burdens, easing other's loads and supplanting empty hearts and lives with generous gifts becomes for us the magic of Christmas.
W. C. Jones

Stewardship is the ordering of one's life so that time, ability, possessions, and all of one's personality are administered as belonging to God.
Unknown

God might want you to extend his love by offering to baby-sit for the single parent down the street. He might want you to prepare a hearty meal for that lonely old man who lost his wife — and to sit and visit with him while he eats. Who knows, he might even want you to reach out and touch the life of a total stranger in some way you can't imagine right now. Are you willing to set aside your own comfort to touch someone else with God's love?
Amy Nappa

Kind words can be short and easy to speak, but their echoes are truly endless.
Mother Teresa

The church as a whole must be concerned with both evangelism and social action. It is not a case of either-or; it is both-and. Anything less is only a partial Gospel, not the whole counsel of God.
Robert De Haan

I choose gentleness... Nothing is won by force. I choose to be gentle. If I raise my voice may it be only in praise. If I clench my fist, may it be only in prayer. If I make a demand, may it be only of myself.
Max Lucado

Make one person happy each day and in forty years you will have made 14,600 human beings happy for a little time at least.
Charley Willey

God appoints our graces to be nurses to other men's weakness.
Henry Ward Beecher

The paradox of Christian leadership is that the way out is the way in, that only by entering into communion with human suffering can relief be found.
Henri Nouwen

I've learned that whenever I decide something with kindness, I usually make the right decision.
Unknown

For the ability to be of service to a fellow creature, we ought to give thanks, not demand it.
W. J. Cameron

Enable me, our Father, to realize that words once spoken, like coins in circulation, pass from person to person along an uncharted course. Grant me the insight so to speak that any words of mine may be repeated without giving hurt. Help me not to criticize but rather to stress the things that are pure, lovely, and of good report. Make my habit of thought gentle and eager to pass along news of kindness and work well done. May my words build, never destroy, faith and confidence. To this end I pray that Thou wilt lead me in the ways of understanding. Amen.
Unknown

Find out how much God has given you and from it take what you need; the remainder is needed by others.
Augustine

I count all that part of my life lost which I spent not in communion with God or in doing good.
John Donne

A story is told about a little boy with a big heart. His next-door neighbor was an older gentleman whose wife had recently died. When the youngster saw the elderly man crying, he climbed up onto his lap and simply sat there. Later, his mother asked the boy what he had said to their saddened neighbor. "Nothing," the child replied. "I just helped him cry." Sometimes that is the best thing we can do for people who are facing profound sorrow. Often, our attempts to say something wise and helpful are far less valuable than just sitting next to the bereaved ones, holding their hand, and crying with them.
Unknown

If you're not using your smile, you're like a man with a million dollars in the bank and no checkbook.
Les Giblin

Kindness is a language the blind can see and the deaf can hear.
L. James Harvey

Our Lord has many weak children in his family, many dull pupils in his school, many raw soldiers in his army, many lame sheep in his flock. Yet he bears with them all, and casts none away. Happy is that Christian who has learned to do likewise with his brethren.
J. C. Ryle

When I see pictures of tragedy,
Don't let it get old to me
When I see hunger and poverty,
Don't let it get old to me
When I see hatred and jealousy,
Don't let it get old to me
When I see shattered integrity,
Don't let it get old to me
Let my heart be broken
Give me eyes of compassion
Don't let my hunger diminish
But let me finish strong
I want to hear you say to me
Well done
Pictures of Tragedy

There's a story that's always meant a lot to Ruth and me. The story was about an African boy who gave his missionary teacher an unusually beautiful seashell as a Christmas gift. The boy had walked a great distance, over rough terrain, to the only place on the coast where these particular shells could be found. The teacher was touched. "You've traveled so far to bring me such a wonderful present," she said. The boy looked puzzled, then his eyes widened with excitement: "Oh, teacher," he explained, "long walk part of gift." Sure, there have been plenty of times over the years when all the pre-holiday shopping and sermon writing and schedule arranging seemed to be too much, and my wife, Ruth, and I have been tempted to throw up our hands and say, "It's just not worth the effort!" But then we've looked at each other and said, "Long walk part of gift." And we've laughed and gotten back to work.
Norman Vincent Peale

Life

Be glad of life because it gives you the chance to love and to work and to play and to look at the stars.
Henry Van Dyke

Everyday happiness means getting up in the morning, and you can't wait to finish your breakfast. You can't wait to do your exercises. You can't wait to put on your clothes. You can't wait to get out- and you can't wait to come home, because the soup is hot.
George Burns

Life is what we are alive to. It is not length but breadth...Be alive to...goodness, kindness, purity, love, history, poetry, music, flowers, stars, God, and eternal hope.
Maltbie D. Babcock

Life passes, riches fly away, popularity is fickle, the senses decay, the world changes. One alone is true to us; One alone can be all things to us; One alone can supply our need.
John Henry Newman

The life I touch for good or ill will touch another life, and in turn another, until who knows where the trembling stops or in what far place my touch will be felt.
Frederick Buechner

The higher goal of spiritual living is not to amass a wealth of information, but to face sacred moments.
Abraham Joshua Heschel

We spend most of our time and energy in a kind of horizontal thinking. We move along the surface of things going from one quick base to another, often with a frenzy that wears us out. We collect data, things, people, ideas, "profound experiences," never penetrating any of them...But there are other times. There are times when we stop. We sit still. We lose ourselves in a pile of leaves or its memory. We listen and breezes from a whole other world begin to whisper. Then we begin our "going down."
James Carroll

I live the perfect imperfect life.
Paul Lore

Your life is to be lived in such a way as to reflect Him, to show the world the character of God- His love, His peace, His mercy, His gentleness. You are to live for Him, to accomplish His will. To miss this purpose is to miss fulfillment. It is to have existed rather than to have lived.
Kay Arthur

Life is short and we have not too much time for gladdening the hearts of those who are traveling the dark way with us. Oh, be swift to love! Make haste to be kind.
Henry Frederick Amiel

Live simply that others may simply live.
Unknown

It's impossible to overestimate the unimportance of most things.
John Lange

He who has the Holy Spirit in his heart and the Scripture in his hands has all he needs.
Alexander MacLaren

Just when I was getting used to yesterday, along came today.
Unknown

Life begins when a person first realizes how soon it will end.
Marcelene Cox

Life without faith in something is too narrow a space to live.
George Lancaster Spalding

He brought my life passion from my life pain.
Beth Moore

Every thought a person dwells upon, whether he expresses it or not, either damages or improves his life.
Lucy Malory

It's terribly amusing how many different climates of feeling one can go through in a day.
Anne Morrow Lindbergh

Think of this- we may live together with Him here and now, a daily walking with Him who loved us and gave Himself for us.
Elisabeth Elliot

If I had my life to live over, I would start barefoot earlier in the spring and stay that way later in the fall. I would go to more dances. I would ride more merry-go-rounds. I would pick more daisies.
Nadine Stair

A monk was asked, "What do you do there in the monastery?" He replied, "We fall and get up, we fall and get up, fall and get up again."
Esther de Waal

Always new.
Always exciting.
Always full of promise.
The mornings of our lives,
Each is a personal daily miracle.
Gloria Gaither

Slow me down, Lord!
Ease the pounding of my heart by the
quieting of my mind.
Steady my hurried pace with a vision of
the eternal reach of time.
Give me, amid the confusion of the day,
the calmness of the everlasting rills.
Break the tensions of my nerves and
muscles, with the soothing music of the
singing streams that live in my memory.
Orin L. Crain

The probability of life originating from
accident is comparable to the probability
of the Unabridged Dictionary resulting
from an explosion in a printing factory.
Edwin Conkin

Let it not be imagined that the life of a
good Christian must be a life of
melancholy and gloominess; for he only
resigns some pleasures to enjoy others
infinitely better.
Blaise Pascal

Isn't it funny how day by day nothing
changes, but when you look back
everything is different.
C. S. Lewis

My life is my message.
Mahatma Gandhi

There is only one basis for really enjoying
life, and that is, to walk in the way in
which God leads you. Then you are
prepared to find delight in all sorts of
wayward incidents....When a man is
drifting through life, seeking nothing
outside of self-gratification, the world
must become increasingly a barren and
forbidding wilderness. But it is wonderful
how many delights fall to the lot of him
who is led by God. For such a one the
clasp of a friend's hand, a cool drink in
the heat of noon, a merry salutation from
a passing traveler, a glimpse of beauty by
the road, a quiet resting place at night, are
all full of unspeakable pleasure.
Leaves of Gold

Is life not full of opportunities for
learning love? Every man and woman
every day has a thousand of them. The
world is not a playground; it is a
schoolroom. Life is not a holiday, but an
education. And the one eternal lesson for
us all is how better we can love.
Henry Drummond

Each of us leads a secret thought life, an
invisible life known only to us- it is not
known to others. This secret life is
usually very different from the visible you-
the you that is known by others. Yet it is
the real you, the you that is known by our
God.
Patrick Morley

Between here and heaven, every minute
that the Christian lives will be a minute of
grace.
C. H. Spurgeon

But whatever you do, find the God-centered, Christ-exalting, Bible-saturated passion of your life, and find your way to say it and live for it and die for it. And you will make a difference that lasts. You will not waste your life.
John Piper

Time, indeed, is a sacred gift, and each day is a little life.
John Lubbock

Too many times we miss so much because we live on the low level of the natural, the ordinary, the explainable.
Vance Havner

There are fathers waiting until other obligations are less demanding to become acquainted with their sons. There are mothers who sincerely intend to be more attentive to their daughters. There are husbands and wives who are going to be more understanding. But time does not draw people closer. When in the world are we going to begin to live as if we understood that this is life? This is our time, our day…and it is passing. What are we waiting for?
Richard L. Evans

That best portion of a good man's life,
His little nameless, unremembered acts
Of kindness and of love.
William Wordsworth

I long to put the experience of fifty years at once into your young lives, to give you at once the key of that treasure chamber every gem of which has cost me tears and struggles and prayers, but you must work for these inward treasures yourselves.
Harriet Beecher Stowe

Your presence is a present to the world.
You're unique and one of a kind.
Your life can be what you want it to be.
Take the days just one at a time.
Don't put limits on yourself.
So many dreams are waiting to be realized.
Decisions are too important to leave to chance.
Reach for your peak, your goal, your prize.
Nothing wastes more energy than worrying.
The longer one carries a problem, the heavier it gets.
Don't take things too seriously.
Live a life of serenity, not a life of regrets.
Count your blessings, not your troubles.
You'll make it through whatever comes along.
Within you are so many answers.
Understand, have courage, be strong.
Douglas Pagels

Each day the first day:
Each day a life.
Dag Hammarskjold

This human life in God is from our point of view a particular period in the history of our world (from His birth to His crucifixion). We therefore imagine it is also a period in the history of God's own existence. But God has no history. He is too completely and utterly real to have one. For, of course, to have a history means losing part of your reality (because it has already slipped away into the past), and not yet having another part (because it is still in the future); in fact, having nothing but the tiny little present, which has gone before you can speak about it. God forbid we should think God was like that! Even we may hope not to be always rationed in that way.
C. S. Lewis

The measure of a life is not its duration but its donation.
Corrie Ten Boom

Life provides losses and heartbreak. But the greatest tragedy is to have the experience and miss the meaning. I am determined not to miss that meaning.
Robin Roberts

Take those road hazards- the potholes, ruts, detours, and all the rest- as evidence that you were on the right route. It's when you find yourself on that big, broad, easy road that you ought to worry.
Joni Eareckson Tada

Thanksgiving is good but thanks-living is better.
Matthew Henry

Life's short and we never have enough time for the hearts of those who travel the way with us. O, be swift to love! Make haste to be kind.
Henri-Frederic Amiel

Some four-letter words that Christians need to revitalize with appropriate action are: give, live, pray, read, hope, help, sing, work, lead, grow, walk, dare, join, lift, talk and love; but the greatest of these is "love."
Unknown

We do not content ourselves with the life we have in ourselves; we desire to live an imaginary life in the minds of others, and for this purpose we endeavor to shine.
Blaise Pascal

Prayer no longer seems like an activity to me; it has become the continuing language of the relationship I believe God designed to fulfill a human life.
Keith Miller

We are all fallen creatures and all very hard to live with.
C. S. Lewis

If he is in a tight spot, he borrows money on the furniture. If he is low, he lights a cigarette. If he is lonely, he goes to a movie. If he is maladjusted, he goes to a psychiatrist. If he has a headache, he takes an aspirin. All from the outside in. The Christian remedy is from the inside out.
E. Stanley Jones

Since 3600 BC the world has known only 292 years of peace. In that period, stretching more than 55 centuries, there have been an incredible 14,531 wars in which over 3.6 billion people have been killed.
John Ankerberg and John Weldon

All too often modern man becomes the plaything of his circumstances because he no longer has any leisure time; he doesn't know how to provide himself with the leisure he needs to stop to take a good look at himself.
Michel Quoist

The tragedy of life is not that it ends so soon, but that we wait so long to begin it.
W. M. Lewis

The trouble with life is that there is no background music.
Unknown

A tried Christian grows rich by his losses, he rises by his falls, he lives by dying, and he becomes full by being emptied.
C. H. Spurgeon

There was a man who heard about a very special ox and determined to have it for his own. He traveled all over the world. He spent his entire fortune. He gave his whole life to the search for this ox. At last, just moments before he died, he realized he had been riding it all the time.
Thomas Aquinas

The moment you wake up each morning, all your wishes and hopes for the day rush at you like wild animals. And the first job each morning consists in shoving it all back; in listening to that other voice, taking that other point of view, letting that other, larger, stronger, quieter life coming flowing in.
C. S. Lewis

Go not abroad for happiness.
For see,
It is a flower that
blossoms at thy door.
Minot J. Savage

You will find, as you look back upon your life, that the moments that stand out, the moments when you have really lived, are the moments when you have done things in the spirit of Love.
Henry Drummond

The problem with spending your life climbing up the ladder is that you will go right past Jesus, for he's coming down.
John Ortberg

No man can estimate what is really happening at the present. All we do know, and that to a large extent by direct experience, is that evil labors with vast power and perpetual success- in vain: preparing always only the soil for unexpected good to sprout in.
J. R. R. Tolkien

To become Christ-like is the only thing in the whole world worth caring for, the thing before which every ambition of man is folly and all lower achievement vain.
Henry Drummond

Live near to God, and all things will appear little to you in comparison with eternal realities.
Robert Murray M'Cheyne

We want to be saints, but we also want to feel every sensation experienced by sinners; we want to be innocent and pure, but we also want to be experienced and taste all of life; we want to serve the poor and have a simple lifestyle, but we also want all the comforts of the rich; we want to have the depth afforded by solitude, but we also do not want to miss anything; we want to pray, but we also want to watch television, read, talk to friends, and go out.
Ronald Rolheiser

If God does not enter your kitchen, there is something wrong with your kitchen. If you can't take God into your recreation, there is something wrong with your play. We all believe in the God of the heroic. What we need most these days is the God of the humdrum, the commonplace, the everyday.
Peter Marshall

To ascertain where you really are with the Lord, recall what saddened you the past month. Was it the realization that you do not love Jesus enough? That you did not seek his face in prayer often enough? That you did not care for his people enough? Or did you get depressed over a lack of respect, criticism from an authority figure, your finances, a lack of friends, fears about the future, or your bulging waistline?
Brennan Manning

Slow down to look and listen. Life happens fast.
David Staal

Each dawn holds a new hope for a new plan, making the start of each day the start of a new life.
Gina Blair

Between us and heaven or hell there is only life, which is the frailest thing in the world.
Blaise Pascal

If we're not telling God and our family that we love them, we just wasted a day of our life.
Ted Roberts

It's not what you did, but what you could have done if you allowed the Lord to work His will in your life.
A. W. Tozer

From our limited vantage point, our lives are marked by an endless series of contingencies. We frequently find ourselves, instead of acting as we planned, reacting to an unexpected turn of events. We make plans but are often forced to change those plans. But there are no contingencies with God. Our unexpected, forced change of plans is a part of His plan. God is never surprised; never caught off guard; never frustrated by unexpected developments. God does as He pleases and that which pleases Him is always for His glory and our good.
Jerry Bridges

Life itself, every bit of health that we enjoy, every hour of liberty and free enjoyment, the ability to see, to hear, to speak, to think, and to imagine- all this comes from the hand of God. We show our gratitude by giving back to Him a part of that which He has given to us.
Billy Graham

The older we get in the Lord, the simpler life becomes as we realize it's all about Jesus.
Jon Courson

Every experience God gives us, every person he puts in our lives, is the perfect preparation for the future that only he can see.
Corrie ten Boom

When Christ came into my life, I came about like a well-handled ship.
Robert Louis Stevenson

We are pilgrims, not settlers; this earth is our inn, not our home.
J. H. Vincent

The ordinary acts we practice every day at home are of more importance to the soul than their simplicity might suggest.
Thomas Moore

If you have so much business to attend to that you have no time to pray, depend upon it, you have more business on hand than God ever intended you should have.
D. L. Moody

If nothing in this world satisfies me, perhaps it is because I was made for another world.
C. S. Lewis

Life does not accommodate you, it shatters you. It is meant to, and couldn't do it better. Every seed destroys its container or there would be no fruition.
F. Scott-Maxwell

I have always been complaining that my work was constantly interrupted, until I slowly discovered that my interruptions were my work.
Henri Nouwen

Plenty of people miss their share of happiness, not because they never found it, but because they didn't stop to enjoy it.
William Feather

Make a list of twenty-five things you want to experience before you die. Carry it in your wallet or purse and refer to it often.
H. Jackson Brown, Jr.

Faith in God – life can never take you by surprise again.
James Dobson

Blessed is the man who has discovered that there is nothing permanent in life but change.
Unknown

I came from God, and I'm going back to God, and I won't have any gaps of death in the middle of my life.
George Macdonald

In the name of God, stop a moment, close your work, and look around you.
Leo Tolstoy

You are what you think about all day long.
Robert Schuller

I was always complaining about the ruts in the road until I realized the ruts are the road.
Unknown

When we understand that He is Lord of our time, we realize that interruptions are of His planning. They become opportunities to serve rather than plagues to keep us from functioning.
Karen Mains

God writes the Gospel not in the Bible alone, but on trees, and flowers, and clouds, and stars.
Martin Luther

I try not to worry about life too much because I read the last page of THE book and it all turns out all right.
Billy Graham

If you have never heard the mountains singing; or seen the trees of the field clapping their hands, do not think because of that they don't. Ask God to open your ears so you may hear it, and your eyes so you may see it, because, though few men ever know it, they do, my friend, they do.
McCandlish Phillips

Every Christian needs a half an hour of prayer each day, except when he is busy, then he needs an hour.
Francis de Sales

Only as man brings his life into harmony with God does that life have balance and meaning. Then man finds that he is not simply a mass of dancing dirt, coming from nowhere and going nowhere.
Henry Schmidt

If you are a Christian, you are not a citizen of this world trying to get to heaven; you are a citizen of heaven making your way through this world.
Vance Havner

My objective in life is not to have a spiritual life that is separate from the rest of my life.
Ed McCraken

Life is deep and simple, and what our society gives us is shallow and complicated.
Fred Rogers

Sometimes when I consider what tremendous consequences come from little things – I am tempted to think – there are no little things.
Ralph Waldo Emerson

Imagine watching all that God might have done with your life if you had let him.
John Ortberg

I still find each day too short for all the thoughts I want to think, all the walks I want to take, all the books I want to read, and all the friends I want to see.
John Burroughs

The early morning hours have gold in their mouth.
Dutch proverb

Hurry means that we gather impressions but have no experiences, that we collect acquaintances but make no friends, that we attend meetings but experience no encounter. We must recover eternity if we are to find time, and eternity is what Jesus came to restore. For without it, there can be no charity.
D. T. Niles

Every day we live is a priceless gift of God, loaded with possibilities to learn something new, to gain fresh insights.
Dale Evans Rogers

Being a Christian is more than just an instantaneous conversion; it is like a daily process whereby you grow to be more and more like Christ.
Billy Graham

I think everybody should get rich and famous and do everything they ever dreamed of so they can see that it's not the answer.
Jim Carrey

Much of what is sacred is hidden in the ordinary, everyday moments of our lives. To see something of the sacred in those moments takes slowing down so we can live our lives more reflectively.
Ken Gire

Beauty is God's handwriting. Welcome it in every fair face, every fair day, every fair flower.
Charles Kingsley

May life's greatest gifts always be yours, Happiness, memories and dreams.
Unknown

It is remarkable that the Holy Spirit has given us very few deathbed scenes in the book of God. We have very few in the Old Testament, fewer still in the New. And I take it that the reason may be, because the Holy Ghost would have us to take more account of how we live than how we die, for life is the main business. He who learns to die daily while he lives will find it no difficulty to breathe out his soul for the last time into the hands of his faithful Creator.
Charles Spurgeon

Lord…give me the gift of faith to be renewed and shared with others each day. Teach me to live this moment only, looking neither to the past with regret, nor the future with apprehension. Let love be my aim and my life a prayer.
Roseann Alexander-Isham

The secret of life is that all we have and are is a gift of grace to be shared.
Lloyd John Ogilvie

Our Lord finds our desires not too strong, but too weak. We are half-hearted creatures, fooling about with drink and sex and ambition when infinite joy is offered us, like an ignorant child who wants to go on making mud pies in a slum because he cannot imagine what is meant by the offer of a holiday at the sea. We are far too easily pleased.
C. S. Lewis

Honesty, or dishonesty, is shown in every little act of life.
Mabel Hale

At different seasons of life, we will be growing in different areas. I try to see where God is at work in my life, and where he is at work in the lives of my friends, and then I pray for and encourage growth in those particular areas.
Alice Fryling

How dangerous it is for our salvation, how unworthy of God and of ourselves, how pernicious even for the peace of our hearts, to want always to stay where we are! Our whole life was only given us to advance us by great strides toward our heavenly country.
Francois Fenelon

We need the whole song, all the verses and the choruses to serve us as our own story unfolds because- trust me- life is hard, but God is good.
Gloria Gaither

Godliness is a life-long business. The working out of the salvation that the Lord, himself, works in you is not a matter of certain hours, or of a limited period of life. Salvation is unfolded throughout our entire sojourn here.
Charles Spurgeon

Don't bother much about your feelings. When they are humble, loving, brave, give thanks for them; when they are conceited, selfish, cowardly, ask to have them altered. In neither case are they you, but only a thing that happens to you. What matters is your intentions and your behaviour.
C. S. Lewis

I came from God, and I'm going back to God, and I won't have any gaps of death in the middle of my life.
George Macdonald

All your life an unattainable ecstasy has hovered just beyond the grasp of your consciousness. The day is coming when you will wake to find, beyond all hope, that you have attained it, or else, that it was within your reach and you have lost it forever.
C. S. Lewis

Many of the world's finest Oriental rugs come from little villages in the Middle East, China, or India. These rugs are hand-produced by crews of men and boys under direction of a master weaver. They work from the underside of the rug-to-be. It frequently happens that a weaver absentmindedly makes a mistake and introduces a color that is not according to the pattern. When this occurs, the master weaver, instead of having the work pulled out in the order to correct the color sequence, will find some way to incorporate the mistake harmoniously into the overall pattern. In weaving our lives, we can lean to take unexpected difficulties and mistakes and weave them advantageously in the greater overall patterns of our lives. There is an inherent good in most difficulties.
Norman Vincent Peale

Everything that happens to me can help me along in my Christian life.
E. Stanley Jones

The master in the art of living makes little distinction between his work and his play, his labor and his leisure, his mind and his body, his information and his recreation, his love and his religion. He hardly knows which is which. He simply pursues his vision of excellence at whatever he does, leaving others to decide whether he is working or playing. To him he's always doing both.
James A. Michener

Pulling weeds and planting seeds. That's the story of life. We are individual lots on which either weeds of selfishness or fruit of the Holy Spirit grows and flourishes.
Dennis and Barbara Rainey

The reflections on a day well spent furnishes us with joys more pleasing than ten thousand triumphs.
Thomas Kempis

Look at everything as though you were seeing it either for the first or last time. Then your time on earth will be filled with glory.
Betty Smith

Yet to live always as though time were a bridge is precisely what the saints do. Their eyes are forever on the eternal, that Beyond which is also here and now and within, because they have cultivated the art of seeing Eternity through that narrow slit- the ever now moment.
Heirlooms

Life is a glorious opportunity, if it is used to condition us for eternity. If we fail in this, though we succeed in everything else, our life will have been a failure. There is no escape for the man who squanders his opportunity to prepare to meet God.
Billy Graham

Who well lives, long lives; for this age of ours should not be numbered by years, days, and hours.
Guillaume de Salluste Du Bartas

Anyone can carry his burden, however hard, until nightfall. Anyone can do his work, however hard, for one day. Anyone can live sweetly patiently, lovingly, purely, till the sun goes down. And this is all that life really means.
Robert Louis Stevenson

The Christian life is a pilgrimage from earth to heaven, and our task is to take as many as possible with us as we make this journey.
Warren Wiersbe

Suddenly I heard the words of Christ and understood them, and life and death ceased to seem to me evil, and instead of despair I experienced happiness and the joy of life undisturbed by death.
Leo Tolstoy

I came from God, and I'm going back to God, and I won't have any gaps of death in the middle of my life.
George Macdonald

As the mother's womb holds us for ten months, making us ready, not for the womb itself, but for life, just so, through our lives, we are making ourselves ready for another birth…Therefore look forward without fear to that appointed hour- the last hour of the body, but not of the soul…That day, which you fear as being the end of all things, is the birthday of your eternity.
Seneca

An advisor of President Lincoln suggested a certain candidate for the Lincoln cabinet. Lincoln refused, saying, "I don't like the man's face." "But, sir, he can't be responsible for his face," insisted his advisor. "Every man over forty is responsible for his face," replied Lincoln, and the subject was dropped.
Abraham Lincoln

You may have living and habitual conversation in heaven, under the aspect of the most simple, ordinary life. Remember that holiness does not consist in doing uncommon things, but in doing every thing with purity of heart.
Henry E. Manning

The Lord of the universe stands ready to pick up your life and give it significance, a sense of fulfillment beyond anything you have ever experienced. Your heart has got eternity in it…and you will not be fulfilled until you know you are making an eternal difference with the one life you have.
Ron Hutchcraft

Once when Ole Bull, the great violinist, was giving a concert in Paris, his "A" string snapped and he transposed the composition and finished it on three strings. That is life- to have your "A" string snap and finish on three strings. How many here have had to test that out! Some of the finest things in human life have been done that way. Indeed, so much the most thrilling part of the human story on this planet lies in such capacity victoriously to handle handicaps that, much as I should have liked to hear Ole Bull with all the resources of a perfect instrument at his command, if I could have heard him only once, I should have liked to hear him when the "A" string snapped and, without rebellion or self-pity or surrender, he finished on three strings.
Harry Emerson Fosdick

Plan your life, budgeting for seventy years…and understand that if your time proves shorter that will not be unfair deprivation but rapid promotion.
J. I. Packer

If life be short, then moderate your worldly cares and projects; do not cumber yourselves with too much provision for a short voyage.
Thomas Manton

If God took time to create beauty, how can we be too busy to appreciate it?
Randall B. Corbin

There were two young boys who were raised in the home of an alcoholic father. As young men, they each went their own way. Years later, a psychologist who was analyzing what drunkenness does to children in the home searched out these two men. One had turned out to be like his father, a hopeless alcoholic. The other had turned out to be a teetotaler. The counselor asked the first man, "Why did you become an alcoholic?" And the second, "Why did you become a teetotaler?" And they both gave the same identical answer in these words, "What else could you expect when you had a father like mine?" It's not what happens to you in life but how you react to it that makes the difference. Every human being in the same situation has the possibilities of choosing how he will react, either positively or negatively.
The West Side Baptist

From heaven even the most miserable life will look like one bad night at an inconvenient hotel.
Teresa of Avila

As a knot appears unexpectedly in a thread, so disappointment blocks the smoothness of life. If a few deft strokes can untangle the skein, life continues evenly; but if it cannot be corrected, then it must be quietly woven into the design. Thus the finished piece can still be beautiful- though not as perfect as planned.
Unknown

I think earth, if chosen instead of Heaven, will turn out to have been, all along, only a region in Hell; and earth, if put second to Heaven, to have been from the beginning a part of Heaven itself.
C. S. Lewis

If you want to live twice as long, eat half as much, sleep twice as much, drink water three times as much, and laugh four times at much.
John H. Cable

There are three important steps to take in preparation for a holy death. And these three principles should be practiced throughout life. (1) Expect that death will come knocking at your gates at any time; this will keep your priorities straight. (2) Value your time for it is the most precious possession you have. (3) Refrain from a soft and easy life; stress the holy life of self-discipline, labor, and alertness. Engage each day in self-examination.
Jeremy Taylor

The only way to live your last day as you would want to, is to live like that all the time.
Vaughan Garwood

If only we knew how to look at life as God sees it, we should realize that nothing is secular in the world, but that everything contributes to the building of the Kingdom of God.
Michel Quoist

God often visits us, but most of the time we are not at home.
French proverb

Life is not given to us that we might live idly without work. No, our life is a struggle and a journey. Good should struggle with evil; truth should struggle with falsehood; freedom should struggle with slavery; love should struggle with hatred. Life is movement, a walk along the way of life to the fulfillment of those ideas which illuminate us, both in our intellect and in our hearts, with divine light.
Giuseppe Mazzini

I should count a life well spent, and the world well lost, if, after tasting all its experiences and facing all its problems, I had no more to show at its close, or to carry with me to another life, than the acquisition of a real, sure, humble, and grateful faith in the Eternal and Incarnate Son of God.
P. T. Forsyth

Our earnest suggestion to the person who feels that she has been hurrying through life a bit too fast and has, in the process, grown a bit indifferent to life: Take the hand of a three-year-old and walk with him two or three blocks. The child can do to a person what any amount of philosophizing cannot.
News-Herald

What are our worst sins? They are chiefly our lost opportunities to grow in wisdom and in nobility of character. They lie in our failure to develop our fullest and best powers given to us by God. They are our missed marks:
The time we wasted.
The education we neglected.
The curiosity we stifled.
The adventures we by-passed.
The excitements of a child which we ignored.
The human relations we treated with indifference.
The entertainment we mistook for culture.
The freedom we left unsupported.
The causes that we scorned.
The books that we did not read.
The wonderful world that we did not penetrate.
Charles Shulman

A man should hear a little music, read a little poetry, and see a fine picture every day of his life, in order that worldly cares may not obliterate the sense of the beautiful which God has implanted in the human soul.
Johann Wolfgang Von Goethe

Shut out suffering, and you see only one side of this strange and fearful thing, the life of man. Brightness and happiness and rest- that is not life. It is only one side of life. Christ saw both sides.
F. W. Robertson

So many of us are blinded to all that is beautiful in life by some ancient hate, fear or sin which haunts us throughout our life. Like Lot's wife, we cease to be human. We dry up like salt and become petrified, imbedded in the ugliness, fright or pain of the past. "Look not behind thee," for behind thee lies Sodom and Gomorrah; before thee the land of promise.
Ahron Opher

The sun is just rising on the morning of another day. What can I wish that this day may bring me? Nothing shall make the world or others poorer, nothing at the expense of other men; but just those few things which in their coming do not stop with me but touch me, rather, as they pass and gather strength. A few friends, who understand me, and yet remain my friends. A work to do which has real value, without which the world would feel the poorer. A return for such work small enough not to tax anyone who pays. A mind unafraid to travel, even through the trail be not blazed. An understanding heart. A sight of the eternal hills, and the unresting sea, and of something beautiful which the hand of man has made. A sense of humor, and the power to laugh. A little leisure with nothing to do. A few moments of quiet, silent meditation. The sense of the presence of God. And the patience to wait for the coming of these things, with the wisdom to know them when they come, and the wit not to change this morning wish of mine.
Walter Hunt

Relying on God has to begin all over again every day as if nothing had yet been done.
C. S. Lewis

How often do we need to see God's face, hear His voice, feel His touch, know His power? The answer to all these questions is the same: Every day!
John Blanchard

Life is a voyage in which we choose neither vessel nor weather, but much can be done in the management of the sails and the guidance of the helm.
Unknown

To see God in everything makes life the greatest adventure there is.
Unknown

Every day is a messenger of God.
Russian proverb

We do ourselves and others a disservice when we make old age something to be feared. Life is not a resource to be used up, so that the older we get, the less life we have left. Life is the accumulation of wisdom, love and experience of people encountered and obstacles overcome. The longer we live, the more life we possess.
Harold Kushner

Never undertake anything for which you wouldn't have the courage to ask the blessings of heaven.
George Lichtenberg

THE BEST THINGS IN LIFE
The best and sweetest things in life are things you cannot buy;
The music of the birds at dawn, the rainbow in the sky.
The dazzling magic of the stars, the miracle of light.
The precious gifts of health and strength, of hearing, speech and sight.
The peace of mind that crowns a busy life of work well done.
A faith in God that deepens as you face the setting sun,
The boon of love, the joy of friendship. As years go by,
You find the greatest blessings are the things you cannot buy.
Patience Strong

The only real life is one lived close to God. This does not happen by itself; you must make an effort to make this happen, and this effort will bring you joy.
Leo Tolstoy

Realize that you must lead a dying life; the more a man dies to himself, the more he begins to live unto God.
Thomas Kempis

It is not in life's chances but in its choices that happiness comes to the heart of the individual.
Unknown

If we live good lives, the times are also good. As we are, such are the times.
Augustine of Hippo

Each day is a storehouse given you
Fresh every morn from God's hand;
Do you stop to think of this
When at its door you stand?
Twenty-four empty, waiting hours,
All ready for you to fill with
Worthwhile thoughts and worthwhile deeds
And service, if you will.
You're given a chance to store
Away treasures of love and joy,
And satisfaction of work well done
That time cannot destroy.
So put your best into all your day
With eyes opened wide to see, and
Eager hands stretched out to grasp
Each opportunity.
Unknown

Our five-year-old Jeanie took to rising at 5:30 each morning and puttering around just long enough to wake the rest of us before climbing back into bed. Her reason was always the same- she had to see if there was a surprise. Finally we told her firmly that she must stop and that there wouldn't be any surprises until Christmas, which was months away. "I wasn't talking about living-room surprises," she said through her tears. "I was talking about like yesterday morning it was raining, and this morning real summer's here, and tomorrow morning I'll probably find some pink in the rosebuds." Jeanie still gets up each morning at 5:30.
Mrs. Roy F. Carter

We do not segment our lives, giving some time to God, some to our business or schooling, while keeping parts to ourselves. The idea is to live all of our lives in the presence of God, under the authority of God, and for the honor and glory of God. That is what the Christian life is all about.
R. C. Sproul

He that lives to live forever, never fears dying.
William Penn

Christ has given us the most glorious interpretation of life's meaning that man has ever had. The fatherhood of God, the fellowship of the Spirit, the sovereignty of righteousness, the law of love, the glory of service, the coming of the Kingdom, the eternal hope- there was never an interpretation of life to compare with that.
Harry Fosdick

One ship drives east and another drives west
With the self-same wind that blows.
'Tis the set of the sail and not the gale
That tells us which way it goes.
Like the winds of the sea are the ways of fate,
As we journey along through life;
'Tis the set of the soul that determines the goal
And neither the calm nor the strife.
Unknown

The waste of life lies in the love we have not given, the powers we have not used, the selfish prudence which will risk nothing and which, shirking pain, misses happiness as well.
Unknown

Stewardship is the ordering of one's life so that time, ability, possessions, and all of one's personality are administered as belonging to God.
Unknown

In the morning hours of a new day we take a moment to give thought to what this day may mean for us. What is a day in a person's life? Isn't it the most precious treasure that can be given to us? If we were denied this day in which to live, you know full well, all of our possessions would mean nothing, our fondest hopes and plans would be of no avail. First and foremost, therefore, is the gift of a new day, one more day of life. Therefore, let us begin the day properly. Let us thank God for this wonderful gift. Let us resolve not to waste one hour of it. Let us resolve to share happiness with those who are closest to us- our family; our neighbors; our associates. This is the greater meaning of the verse we read in the Holy Bible: "So teach us to number our days that we may get us a heart of wisdom."
Morris Goldstein

We may be certain that whatever God has made prominent in his word, he intended to be conspicuous in our lives.
Charles Spurgeon

How life catches up with us and teaches us to love and forgive each other.
Judy Collins

Enjoy the little things in life, for one day you may look back and realize they were the big things.
Antonio Smith

An Outline for Life…
1. Set high goals for yourself.
2. Prepare as thoroughly as you can.
3. Never give into discouragement
4. Strive for self control.
5. Go for absolute honesty.
6. Chose Jesus as a role model.
7. Look for God's purpose in your life.
"The chief cause of failure and unhappiness is trading what we want most, for what we want now."
Nancy Mochel

Life is a big canvas, throw all the paint on it you can.
Danny Kaye

The probability of life originating from accident is comparable to the probability of the unabridged dictionary resulting from an explosion in a printing shop.
Edwin Conklin

One-half the troubles of this life can be traced to saying yes too quickly and not saying no soon enough.
Josh Billings

When Jesus is truly our Lord, he directs our lives and we gladly obey him. Indeed, we bring every part of our lives under his lordship- our home and family, our sexuality and marriage, our job or unemployment, our money and possessions, our ambitions and recreations.
John Stott

As we begin to see the package God is putting together in our lives and discover his purposes for bringing us to our world, it will provide us with the framework we need to make wise choices. In addition, we will find that a sense of purpose gives hope in the midst of tragedy and difficulty, gives meaning to the mundane aspects of our lives, and helps us to make our lives count for God.
R. Ruth Barton

Instead of living a black-and-white existence, we'll be released into a Technicolor world of vibrancy and emotion when we more accurately reflect His nature to the world around us.
Bill Hybels

If you're going through difficult times today, hold steady. It will change soon. If you are experiencing smooth sailing and easy times now, brace yourself. It will change soon. The only thing you can be certain of is change.
James Dobson

There is only one way to bring peace to the heart, joy to the mind, and beauty to the life; it is to accept and do the will of God.
William Barclay

Loneliness

The best remedy for those who are afraid, lonely or unhappy is to go outside, somewhere where they can be quiet, alone with the heavens, nature and God. Because only then does one feel that all is as it should be and that God wishes to see people happy, amidst the simple beauty of nature. As long as this exists, and it certainly always will, I know that then there will always be comfort for every sorrow, whatever the circumstances may be. And I firmly believe that nature brings solace in all troubles.
Anne Frank

In the diary of an elderly woman who lived alone, she often penned: "No one called today."
Unknown

What makes loneliness an anguish is not that I have no one to share my burden, but this: I have only my own burden to bear.
Dag Hammarskjold

Don't forget, a person's greatest emotional need is to feel appreciated.
Unknown

Never lose sight of the fact that old age needs so little but needs that little so much.
Margaret Willour

You have it easily in your power to increase the sum total of this world's happiness now. How? By giving a few words of sincere appreciation to someone who is lonely or discouraged. Perhaps you will forget tomorrow the kind words you say today, but the recipient may cherish them over a lifetime.
Dale Carnegie

There is a treasury of blessing to be found in sharing with shut-ins; they have much to give and often no one to give it to.
William J. Johnston

The loneliest place in the world is the human heart when love is absent.
Unknown

What a pity that so many people are living with so few friends when the world is full of lonesome strangers who would give anything just to be somebody's friend.
Milo L. Arnold

It is not darkness you are going to, for God is Light. It is not lonely, for Christ is with you. It is not unknown country, for Christ is there.
Charles Kingsley

Not many sounds in life, and I include all urban and all rural sounds, exceed in interest a knock at the door.
Charles Lamb

Prayer is an end to isolation. It is living our daily life with someone; with Him who alone can deliver us from solitude.
Georges Lefevre

Love

Be glad of life because it gives you the chance to love and to work and to play and to look at the stars.
Henry Van Dyke

Through the centuries men have displayed many different symbols to show that they are Christians. They have worn crosses in the lapels of their coats, hung chains about their necks, even had special haircuts. Of course, there is nothing intrinsically wrong with any of this, if one feels it is his calling. But there is a much better sign, a universal mark that is to last through all the ages of the church until Jesus comes back...Love- and the unity it attests to- is the mark Christ gave Christians to wear before the world. Only with this mark may the world know that Christians are indeed Christians and that Jesus was sent by the Father.
Francis Schaeffer

Insomuch as love grows in you, so in you beauty grows. For love is the beauty of the soul.
Augustine

No man truly has joy unless he lives in love.
Thomas Aquinas

We all long for heaven where God is, but we have it in our power to be in heaven with Him right now- to be happy with Him at this very moment. But being happy with Him now means loving like He loves, helping like He helps, giving as He gives, serving as He serves, rescuing as He rescues, being with Him twenty-four hours a day- touching Him in His distressing disguise.
Mother Teresa

Somehow, somewhere, I know that God loves me, even though I do not feel that love as I can feel a human embrace, even though I do not hear a voice as I hear human words...God is greater than my senses, greater than my thoughts, greater than my heart. I do believe that He touches me in places that are unknown even to myself.
Henri J. M. Nouwen

Love is an act of endless forgiveness, a tender look which becomes a habit.
Peter Ustinov

Love and trust, in the space between what's said and what's heard in our life, can make all the difference in the world.
Fred Rogers

People often say, "I do not understand love of God; what is love of God?" It would be more exact to say, "cannot understand love in this world without love of God."
Leo Tolstoy

I can understand the greatness of God but I cannot understand his humility. It becomes so clear in him being in love with each one of us separately and completely. It is as if there is no one but me in the world. He loves me so much. Each one of us can say this with great conviction.
Mother Teresa

Life is short and we have not too much time for gladdening the hearts of those who are traveling the dark way with us. Oh, be swift to love! Make haste to be kind.
Henry Frederick Amiel

Prayer is the sum of our relationship with God. We are what we pray. The degree of our faith is the degree of our prayer. Our ability to love is our ability to pray.
Carlo Carretto

Love is a fruit, in season at all times and within the reach of every hand. Anyone may gather it and no limit is set. Everyone can reach this love through mediation, the spirit of prayer, and sacrifice.
Mother Teresa

The love of Christ becomes the mightiest force in the world to the man who is yielded to it.
E. W. Kenyon

Try to live with the part of your soul which understands eternity, which is not afraid of death. And that part of your soul is love.
Leo Tolstoy

If we demonstrate unconditional love, daily prayer, persistent faith, and adherence to God's laws, we give our children a gift. If we teach them that good deeds and kind words are expressions of the Spirit, we are on track toward living more like Jesus.
Jane Jarrell

Our life of poverty is as necessary as the work itself. Only in heaven will we see how much we owe to the poor for helping us to love God better because of them.
Mother Teresa

Engrave this upon my heart: There isn't anyone you couldn't love once you've heard their story.
Mary Lou Kownacki

The capacity for grief is as much from God as the capacity for love- and we have not really lived until we have sounded them both.
Unknown

It matters not how much Bible reading and prayer and catechism saying and godly teaching there may be in a home, if gentleness is lacking; that is lacking which most of all the young need in the life of a home. A child must have love. Love is to its life what sunshine is to plants and flowers. No young life can ever grow to its best in a home without gentleness. The lack is one which leaves an irreparable hurt in the lives of children.
Unknown

The springs of love are in God, not in us.
Oswald Chambers

Homes that are built on anything other than love are bound to crumble.
Billy Graham

Every single act of love bears the imprint of God.
Unknown

Love is never lost. If not reciprocated, it will flow back and soften and purify the heart.
Washington Irving

Every time you smile at someone, it is an action of love, a gift to that person, a beautiful thing.
Mother Teresa

We are only as good as what we love.
Sam Bellow

Four stages of growth in Christian maturity...
Love of self for self's sake
Love of God for self's sake
Love of God for God's sake
Love of self for God's sake.
Bernard of Clairvaux

There is a wealth of unexpressed love in the world. It is one of the chief causes of sorrow evoked by death: what might have been said or might have been done that never can be said or done.
Arthur Hopkins

The most vivid memories of Christmases past are usually not of gifts given or received, but of the spirit of love; the cherished little habits of the home.
Lois Rand

God does not have to come and tell me what I must do for Him, He brings me into a relationship with Himself where I hear His call and understand what He wants me to do, and I do it out of sheer love to Him... When people say they have had a call to foreign service, or to any particular sphere of work, they mean that their relationship to God has enabled them to realize what they can do for God.
Oswald Chambers

What the heart gives away is never gone. It is kept in the hearts of others.
Robin St. John

Is life not full of opportunities for learning love? Every man and woman every day has a thousand of them. The world is not a playground; it is a schoolroom. Life is not a holiday, but an education. And the one eternal lesson for us all is how better we can love.
Henry Drummond

Many do not advance in Christian progress because they stick in penances and particular exercises, while they neglect the love of God, which is the end.
Brother Lawrence

The three hardest tasks in the world are neither physical feats nor intellectual achievements, but moral acts: to return love for hate, to include the excluded, and to say, "I was wrong."
Sydney J. Harris

That best portion of a good man's life, His little nameless, unremembered acts Of kindness and of love.
William Wordsworth

When a man sees that his neighbour hates him, then he must love him more than he did before to fill up the gap.
Rabbi Rafael

Family matters. Family are the only people who will tell you when you're getting off the tracks a little. Surround yourself with people who love the Lord, love themselves and love you, and you can't really fail.
A. J. Michalka

Every single person in our lives will disappoint us at some level. Some days they'll be busy when we need them to be still; other days they'll be self-centered when we need them to concentrate on us. Sometimes they'll bruise us with hard words aimed right for the soft places in our soul. They won't meet all our emotional needs. They can't; they have too many needs of their own. They're sinners just like us. Only our Creator can love us perfectly, the way He created us to be loved. His love is the only thing that can define us without destroying us.
Lisa Harper

The measure of our love for others can largely be determined by the frequency and earnestness of our prayers for them.
A. W. Pink

Nothing can separate you from His love, absolutely nothing. God is enough for time, and God is enough for eternity. God is enough!
Hannah Whitall Smith

Life's short and we never have enough time for the hearts of those who travel the way with us. O, be swift to love! Make haste to be kind.
Henri-Frederic Amiel

Some four-letter words that Christians need to revitalize with appropriate action are: give, live, pray, read, hope, help, sing, work, lead, grow, walk, dare, join, lift, talk and love; but the greatest of these is "love."
Unknown

Forgiveness is the precondition of love.
Catherine Marshall

You will find, as you look back upon your life, that the moments that stand out, the moments when you have really lived, are the moments when you have done things in the spirit of Love.
Henry Drummond

Always, love is a choice. You come up against scores of opportunities every day to love or not to love. You encounter hundreds of small chances to please your friends, delight your Lord, and encourage your family. That's why love and obedience are intimately linked- you can't have one without the other.
Joni Eareckson Tada

The first command in Ephesians 5 tells us to be imitators of God by reflecting the way he loves us. Our love for others flows out of our sense of being deeply loved. Instead of constantly looking for the right person, God tells us to become the right person. Instead of looking for love, God tells us to realize that love has already found us! God loves as no one else ever can.
Chip Ingram

The main evidence that we are growing in Christ is not exhilarating prayer experiences, but steadily increasing, humble love for other people.
Frederica Mathewes-Green

To love means loving the unlovable. To forgive means pardoning the unpardonable. Faith means believing the unbelievable. Hope means hoping when everything seems hopeless.
Gilbert Keith Chesterton

People are unreasonable, illogical, and self-centered. Love them anyway.
Mother Teresa

Trust God's love. His perfect love. Don't fear he will discover your past. He already has. Don't fear disappointing him in the future. He can show you the chapter in which you will. With perfect knowledge of the past and perfect vision of the future, he loves you perfectly in spite of both.
Max Lucado

Allowing ourselves to be more loving is a most beautiful journey.
Barry Neil Kaufman

If we're not telling God and our family that we love them, we just wasted a day of our life.
Ted Roberts

Because of God's grace, there is nothing we can do that will make Him love us more than He already does. And there is nothing we can do or have done that will cause Him to love us any less.
Steven Curtis Chapman

If you were going to die soon and had only one phone call you could make, who would you call and what would you say? And why are you waiting?
Stephen Levine

Authentic religion is not a theology test. It's a love test.
Oliver Thomas

I never knew how to worship until I knew how to love.
Henry Ward Beecher

The supreme happiness of life is the conviction of being loved for yourself, or more correctly, being loved in spite of yourself.
Unknown

Love me when I least deserve it, because that's when I really need it.
Swedish proverb

We are all pencils in the hand of a writing God, who is sending love letters to the world.
Mother Teresa

Tell me how much you know of the sufferings of your fellow men and I will tell how much you have loved them.
Unknown

It is love, not reason, that is stronger than death.
Thomas Mann

My weight is my love.
Augustine

Looking back, I have this to regret, that too often when I loved, I did not say so.
David Grayson

To love and be loved is to feel the sun from both sides.
David Viscott

God loves us the way we are, but He loves us too much to leave us that way.
Leighton Ford

The love of God is like the Amazon River flowing down to water one daisy.
Unknown

There is nothing that will not reveal its secrets if you love it enough. *George Washington Carver*

When we come to the last moment of this lifetime, and we look back across it, the only thing that's going to matter is "what was the quality of our love?"
Richard Bach

Others may argue your beliefs, but they can't refuse your love.
Unknown

Not where I breathe,
But where I love, I live.
Robert Southey

When Jesus tells us to love our enemies, He Himself will give us the love with which to do it. We are neither factories nor reservoirs of His love, only channels. When we understand that, all excuse for pride is eliminated.
Corrie ten Boom

Grace means that God already loves us as much as an infinite God can possibly love.
Philip Yancey

God has not promised skies always blue, flower-strewn pathways all our lives through;
God has not promised sun without rain, joy without sorrow, peace without pain.
But God has promised strength for the day,
rest for the labor, light for the way, grace for the trials, help from above, unfailing sympathy, undying love.
Annie Johnson Flint

Get yourself into the presence of the loving Father. Just place yourself before Him, and look up into His face; think of His love, His wonderful, tender, pitying love.
Andrew Murray

Lord…give me the gift of faith to be renewed and shared with others each day. Teach me to live this moment only, looking neither to the past with regret, nor the future with apprehension. Let love be my aim and my life a prayer.
Roseann Alexander-Isham

Lord, give me an open heart to find You everywhere, to glimpse the heaven enfolded in a bud, and to experience eternity in the smallest act of love.
Mother Teresa

To worship rightly is to love each other, Each smile a hymn, each kindly deed a prayer.
John Greenleaf Whittier

Love is of utmost importance. Once you have set your will that you will learn the way of love, then there is no flaw or irritation in another person that you cannot bear…If this one commandment were kept- "Love one another"- I know that it would carry us a long way toward keeping all the rest of our Lord's commands.
Teresa of Avila

To be really truthful, we have to do more than stop lying. Really, most of the work is positively learning how to speak the whole truth in love.
Tim Stafford

You are more evil than you have ever feared, and more loved than you have ever hoped.
Mark Driscoll

Goodness is love in action, love with its hands to the plow, love with the burden on its back, love following His footsteps who went about continually doing good.
James H. Hamilton

Is it a small thing in your eyes to be loved by God- to be the son, the spouse, the love, the delight of the King of glory? Christian, believe this, and think about it: you will be eternally embraced in the arms of the love which was from everlasting, and will extend to everlasting- of the love which brought the Son of God's love from heaven to earth, from earth to the cross, from the cross to the grave, from the grave to glory- that love which was weary, hungry, tempted, scorned, scourged, buffered, spat upon, crucified, pierced- which fasted, prayed, taught, healed, wept, sweated, bled, died. That love will eternally embrace you.
Richard Baxter

The love of God is like the Amazon River flowing down to water one daisy.
Unknown

To please God...to be a real ingredient in the divine happiness...to be loved by God, not merely pitied, but delighted in, as an artist delights in this work or a father in a son...it seems impossible, a weight or burden of glory which your thoughts can hardly sustain. But it is so!
C. S. Lewis

Forgiveness is the greatest expression of love.
Unknown

Tears are liquid love.
Faye Landrum

Perfect prayer is only another name for love.
François Fénelon

Hatred and bitterness can never cure the disease of fear; only love can do that. Hatred paralyses life; love releases it. Hatred confuses life; love harmonizes it. Hatred darkens life; love illumines it.
Martin Luther King, Jr.

When we are humble enough to allow God to fill us with His love, a miracle happens.
Kim Moore

People are unreasonable, illogical, and self-centered. Love them anyway.
Mother Teresa

Faith, like light, should always be simple and unbending; while love, like warmth, should beam forth on every side, and bend to every necessity of our brethren.
Martin Luther

Live your human task in the liberating certainty that nothing in the world can separate you from God's love for you.
Brakkenstein Community of Blessed Sacrament Fathers

Love is an act of endless forgiveness, a tender look which becomes a habit.
Peter Ustinov

Not tongues nor faith nor prophecy nor knowledge nor martyrdom nor philanthropy, but love is the Christian's mark of distinction.
Vance Havner

To understand is not only to pardon, but in the end to love.
Walter Lippmann

To love what is below the human is degradation; to love what is human for the sake of the human is mediocrity; to love the human for the sake of the Divine is enriching; to love the Divine for its own sake is sanctity.
Fulton J. Sheen

There is no greater love than the love that holds on where there seems nothing left to hold on to.
G. W. C. Thomas

The holy heart can be hurt. But it answers injury with love and prayer and forgiveness.
W. E. McCumber

The loneliest place in the world is the human heart when love is absent.
Unknown

A loving heart is the truest wisdom.
Charles Dickens

All love is lost but upon God alone.
William Dunbar

The problem of reconciling human suffering with the existence of a God who loves, is only insoluble so long as we attach a trivial meaning to the word "love."
C. S. Lewis

Love has hands to help others. It has feet to hasten to the poor and needy. It has eyes to see misery and want. It has ears to hear the sighs and sorrows of men. This is what love looks like.
Augustine

Love is the one business in which it pays to be an absolute spendthrift: give it away; throw it away; splash it over; empty your pockets; shake the basket; and tomorrow you'll have more than ever.
Unknown

Grace means primarily the free, forgiving love of God in Christ to sinners and the operation of that love in the lives of Christians.
A. M. Hunter

The truth about man is that he needs to be loved the most when he deserves it the least. Only God can fulfill this incredible need. Only God can provide a love so deep it saves from the depths.
Unknown

If there is love in your heart Christmas can last forever.
Marion Schoeberlein

Joy is love exalted; peace is love in repose; long-suffering is love enduring; gentleness is love in society; goodness is love in action; faith is love on the battlefield; meekness is love in school; and temperance is love in training.
Dwight L. Moody

To live in prayer together is to walk in love together.
Margaret Moore Jacobs

Without Christ I was like a fish out of water. With Christ I am in the ocean of love.
Sadhu Singh

I love little children, and it is not a slight thing when they, who are fresh from God, love us.
Charles Dickens

Christ revealed to humanity those things which their best selves already knew: that people are equal because the same spirit lives in all of them…Learn from the small children, behave like children, and treat all people on an equal basis, with love and tenderness.
Leo Tolstoy

We grasp for truth and lose it till it comes to us by love.
Madeleine L'Engle

While faith makes all things possible, it is love that makes all things easy.
Evan Hopkins

Perhaps with charity one shouldn't think. Charity like love should be blind.
Graham Greene

God is perfect love and perfect wisdom. We do not pray in order to change His Will, but to bring our wills into harmony with His.
William Temple

A deep plunge into the waters of sorrow is the hopefullest way of getting through them on one's daily road of life again. No one can help another very much in these crises of life; but love and sympathy count for something.
Thomas Henry Huxley

There is no surprise more magical than the surprise of being loved. It is the finger of God on a man's shoulder.
Charles Morgan

Say to yourself, "I am loved by God more than I can either conceive or understand." Let this fill all your soul and all your prayers and never leave you. You will soon see that this is the way to find God.
Henri De Tourville

To live well is nothing other than to love God with all one's heart, with all one's soul and with all one's efforts; from this it comes about that love is kept whole and uncorrupted. No misfortune can disturb it. It obeys only [God] and is careful in discerning things, so as not to be surprised by deceit or trickery.
Augustine of Hippo

Family life is too intimate to be preserved by the spirit of justice. It can be sustained by a spirit of love which goes beyond justice.
Reinhold Niebahr

God might want you to extend his love by offering to baby-sit for the single parent down the street. He might want you to prepare a hearty meal for that lonely old man who lost his wife — and to sit and visit with him while he eats. Who knows, he might even want you to reach out and touch the life of a total stranger in some way you can't imagine right now. Are you willing to set aside your own comfort to touch someone else with God's love?
Amy Nappa

Love is an act of endless forgiveness.
Jean Vanier

When you pray, you open yourself to the influence of the power which has revealed itself as love. The power gives you freedom and independence. Once touched by this power, you are no longer swayed back and forth by the countless opinions, ideas, and feelings which flow through you. You have found a center for your life that gives you a creative distance so that everything you see, hear, and feel can be tested against the source.
Henri Nouwen

Throw your heart over the fence and the rest will follow.
Norman Vincent Peale

The proof of who we are in Christ isn't how many folks have come to the Lord through us. It isn't how much we've contributed to the Lord's work. It isn't how sweetly we've sung his praises. It is, pure and simple, how we have loved each other.
Gayle Roper

The essential truth is that discernment is a function of a loving, personal relationship to the Lord. It can normally be only as deep and as solid as that relationship itself. The true discerner must be a praying, loving person.
Unknown

I have found the paradox that if I love until it hurts, then there is no hurt, but only more love.
Mother Teresa

One day, a child of mine came home in tears. Another child had been mean to him and hurt his feelings. I want to say now, as I said then, "When a person doesn't like you, or is mean to you, it has more to do with them than it does with you. Dry your tears. You cannot be loved by everyone, because everyone cannot love themselves. You can know that I will always love you. And the greatest gift you can give to others is to love yourself. If you do that, you can love others without worrying whether they love you back. You will have enough love for both of you."
Dorothy Dupont

One forgives as much as one loves.
Francois Rochefoucauld

Miracles

As for me, I know of nothing else but miracles.
Walt Whitman

I believe praise is a powerful weapon against the enemy. Breakthroughs happen as we praise God. He can work a miracle in whatever situation we face regarding our health, finances, family, or career.
Arah Wehrli

Too many times we miss so much because we live on the low level of the natural, the ordinary, the explainable.
Vance Havner

We do not hug our miracles close. We put them hastily away, preferring the commonplace to live with.
Fulton Oursler

Grant me God and miracles take care of themselves!
A. W. Tozer

The divine art of miracle is not an art of suspending the pattern to which events conform, but of feeding new events into that pattern.
C. S. Lewis

The miracles of Jesus were the ordinary works of his Father, wrought small and swift that we might take them in.
George MacDonald

When we are humble enough to allow God to fill us with His love, a miracle happens.
Kim Moore

There are two ways to live: you can live as if nothing is a miracle; you can live as if everything is a miracle.
Albert Einstein

The miracles of Jesus were the ordinary works of his Father, wrought small and swift that we might take them in.
George Macdonald

In order to be a realist you must believe in miracles.
Unknown

If there is a Creator God, there is nothing illogical at all about the possibility of miracles. After all, if he created everything out of nothing, it would hardly be a problem for him to rearrange parts of it as and when he wishes.
Timothy Keller

Money & Greed

Because we lack a divine Center our need for security has led us into an insane attachment to things. We really must understand that the lust for affluence in contemporary society is psychotic. It is psychotic because it has completely lost touch with reality. We crave things we neither need nor enjoy…We are made to feel ashamed to wear clothes or drive cars until they are worn out. The mass media have convinced us that to be out of step with fashion is to be out of step with reality. It is time we awaken to the fact that conformity to a sick society is to be sick.
Richard Foster

Never try to save out of God's cause; such money will canker the rest. Giving to God is no loss; it is putting your substance in the best bank. Giving is true having.
Charles Haddon Spurgeon

My children, the three acts of faith, hope, and charity contain all the happiness of man upon the earth.
John Vianney

I remember a friend of mine telling a story about one of his first paying jobs. When he was in seminary, he and his wife pastored a small church in a rough part of Houston. They lived in the parsonage and received a salary of one hundred dollars a week. One day a college friend of his passed through town and stopped by for a visit. The friend's career was in sales, and at the time, 1972, he was doing quite well, with a six-figure salary. He said to the young pastor, "You were pretty sharp in school. You know, you could be doing a lot better financially if you had chosen a different profession. For instance, if you were with my company, you could be making a hundred thousand dollars a year." My friend eyed his buddy and said, " Well, I don't know if I could live on that." "What do you mean, you don't know if you could live on that? You don't look like you're making half that much now." My friend said, "Well, I don't right now, but I work for someone who promised to pay me whatever I need. This last year I didn't need much, but what if next year I needed more? I sure would be in a mess if all I had was a hundred thousand dollars."
Amy Grant

God comes right out and tells us why He gives us more money than we need. It's not so we can find more ways to spend it. It's not so we can indulge ourselves and spoil our children. It's not so we can insulate ourselves from needing God's provision. It's so we can give and give generously.
Randy Alcorn

Live simply that others may simply live.
Unknown

Laughter is an instant vacation. Giving is a two-week cruise- with pay.
Bob Hope

When you serve God, you are using God's money to accomplish His wishes. But when you serve money, you are using God's money to accomplish your wishes.
Bruce Wilkinson

Prosperity knits a man to the World. He feels that he is "finding his place in it," while really it is finding its place in him.
C. S. Lewis

There is absolutely no evidence that complexity and materialism lead to happiness. On the contrary, there is plenty of evidence that simplicity and spirituality lead to joy, a blessedness that is better than happiness.
Dennis Swanberg

In the name of God, stop a moment, close your work, and look around you.
Leo Tolstoy

No man can tell whether he is rich or poor by turning to his ledger. It is the heart that makes a man rich. He is rich or poor according to what he is, not according to what he has.
Henry Ward Beecher

The problem with spending your life climbing up the ladder is that you will go right past Jesus, for he's coming down.
John Ortberg

Who is a wise man? -He who studies all the time.
Who is strong? -He who can limit himself.
Who is rich? -He who is happy with what he has.
The Talmud

Have you noticed, it's difficult, if not impossible, to save money when your neighbors keep buying things you can't afford?
Unknown

One of the dangers of having a lot of money is that you may be quite satisfied with the kinds of happiness money can give and so fail to realize your need for God. If everything seems to come simply by signing checks, you may forget that you are at every moment totally dependent on God.
C. S. Lewis

Hold everything you own with an open hand.
Terri Green

Save some before you spend, spend less than you earn, and honor the Lord by your tithing.
R. R. Ball

The bread that you store up belongs to the hungry; the cloak that lies on your chest belongs to the naked; and the gold that you have hidden in the ground belongs to the poor.
Basil of Caesarea

Learn to hold loosely all that is not eternal.
A. Maude Royden

We can stand affliction better than we can prosperity, for in prosperity we forget God.
D. L. Moody

There is no dignity quite so impressive, and no independence quite so important, as living within your means.
Calvin Coolidge

I think everybody should get rich and famous and do everything they ever dreamed of so they can see that it's not the answer.
Jim Carrey

We must teach our children that the real measure of their success in life is how much they'd be worth if they had absolutely nothing.
Walt Mueller

A lad who heard his father pray for missions, and especially for the needs of missionaries, that they might be supplied, and that their institutions might be amply sustained, said to him, "Father, I wish I had your money." "Why, my son, what would you do with it?" asked the father. "I would answer your prayers," was the reply.
Unknown

Contentment is natural wealth; luxury, artificial poverty.
Socrates

In Tolstoy's "Man and Dame Fortune," the hero is told he can have the right to all the land around which he can plow a furrow in a single day. The man started off with great vigor, and was going to encompass only that which he could easily care for. But as the day progressed, he desired more and more rights. He plowed and plowed, until at the end of the day he could in no possible way return to his original point of departure, but struggling to do so, he fell, the victim of a heart attack. The only right he secured was the right to 18 square feet of land in which to be buried.
Russell T. Loesch

If all the gold in the world were melted down into a solid cube it would be about the size of an eight-room house. If a man got possession of all that gold- billions of dollars' worth- he could not buy a friend, character, peace of mind, clear conscience, or a sense of eternity.
Charles F. Banning

Ironically, many people can't afford to give precisely because they're not giving. If we pay our debt to God first, then we will incur His blessing to help us pay our debts to men. But when we rob God to pay men, we rob ourselves of God's blessing.
Randy Alcorn

Watch lest prosperity destroy generosity.
Henry Ward Beecher

Some people are so poor they only have money!
Ivor Powell

To possess money is very well; it may be a most valuable servant; to be possessed by it is to be possessed by a devil, and one of the meanest and worst kinds of devils.
Tryon Edwards

Money has never yet made anyone rich.
Seneca

Wealth is a pre-payment for a task to be performed.
Jay Kaufman

Contentment is natural wealth; luxury is artificial poverty.
Socrates

The evils of riches, to the Christian, are the evils of distraction (the distraction that keeps men from thinking about God), the evils of a false dependence on the created order, and a would-be security that fails to take account o the inevitable fragility of human destiny on this earth.
D. L. Munby

Economy is half the battle of life; it is not so hard to earn money as to spend it well.
Charles Haddon Spurgeon

Perhaps with charity one shouldn't think. Charity like love should be blind.
Graham Greene

THE BEST THINGS IN LIFE
The best and sweetest things in life are things you cannot buy;
The music of the birds at dawn, the rainbow in the sky.
The dazzling magic of the stars, the miracle of light.
The precious gifts of health and strength, of hearing, speech and sight.
The peace of mind that crowns a busy life of work well done.
A faith in God that deepens as you face the setting sun,
The boon of love, the joy of friendship. As years go by,
You find the greatest blessings are the things you cannot buy.
Patience Strong

Stewardship is the ordering of one's life so that time, ability, possessions, and all of one's personality are administered as belonging to God.
Unknown

There is nothing more harmful to you than improving only your material, animal side of life. There is nothing more beneficial, both for you and for others, than activity directed to the improvement of your soul.
Leo Tolstoy

Money is the longest route to happiness.
Evangeline Lilly

Simplicity is the real luxury.
Unknown

I am happy in having learned to distinguish between ownership and possession. Books, pictures, and all the beauty of the world belong to those who love and understand them- not usually to those who possess them. All of those things that I am entitled to have I have- I own by divine right. So I care not a bit who possesses them.
Unknown

Find out how much God has given you and from it take what you need; the remainder is needed by others.
Augustine

He is no fool who gives what he cannot keep to gain what he cannot lose.
Jim Elliot

Pain, Suffering & Grief

The best remedy for those who are afraid, lonely or unhappy is to go outside, somewhere where they can be quiet, alone with the heavens, nature and God. Because only then does one feel that all is as it should be and that God wishes to see people happy, amidst the simple beauty of nature. As long as this exists, and it certainly always will, I know that then there will always be comfort for every sorrow, whatever the circumstances may be. And I firmly believe that nature brings solace in all troubles.
Anne Frank

Tears are part of existence on this earth. They have flowed from Eden right down through history to the present day.
Wayne Detzler

There are such things as consecrated griefs, sorrows that may be common to everyone but which take on a special character when accepted intelligently and offered to God in loving submission.
A. W. Tozer

In the prison house I sung praises to my God, and esteemed the bolts and locks put upon me as jewels.
William Dewsbury

O God, my God, the night has values that the day never dreamed of.
Thomas Merton

Often, in the midst of great problems, we stop short of the real blessing God has for us, which is a fresh vision of who He is.
Anne Graham Lotz

The capacity for grief is as much from God as the capacity for love- and we have not really lived until we have sounded them both.
Unknown

Mankind wants glory. We want health. We want wealth. We want happiness. We want all our felt needs met, all our little human itches scratched. We want a painless life. We want the crown without the cross. We want the gain without the pain. We want the words of Christ's salvation to be easy.
John MacArthur

We need to remind each other that the cup of sorrow is also the cup of joy, that precisely what causes us sadness can become the fertile ground for gladness.
Henri Nouwen

He brought my life passion from my life pain.
Beth Moore

It is a remarkable thing that some of the most optimistic and enthusiastic people you will meet are those who have been through intense suffering.
Warren Wiersbe

There is a wealth of unexpressed love in the world. It is one of the chief causes of sorrow evoked by death: what might have been said or might have been done that never can be said or done.
Arthur Hopkins

For Jesus, prayer was a vital element in making God's power available to people in need.
Jim Reapsome

A spirit of thankfulness is one of the most distinctive marks of a Christian whose heart is attuned to the Lord. Thank God in the midst of trials and every persecution.
Billy Graham

Great grief makes sacred those upon whom it is laid. Joy may elevate, ambition glorify, but only sorrow can consecrate.
Horace Greeley

The sermon of your life in tough times ministers to people more powerfully than the most eloquent speaker.
Bill Bright

There are wounds of the spirit which never close and are intended in God's mercy to bring us nearer to Him, and to prevent us leaving Him by their very perpetuity. Such wounds then may almost be taken as a pledge, or at least as a ground for a humble trust, that God will give us the great gift of perseverance to the end. This is how I comfort myself in my own great bereavements.
John Henry Newman

A wise man once said, "Whatever came to me, I looked on as God's gift for some special purpose. If it was a difficulty, I knew He gave it to me to struggle with, to strengthen my mind and my faith." That idea has sweetened and helped me all of my life.
Unknown

God Almighty would in no way permit evil in His works were He not so omnipotent and good that even out of evil He could work good.
Augustine

If suffering went out of life, courage, tenderness, pity, faith, patience and love in its divinity would go out of life too.
Father Andrew

To follow Jesus doesn't remove us from the stuff of life. It is not resolution. It is tension and journey.
David Crowder

Life provides losses and heartbreak. But the greatest tragedy is to have the experience and miss the meaning. I am determined not to miss that meaning.
Robin Roberts

Take those road hazards- the potholes, ruts, detours, and all the rest- as evidence that you were on the right route. It's when you find yourself on that big, broad, easy road that you ought to worry.
Joni Eareckson Tada

Worship God in the difficult circumstances, and when He chooses, He will alter them in two seconds.
Oswald Chambers

A tried Christian grows rich by his losses, he rises by his falls, he lives by dying, and he becomes full by being emptied.
C. H. Spurgeon

The dark moments of our life will last only as long as is necessary for God to accomplish His purpose in us.
Charles Stanley

No man can estimate what is really happening at the present. All we do know, and that to a large extent by direct experience, is that evil labors with vast power and perpetual success- in vain: preparing always only the soil for unexpected good to sprout in.
J. R. R. Tolkien

World poverty is a hundred million mothers weeping…because they cannot feed their children.
Ronald Sider

Only God can turn a mess into a message, a test into a testimony.
Joyce Meyer

Before every great opportunity God gave me a great trial.
Martin Luther

Being a Christian doesn't mean that our struggles are necessarily different from those of non-Christians; it's just that our solution to the struggles is different.
Bobby Richardson

The best place any Christian can ever be in is to be totally destitute and totally dependent upon God, and know it.
Alan Redpath

When you are in the dark, listen, and God will give you a very precious message for someone else when you get into the light.
Oswald Chambers

Life does not accommodate you, it shatters you. It is meant to, and couldn't do it better. Every seed destroys its container or there would be no fruition.
F. Scott-Maxwell

There are certainly things in this life that God can reveal to us only in the midst of adversity. There are hidden places deep in our souls He can reach only through our suffering.
Mary Nelson

In the midst of winter, I finally learned there was within me an invincible summer.
Albert Camus

Afflictions are the steps to heaven.
Elizabeth Seton

We turn to God for help when our foundations are shaking only to learn that it is God shaking them.
Charles West

Have courage for the great sorrows of life and have patience for the small ones. Go to sleep in peace. God is awake.
Victor Hugo

If a bird is flying for pleasure, it flies with the wind, but if it meets danger it turns and faces the wind, in order that it may rise higher.
Corrie ten Boom

Remember that everyone you meet is afraid of something, loves something, and has lost something.
Unknown

Our little time of suffering is not worthy of our first night's welcome home to Heaven.
Samuel Rutherford

The next time you are called to suffer, pay attention. It may be the closest you'll ever get to God.
Max Lucado

The most fruitful and the most joy-filled Christians are the most pruned Christians.
Bruce Wilkinson

The brook would lose its song if the rocks were removed.
Unknown

God's Heart is especially tender toward the downtrodden and the defeated. He knows your name and He has seen every tear you have shed.
James Dobson

Only when we are brought to the end of ourselves are we in a position to see more of God than we have seen.
Unknown

Every tear from every eye becomes a babe in eternity.
William Blake

Afflictions are but the shadow of God's wings.
George Macdonald

Our real blessings often appear to us in the shapes of pains, losses, and disappointments; but let us have patience, and we soon shall see them in their proper figures.
Joseph Askinas

God whispers to us in our pleasures, speaks in our conscience, but shouts in our pains; it is His megaphone to rouse a deaf world.
C.S. Lewis

God has not promised skies always blue,
flower-strewn pathways all our lives through;
God has not promised sun without rain,
joy without sorrow, peace without pain.
But God has promised strength for the day,
rest for the labor, light for the way,
grace for the trials, help from above,
unfailing sympathy, undying love.
Annie Johnson Flint

God permits troubles to beset His children, but He also refreshes them. He grants them respite when the heart is still and the soul joyous, and you will agree with me that such moments of the secret joy of the Spirit are far more precious than the highest pleasures this world can offer.
The Lutheran Witness

Nothing transcends the power of God. Whether our difficulty is from Satan, others, self-inflicted, or experienced in the process of our obedience, it is God's prerogative to rearrange, reconstruct, reinterpret, and realign the situation to bring glory and praise to His name.
Joseph Stowell

No storm is so great, no wave is so high, no sea is so deep, no wind is so strong, that Jesus cannot either calm it or carry us through it.
Anne Graham Lotz

It is said an eastern monarch once charged his wise men to invent a sentence, to be ever in view, and which should be true and appropriate in all times and situations. They presented him with the words, "And this, too, shall pass away." How much it expresses! How chastening in the hour of pride! How consoling in the depths of affliction!
Abraham Lincoln

Beethoven once said of Rossini that he had in him the making of a great musician if only he had some difficulties to struggle with and some failures. Beethoven understood from his own experience that struggle produces greatness.
Ludwig van Beethoven

A man was carrying a heavy basket. His son asked to help him. The father cut a stick and placed it through the handle of the basket so that the end toward himself was very short; while the end toward the boy was three or four times as long. Each took hold of his end of the stick, and the basket was lifted and easily carried. The son was bearing the burden with the father, but he found his work easy and light because his father assumed the heavy end of the stick. Just so it is when we bear the yoke with Christ; He sees to it that the burden laid on us is light; He carries the heavy end.
John T. Faris

I walked a mile with pleasure,
She chattered all the way;
But left me none the wiser,
For all she had to say.
I walked a mile with sorrow,
Not a word, said she;
But oh the things I learned
When sorrow walked with me.
Robert Browning Hamilton

A soul untried by sorrows is good for nothing.
Theophan the Recluse

Ten thousand difficulties do not make one doubt.
John Henry Newman

Some of the world's greatest men and women have been saddled with disabilities and adversities but have managed to overcome them. Cripple him, and you have a Sir Walter Scott. Lock him in a prison cell, and you have a John Bunyan. Bury him in the snows of Valley Forge, and you have a George Washington. Raise him in abject poverty, and you have an Abraham Lincoln. Subject him to bitter religious prejudice, and you have a Benjamin Disraeli. Strike him down with infantile paralysis, and he becomes a Franklin D. Roosevelt. Burn him so severely in a schoolhouse fire that the doctors say he will never walk again, and you have a Glenn Cunningham, who set a world's record in 1934 for running a mile in 4 minutes, 6.7 seconds. Deafen a genius composer, and you have a Ludwig van Beethoven. Have him or her born Black in a society filled with racial discrimination, and you have a Booker T. Washington, a Harriet Tubman, a Marian Anderson, or a George Washington Carver. Make him the first child to survive in a poor Italian family of eighteen children, and you have an Enrico Caruso. Have him born of parents who survived a Nazi concentration camp, paralyze him from the waist down when he is four, and you have an incomparable concert violinist, Itzhak Perlman. Call him a slow learner, "retarded," and write him off as ineducable, and you have an Albert Einstein.
Unknown

God uses broken things. It takes broken soil to produce a crop, broken clouds to give rain, broken grain to give bread, broken bread to give strength. It is the broken alabaster box that gives forth perfume…it is Peter, weeping bitterly, who returns to greater power than ever.
Vance Havner

A violin-maker in the old days always chose the wood for his violins from the north side of the trees; it was the side upon which the wind and the storms had beaten. So he said when he heard the groaning of the trees in the forest at night he didn't feel sorry for them, for they were just learning to be violins.
Unknown

There are certainly things in this life that God can reveal to us only in the midst of adversity. There are hidden places deep in our souls He can reach only through our suffering.
Mary Nelson

We all come up against our own version of the Red Sea- Seas of Divorce, Debt, Death, Depression, Guilt, Fear, Loneliness or Hopelessness. And hey, if you're anything like me, you might look around for a boat when God wants to display His glory by parting the Sea instead.
Rebecca Lusignolo

God prepares great men for great tasks by great trials.
J. K. Gressett

Sometimes we are helped by being hurt. A skilled physician about to perform a delicate operation upon the ear said reassuringly, "I may hurt you, but I will not injure you." How often the Great Physician speaks to us the same message if we would only listen! Richer life, more abundant health for every child of His- that is His only purpose. Why defeat that purpose?
The Sunday School Times

If a man carries his cross beautifully and makes it radiant with glory of a meek and gentle spirit, the time will come when the things that now disturb will be the events for which he will most of all give gratitude to God.
Unknown

Too often we forget that the great men of faith reached the heights they did only by going through the depths.
Os Guinness

Pain is pain and sorrow is sorrow. It hurts. It limits. It impoverishes. It isolates. It restrains. It works devastation deep within the personality. It circumscribes in a thousand different ways. There is nothing good about it. But the gifts God can give with it are the richest the human spirit can know.
Margaret Clarkson

When God would make a pearl, He allows a grain of sand to hurt the oyster. When God would make a saint, He buries a sorrow in the life.
George E. Failing

The problem of reconciling human suffering with the existence of a God who loves, is only insoluble so long as we attach a trivial meaning to the word "love."
C. S. Lewis

Who would complain if God allowed one hour of suffering in an entire lifetime of comfort? Why complain about a lifetime that includes suffering when that lifetime is a mere hour of eternity?
Philip Yancy

The past is never completely lost, however extensive the devastation. Your sorrows are the bricks and mortar of a magnificent temple. What you are today and what you will be tomorrow are because of what you have been. Your faith of yesterday is built into your faith today.
Gordon Wright

A Christian lady was complaining to a friend about the hardness of life and the circumstances that buffeted her and in anger said: "Oh, I wish to God that I had never been made!" "My dear child," replied the friend," you are not yet made; you are only being made, and you are quarreling with God's processes."
Unknown

In sorrow and suffering, go straight to God with confidence, and you will be strengthened, enlightened and instructed.
John of the Cross

He who would live a life without pain has come to the wrong world. There is no such choice here on this earth. But we can choose, at least to some extent, the kind of pain we want to have. We can choose between creative pain and pointless pain, between holy pain and petty pain, between pain for a purpose and pain that has no purpose.
Jack Riemer

I wish you could convince yourself that God is often nearer to us, and more effectually present with us, in sickness than in health.
Brother Lawrence

Shut out suffering, and you see only one side of this strange and fearful thing, the life of man. Brightness and happiness and rest- that is not life. It is only one side of life. Christ saw both sides.
F. W. Robertson

God doesn't build a fence around his children to protect us from the suffering common to all humanity. It is clear from the Bible and from the lives of Christians in every generation that God uses suffering in some form in the life of every believer.
Martha Reapsome

A person who lives a spiritual life cannot help but see that suffering brings him closer to God. Seen in this light, suffering loses its bitter side and becomes bliss.
Leo Tolstoy

A deep plunge into the waters of sorrow is the hopefullest way of getting through them on one's daily road of life again. No one can help another very much in these crises of life; but love and sympathy count for something.
Thomas Henry Huxley

Many men owe the grandeur of their lives to their tremendous difficulties.
Charles Haddon Spurgeon

Like Buddha under the Bo tree, Jesus, on his tree, has his eyes closed too. The difference is this. The pain and sadness of the world that Buddha's eyes close out is the pain and sadness of the world that the eyes of Jesus close in.
Frederick Buechner

I know well there is no comfort for this pain of parting: the wound always remains, but one learns to bear the pain, and learns to thank God for what He gave, for the beautiful memories of the past, and the yet more beautiful hope for the future.
Max Muller

When you suffer and lose, that does not mean you are being disobedient to God. In fact, it might mean you're right in the center of His will. The path of obedience is often marked by times of suffering and loss.
Chuck Swindoll

I thank thee more that all our joy is touched with pain;
That shadows fall on brightest hours, that thorns remain;
So that earth's bliss may be our guide, and not our chain.
For thou, who knowest, Lord, how soon our weak heart clings,
Hast given us joys, tender and true, yet all with wings;
So that we see, gleaming on high, diviner things.
Adelaide Anne Proctor

Sometimes your medicine bottle has on it, "shake well before using." That is what God has to do with some of His people. He has to shake them well before they are ever usable.
Vance Havner

The only way to meet affliction is to pass through it solemnly, slowly, with humility and faith, as the Israelites passed through the sea. Then its very waves of misery will divide, and become to us a wall, on the right side and on the left, until the gulf narrows before our eyes, and we land safe on the opposite shore.
Dinah Craik

Just as there comes a warm sunbeam into every cottage window, so comes a love born of God's care for every separate need.
Unknown

A lone shipwreck survivor on an uninhabited island managed to build a rude hut in which he placed all that he had saved from the sinking ship. He prayed to God for deliverance, and anxiously scanned the horizon each day to hail any passing ship. One day he was horrified to find his hut in flames. All that he had was gone. To the man's limited vision, it was the worst that could happen and he cursed God. Yet the very next day a ship arrived. "We saw your smoke signal," the captain said.
Walter Heiby

So what if my stroke left me with a speech impediment? Moses had one, and he did all right.
Kirk Douglas

Do not cheat thy Heart and tell her,
"Grief will pass away,
Hope for fairer times in future,
And forget to-day."
Tell her, if you will, that sorrow
Need not come in vain;
Tell her that the lesson taught her
far outweighs the pain.
Adelaide Procter

God promises a safe landing, not a calm passage.
Unknown

You have done everything you know to do to bring it to pass, and now it has brought you to your knees and you are desperate. You have finally arrived in the ultimate posture of worship- desperate despondency!
Tommy Tenney

We have to pray with our eyes on God, not on the difficulties.
Oswald Chambers

Peace does not dwell in outward things, but within the soul; we may preserve it in the midst of the bitterest pain, if our will remain firm and submissive. Peace in this life springs from acquiescence to, not in an exemption from, suffering.
François de Fendon

In the Divine economy misery becomes a sacramental thing to the man who follows God- to the righteous man. God utilizes suffering to man's benefit. Taken God's way- it has healing- strengthening- maturing qualities.
Richard Halverson

Those who do not know how to weep with their whole heart don't know how to laugh either.
Golda Meir

A story is told about a little boy with a big heart. His next-door neighbor was an older gentleman whose wife had recently died. When the youngster saw the elderly man crying, he climbed up onto his lap and simply sat there. Later, his mother asked the boy what he had said to their saddened neighbor. "Nothing," the child replied. "I just helped him cry." Sometimes that is the best thing we can do for people who are facing profound sorrow. Often, our attempts to say something wise and helpful are far less valuable than just sitting next to the bereaved ones, holding their hand, and crying with them.
Unknown

One thing we may be sure of, however: For the believer all pain has meaning; all adversity is profitable. There is no question that adversity is difficult. It usually takes us by surprise and seems to strike where we are most vulnerable. To us it often appears completely senseless and irrational, but to God none of it is either senseless or irrational. He has a purpose in every pain He brings or allows in our lives. We can be sure that in some way He intends it for our profit and His glory.
Jeff Bridges

Things aren't always as they appear to be on the surface. Sometimes the people who most trouble us are the ones facing trouble in their own lives.
C. Hosher

One day, a child of mine came home in tears. Another child had been mean to him and hurt his feelings. I want to say now, as I said then, "When a person doesn't like you, or is mean to you, it has more to do with them than it does with you. Dry your tears. You cannot be loved by everyone, because everyone cannot love themselves. You can know that I will always love you. And the greatest gift you can give to others is to love yourself. If you do that, you can love others without worrying whether they love you back. You will have enough love for both of you."
Dorothy Dupont

Whenever pain is so borne as to be prevented from breeding bitterness or any other evil fruit, a contribution is made to rescuing God's creation from the devil's grip.
Leonard Hodgson

Our real blessings often appear to us in the shape of pains, losses and disappointments; but let us have patience, and we soon shall see them in their proper figures.
Joseph Addison

Once we begin to flee the things that threaten and burden us, there is no end to fleeing. God's solution is surprising. He offers rest. But it's a unique form of rest. It's to rest in him in the midst of our threats and our burdens. It's discovering, as David did in seasons of distress, that God is our rock and refuge right in the thick of our situation.
Mark Buchanan

In this life, the Lord allows His saints to
enjoy many sweet blessings, but none are
more precious than those which occur
deep in the valleys of disappointment,
pain and heartache, where He without fail
draws near.
George S. Lauderdale

Peace

If it happens that you are well off, in your heart be tranquil about it- if you can be just as glad and willing for the opposite condition. So let it be with food, friends, kindred, or anything else that God gives or takes away.
Meister Eckhart

Where the soul is full of peace and joy, outward surroundings and circumstances are of comparatively little account.
Hannah Witall Smith

Do not lose your inward peace for anything whatsoever, even if your whole world seems upset. Commend all to God, and then lie still and be at rest in His bosom. Whatever happens, abide steadfast in a determination to cling simply to God, trusting to His eternal love for you.
Francis de Sales

Those who are God's without reserve are, in every sense, content.
Hannah Whitall Smith

Have peace in your heart, and thousands will be saved around you.
Seraphim of Sarov

Slow me down, Lord!
Ease the pounding of my heart by the quieting of my mind.
Steady my hurried pace with a vision of the eternal reach of time.
Give me, amid the confusion of the day, the calmness of the everlasting rills.
Break the tensions of my nerves and muscles, with the soothing music of the singing streams that live in my memory.
Orin L. Crain

Deep peace of the running wave to you.
Deep peace of the flowing air to you.
Deep peace of the quiet earth to you.
Deep peace of the shining stars to you.
Deep peace of the Son of Peace to you.
Celtic blessing

If we have no peace, it is because we have forgotten that we belong to each other.
Mother Teresa

Just think: Every promise God has ever made finds its fulfillment in Jesus. God doesn't just give us grace; he gives us Jesus, the Lord of grace. If it's peace, it's only found in Jesus, the Prince of Peace. Even life itself is found in the Resurrection and the Life. Christianity isn't all that complicated…it's Jesus.
Joni Eareckson Tada

God's peace is joy resting.
His joy is peace dancing.
F. F. Bruce

God's in His Heaven – All's right with the world.
Robert Browning

Lord, make me an instrument of Your peace. Where there is hatred let me sow love; where there is injury, pardon; where there is despair, hope; where there is darkness, light; and where there is sadness, joy.
Francis of Assisi

Peace is seeing a sunrise or a sunset and knowing whom to thank.
Unknown

The peace of God is that eternal calm which lies far too deep down to be reached by any external trouble or disturbance.
Arthur T. Pierson

Peace does not dwell in outward things, but within the soul; we may preserve it in the midst of the bitterest pain, if our will remain firm and submissive. Peace in this life springs from acquiescence to, not in an exemption from, suffering.
François de Fendon

There is only one way to bring peace to the heart, joy to the mind, and beauty to the life; it is to accept and do the will of God.
William Barclay

To be glad of life, because it gives you the chance to love and to work and to play and to look up at the stars; to be satisfied with your possessions, but not contented with yourself until you have made the best of them; to despise nothing in the world except falsehood and meanness, and to fear nothing except cowardice; to be governed by your admirations rather than by your disgusts; to covet nothing that is your neighbor's except his kindness of heart and gentleness of manners; to think seldom of your enemies, often of your friends, and every day of Christ; and to spend as much time as you can, with body and with spirit, in God's out-of-doors- these are little guideposts on the footpath to peace
Henry Van Dyke

This is the secret of joy. We shall no longer strive for our own way; but commit ourselves, easily and simply, to God's way, acquiesce in his will and in so doing find our peace.
Evelyn Underhill

All men who live with any degree of serenity live by some assurance of grace.
Reinhold Niebuhr

My son, now will I teach thee the way of peace and inward liberty. Be desirous to do the will of another rather than thine own. Choose always to have less rather than more. Seek always the lowest place, and to be inferior to everyone. Wish always, and pray, that the will of God may be wholly fulfilled in thee.
Thomas Kempis

Now, once again loaded with responsibilities- two orphaned teenage boys, an elderly alcoholic brother, and a household- bereaved and sorrowing, ill and tired, Jack [C. S. Lewis] discovered one of the greatest secrets of life: that no matter what is actually happening around you, you can still be content if you hand your life over entirely to Christ. Jack settled into a contentment that is hard to understand. He had to retire from Cambridge University. He was no longer able to go for the long walks he had delighted in. He was not allowed to drink wine or beer, not allowed to eat anything other than a strict diet prescribed by his doctors. All the pleasures of his life had been taken away from him as also had been the love of his life [the loss of his wife], and yet he was content. He was in that rare stature in which his physical disabilities and his emotional distresses no longer affected his happiness or lack of it. He had finally become able to make God the center of his life and to regard himself as merely a bit player in the drama. He was not exactly happy; he had merely come to the conclusion that his happiness was not what he should be seeking at all. In fact it was completely irrelevant, and therefore he was content to be without it.
Douglas Gresham

Peace is not the absence of conflict, but the presence of God no matter what the conflict.
Unknown

Praise

The morning is the gate of the day, and should be well guarded with prayer. It is one end of the thread on which the day's actions are strung, and should be well knotted with devotion. If we felt more the majesty of life we should be more careful of its mornings. He who rushes from his bed to his business and without worship is as foolish as though he had not put on his clothes, or washed his face, and as unwise as thought he dashed into battle without arms or armor.
Charles Haddon Spurgeon

How hard is it for God to get your attention? Do you regularly practice turning aside in your day? That is, taking a moment to listen to God- because God, through the Holy Spirit, really is speaking, because we know, every place is filled with the presence of God. There is not an inch of space, not a moment of time, that God does not inhabit.
John Ortberg

I believe praise is a powerful weapon against the enemy. Breakthroughs happen as we praise God. He can work a miracle in whatever situation we face regarding our health, finances, family, or career.
Arah Wehrli

If you're a believer- if you're "in Christ" – then kick up your heels! Celebrate the Lord! Celebrate yourself! Discover a life of pleasure you never dreamed possible.
Anne Ortlund

God created the universe in order to hear music, and everything has a song of praise for God.
Louis Ginsberg

Every little blessing is far too precious to ever forget to say "thank you!"
Laura Regis

Never say there is nothing beautiful in the world anymore. There is always something to make you wonder in the shape of a tree, the trembling of a leaf.
Albert Schweitzer

By reading the scriptures I am so renewed that all nature seems renewed around me and with me. The sky seems to be a pure, a cooler blue, the trees a deeper green. The whole world is charged with the glory of God and I feel fire and music under my feet.
Thomas Merton

The whole duty and blessedness of waiting on God has its root in this, that He is such a blessed Being, full, to overflowing, of goodness and power and life and joy, that we, however wretched, cannot for any time come into contact with Him, without that life and power secretly, silently, beginning to enter into us and blessing us. God is Love! God's love is just His delight to impart Himself and His blessedness to His children. Come, and however feeble you feel, just wait in His presence. As a feeble invalid is brought out into the sunshine to let its warmth go through him, come with all that is dark and cold in you into the sunshine of God's holy, omnipotent love, and sit and wait there, with the one thought: Here I am, in the sunshine of His love. As the sun does its work in the weak one who seeks its rays, God will do His work in you.
Andrew Murray

Fire. God of Abraham, God of Isaac, God of Jacob, not of the philosophers and scholars. Certainty. Certainty. Feeling. Joy. Peace.
Blaise Pascal, written on a sheet of paper and sewed into his jacket.

Nature is too thin a screen; the glory of the omnipresent God bursts through everywhere.
Ralph Waldo Emerson

There is not one blade of grass, there is no color in this world, that is not intended to make us rejoice.
John Calvin

A dining room table with children's eager, hungry faces around it, ceases to be a mere dining room table, and becomes an altar.
Simeon Strunsky

The world is charged with the grandeur of God.
Gerard Hopkins

The Lord's goodness surrounds us at every moment. I walk through it almost with difficulty, as through thick grass and flowers.
R. W. Barbour

All this and heaven too.
Matthew Henry

The early morning hours have gold in their mouth.
Dutch proverb

What can God have that gives him greater satisfaction than that a thousand times a day all his creatures should thus pause to withdraw and worship him in the heart.
Brother Lawrence

If anyone would tell you the shortest, surest way to happiness and all perfection, he must tell you to make it a rule to yourself to thank and praise God for everything that happens to you. For it is certain that whatever happens to you, if you thank and praise God for it, you turn it into a blessing.
William Law

We can be tired, weary and emotionally distraught, but after spending time alone with God, we find that He injects into our bodies energy, power and strength.
Charles Stanley

Everything that God has created is like an orchestra praising Him.
Oswald Chambers

If I were to wake up one morning and find I was an atheist with my faith in God completely gone, I think I would miss almost more than anything else having someone to thank...I can hardly conceive what it would be like never, never being able to say in a moment of exhilaration or of unexpected happiness or of rescue from deep distress, "O God, you're good to me!"
David Read

Doth not all nature around me praise God? If I were silent, I should be an exception to the universe. Doth not the thunder praise Him as it rolls like drums in the march of the God of armies? Do not the mountains praise Him when the woods upon their summits wave in adoration? Does not the lightning write His name in letters of fire? Hath not the whole earth a voice? And shall I, can I, silent be?
Charles H. Spurgeon

There is a loyalty which turns into idolatry. The very thing which once freed us can turn into the very thing that enslaves us: a method of prayer, a technique of mediation, a way of expressing ourselves through art, music, writing or speaking, which was once the channel through which God reaches us, may have become the very thing which prevents our continued growth. We may confuse the channels of God with God himself!! This turns us into idolators of a certain system. We become fixed and petrified. It's natural to thrill at each new level of growth and feel that we've arrived. But God, the living God, keeps breaking our old molds; He constantly enlarges us, presenting new challenges and new sacraments.
Paul Tournier

Let us see God before man every day.
Robert Murray M'Cheyne

Prayer in the sense of petition, asking for things, is a small part of it; confession and penitence are its threshold, adoration its sanctuary, the presence and vision and enjoyment of God its bread and wine.
C. S. Lewis

Prayer

The morning is the gate of the day, and should be well guarded with prayer. It is one end of the thread on which the day's actions are strung, and should be well knotted with devotion. If we felt more the majesty of life we should be more careful of its mornings. He who rushes from his bed to his business and without worship is as foolish as though he had not put on his clothes, or washed his face, and as unwise as thought he dashed into battle without arms or armor.
Charles Haddon Spurgeon

I have found silence to be a powerful element in prayer. To learn to be alone with God even in the presence of others is something we Christians should try to do. There are innumerable times during the day when we can turn our thoughts, even for a moment, from business affairs and center them on God's goodness, Christ's love, our fellow man's needs.
J. C. Penney

Every day you have another opportunity to affect your future with the words you speak to God.
Stormie Omartian

If a care is too small to be turned into a prayer it is too small to be made into a burden.
Corrie ten Boom

Get into the habit of dealing with God about everything. Unless in the first waking moment of the day you learn to fling the door wide back and let God in, you will work on a wrong level all day; but swing the door wide open and pray to your Father in secret, and every public thing will be stamped with the presence of God.
Oswald Chambers

Beware in your prayer, above everything, of limiting God- not only by unbelief, but by fancying that you know what he can do.
Andrew Murray

The best reason to pray is that God is really there. In praying our unbelief starts to melt. God moves smack into the middle of even an ordinary day.
Emily Griffin

How hard is it for God to get your attention? Do you regularly practice turning aside in your day? That is, taking a moment to listen to God- because God, through the Holy Spirit, really is speaking, because we know, every place is filled with the presence of God. There is not an inch of space, not a moment of time, that God does not inhabit.
John Ortberg

God is bigger than all of us, beyond all of us. When I pray, I don't really pray for anything, I just try to understand God's will and do the best I can.
Harry Connick, Jr.

The only certainties that don't break down are those acquired in prayer.
Reinhold Schneider

Make a plan now to keep a daily appointment with God. The enemy is going to tell you to set it aside, but you must carve out the time. If you're too busy to meet with the Lord, friend, then you are simply too busy.
Charles Swindoll

Prayer gives a man the opportunity of getting to know a gentleman he hardly ever meets. I do not mean his maker, but himself.
William Inge

Who goes to bed and does not pray
Maketh two nights to every day.
George Herbert

Prayer is the sum of our relationship with God. We are what we pray. The degree of our faith is the degree of our prayer. Our ability to love is our ability to pray.
Carlo Carretto

God wants us to pray and will tell us how to begin where we are.
The Cloud of Unknowing

Love is a fruit, in season at all times and within the reach of every hand. Anyone may gather it and no limit is set. Everyone can reach this love through mediation, the spirit of prayer, and sacrifice.
Mother Teresa

Give rest to the weary, visit the sick, support the poor; for this also is prayer.
Aphrahat

If Jesus had to take time alone with God, then we surely need to.
Sharon Daugherty

I remember my mother's prayers and they have always followed me. They have clung to me all my life.
Abraham Lincoln

If we demonstrate unconditional love, daily prayer, persistent faith, and adherence to God's laws, we give our children a gift. If we teach them that good deeds and kind words are expressions of the Spirit, we are on track toward living more like Jesus.
Jane Jarrell

Nothing lies beyond the reach of prayer except that which lies outside the will of God.
Unknown

Prayer is the peace of our spirit, the stillness of our thoughts, the evenness of our recollection, the seat of mediation, the rest of our cares, and the calm of our tempest.
Jeremy Taylor

One of our consistent prayers should be for God to reveal the hypocrite in our hearts.
Lisa Harper

As I work through my day, I often find myself praying after each task. "What's next, Lord?" And before I walk into any room for a meeting, I always say a silent prayer, asking God to give me wisdom for that meeting. Prayer is the key to staying connected to God, and staying connected is the key to God's power and effectiveness. I recently tweeted this: "Much prayer- much power. Little prayer- little power. No prayer- no power." If I am not quietly talking to God as I do my work, I am not depending on him at that moment. And if I don't talk to God about what I'm doing, it shows that I'm doing it on my own power.
Rick Warren

How far away is heaven? It is not so far as some imagine. It wasn't very far for Daniel. It was not so far off that Elijah's prayer, and those of others could not be heard there. Men full of the Spirit can look right into heaven.
Dwight L. Moody

Prayer is striking the winning blow at the concealed enemy. Service is gathering up the results of that blow among the men we see and touch.
Samuel Gordon

Pray for a strong and lively sense of sin; the greater the sense of sin, the less sin.
Samuel Rutherford

In the soul-searching of our lives, we are to stay quiet so we can hear Him say all that He wants to say to us in our hearts.
Charles Swindoll

For Jesus, prayer was a vital element in making God's power available to people in need.
Jim Reapsome

The measure of our love for others can largely be determined by the frequency and earnestness of our prayers for them.
A. W. Pink

The whole duty and blessedness of waiting on God has its root in this, that He is such a blessed Being, full, to overflowing, of goodness and power and life and joy, that we, however wretched, cannot for any time come into contact with Him, without that life and power secretly, silently, beginning to enter into us and blessing us. God is Love! God's love is just His delight to impart Himself and His blessedness to His children. Come, and however feeble you feel, just wait in His presence. As a feeble invalid is brought out into the sunshine to let its warmth go through him, come with all that is dark and cold in you into the sunshine of God's holy, omnipotent love, and sit and wait there, with the one thought: Here I am, in the sunshine of His love. As the sun does its work in the weak one who seeks its rays, God will do His work in you.
Andrew Murray

Prayer no longer seems like an activity to me; it has become the continuing language of the relationship I believe God designed to fulfill a human life.
Keith Miller

The severe drought this summer in the south prompted a visiting pastor to pray for rain. The next day there was a torrential downpour that ruined the crops. "Well that's what happens," said one of the farmers wryly, "When you get a pastor that ain't familiar with agriculture."
Unknown

Since marriage is a spiritual relationship involving husband, wife, and God, prayer together keeps communication flowing among all three.
Dennis and Barbara Rainey

To try to pray is to pray. You can't fail at it. It's the only human endeavor I can think of where trying is doing. Reaching out is holding on. Joining in is letting go.
Rick Hamlin

Certain thoughts are prayers. There are certain moments when, whatever the attitude of the body, the soul is on its knees.
Victor Hugo

Fight all your battles on your knees and you win every time.
Charles Stanley

I live in the spirit of prayer. I pray as I walk about, when I lie down, and when I rise up. And the answers are always coming.
George Muller

Go where your best prayers take you.
Frederick Buechner

Have you ever thought what a wonderful privilege it is that every one each day and each hour of the day has the liberty of asking God to meet him in the inner chamber and to hear what He has to say?
Andrew Murray

I have often learned much more in one prayer than I have been able to glean from much reading and reflection.
Martin Luther

Our prayers lay the track down on which God's power can come. Like a mighty locomotive, his power is irresistible, but it cannot reach us without rails.
Watchman Nee

If you are a stranger to prayer, you are a stranger to the greatest source of power known to human beings.
Billy Sunday

If you have so much business to attend to that you have no time to pray, depend upon it, you have more business on hand than God ever intended you should have.
D. L. Moody

People who are in the habit of praying – and they include the mystics of the Christian tradition – know that when a prayer is answered, it is never answered in a way that you expect.
Kathleen Norris

Prayer is the mortar that holds our house together.
Mother Teresa

Prayer is the very highest energy of which the mind is capable.
Samuel Taylor Coleridge

The self-sufficient does not pray, the self-satisfied will not pray, the self-righteous cannot pray. No man is greater than his prayer life.
Leonard Ravenhill

What a man is on his knees before God, that he is – and nothing more.
Robert McCheyne

It is more effective to spend time talking to Christ about a man than talking to a man about Christ, because if you are talking to Christ about a man earnestly, trustingly, in the course of time you cannot help talking to the man effectively about Christ.
Robert Munger

Prayer enlarges the heart until it is capable of containing God's gift of himself.
Mother Teresa

When a Christian shuns fellowship with other Christians, the devil smiles. When he stops studying the Bible, the devil laughs. When he stops praying, the devil shouts for joy.
Corrie Ten Boom

God often gives in one brief moment that which he has for a long time denied.
Thomas Kempis

God's gifts put man's best dreams to shame.
Unknown

Silence is the first language of God; all else is a poor translation.
Thomas Merton

A day without prayer is a boast against God.
Owen Carr

In intercessory prayer, one seldom ends where one began.
Douglas Steere

God always answers our prayer. Either he changes the circumstances, or he supplies sufficient power to overcome them.
Unknown

Some prayers are followed by silence because they are wrong, others because they are bigger than we can understand.
Oswald Chambers

Every Christian needs a half an hour of prayer each day, except when he is busy, then he needs an hour.
Francis de Sales

The way to worry about nothing is to pray about everything.
Unknown

Prayer is the slender nerve that moves the muscle of Omnipotence.
J. Edwin Hartill

I have so many things to do today, I dare not ignore my time with God.
Martin Luther

He who has learned to pray has learned the greatest secret of a holy and happy life.
William Law

I have been driven many times to my knees by the overwhelming conviction that I had nowhere else to go.
Abraham Lincoln

A man prayed, and at first he thought that prayer was talking. But he became more and more quiet until in the end he realized that prayer is listening.
Soren Kierkegaard

Many a fellow is praying for rain with his tub the wrong side up.
Sam Jones

Some prayers have a longer voyage than others, but they return with the richer lading at last, so that the praying soul is a gainer by waiting for an answer.
William Gurnall

How can you expect God to speak in that gentle and inward voice which melts the soul, when you are making so much noise with your rapid reflections? Be silent, and God will speak again.
Francois Fenelon

We lie to God in prayer if we do not rely on him afterwards.
Robert Leighton

I have had prayers answered – most strangely so sometimes – but I think our heavenly Father's loving kindness has been even more evident in what He has refused me.
Lewis Carroll

Pray the largest prayers. You cannot think a prayer so large that God, in answering it, will not wish you had made it larger. Pray not for crutches but for wings.
Phillips Brooks

Most commit the same mistake with God that they do with their friends: they do all the talking.
Fulton J. Sheen

Heaven is full of answers to prayers for which no one ever bothered to ask.
Billy Graham

We never pray for folks we gossip about, and we never gossip about the folk for whom we pray!
Leonard Ravenhill

Have you ever learned the beautiful art of letting God take care of you and giving all your thought and strength to pray for others and for the kingdom of God? It will relieve you of a thousand cares.
A. B. Simpson

What can God have that gives him greater satisfaction than that a thousand times a day all his creatures should thus pause to withdraw and worship him in the heart.
Brother Lawrence

There is no greater intimacy with another than that which is built through holding him or her up in prayer.
Douglas Steere

Every time we pray our horizon is altered, our attitude to things is altered, not sometimes but every time, and the amazing thing is that we don't pray more.
Oswald Chambers

Lord…give me the gift of faith to be renewed and shared with others each day. Teach me to live this moment only, looking neither to the past with regret, nor the future with apprehension. Let love be my aim and my life a prayer.
Roseann Alexander-Isham

To pray is to change. This is a great grace. How good of God to provide a path whereby our lives can be taken over by love and joy and peace and patience and kindness and goodness and faithfulness and gentleness and self-control.
Richard J. Foster

To worship rightly is to love each other, Each smile a hymn, each kindly deed a prayer.
John Greenleaf Whittier

Oh, men and women, pray through; pray through! Do not just begin to pray and pray a little while and throw up your hands and quit, but pray and pray and pray until God bends the heavens and comes down!
R. A. Torrey

Whenever the insistence is on the point that God answers prayer, we are off the track. The meaning of prayer is that we get hold of God, not of the answer.
Oswald Chambers

In order to grow in grace, we must be much alone. It is not in society that the soul grows most vigorously. In one single quite hour of prayer it will often make more progress than in days of company with others. It is in the desert that the dew falls freshest and the air ifs purest.
Horatius Bonar

It is by no haphazard chance that in every age men have risen early to pray. The first thing that marks decline in spiritual life is our relationship to the early morning.
Oswald Chambers

We can be tired, weary and emotionally distraught, but after spending time alone with God, we find that He injects into our bodies energy, power and strength.
Charles Stanley

It is very proper for friends, when they part, to part with prayer.
Matthew Henry

A guest at a country house coming down to breakfast one morning was met by the child of the house, who running up to him and putting his hand in his, looked up into his face with a smile, saying, "I'm your friend now; I put you in my prayer last night!"
Unknown

I ought to pray before seeing anyone. Often when I sleep long, or meet with others early, it is eleven or twelve o'clock before I begin secret prayer. This is a wretched system. It is unscriptural. Christ arose before day and went into solitary place. David says: "Early will I seek thee; Thou shalt early hear my voice." Family prayer loses much of its power and sweetness, and I can do no good to those who come to seek from me. The conscience feels guilty, the soul unfed, the lamp not trimmed. Then when I secure prayer the soul is often out of tune. I feel it is far better to begin with God- to see his face first, to get my soul near him before it is near another.
Robert Murray McCheyne

Prayer crowns God with the honor and glory due to His name, and God crowns prayer with assurance and comfort. The most praying souls are the most assured souls.
Thomas Brooks

Perfect prayer is only another name for love.
François Fénelon

We impoverish God in our minds when we say there must be answers to our prayers on the material plane; the biggest answers to our prayers are in the realm of the unseen.
Oswald Chambers

I thank Thee first because I was never robbed before; second, because although they took my purse they did not take my life; third, although they took my all, it was not much; and fourth, because it was I who was robbed and not I who robbed.
Henry Matthey, on the night he was robbed, he prayed this prayer

Faith gathers strength by waiting and praying.
E. M. Bounds

Prayer does not mean simply to pour out one's heart. It means rather to find the way to God and to speak with him, whether the heart is full or empty.
Dietrich Bonhoeffer

Our prayer will be most like the prayer of Christ if we do not ask God to show us what is going to be, or to make any particular thing happen, but only pray that we may be faithful in whatever happens.
Father Andrew

What isn't won in prayer first, is never won at all.
Malcolm Cronk

Prayerless people cut themselves off from God's prevailing power, and the frequent result is the familiar feeling of being overwhelmed, overrun, beaten down, pushed around, defeated. Surprising numbers of people are willing to settle for lives like that.
Bill Hybels

There is a story about trust in God's promises that comes from F. W. Boreham. Boreham tells about an episode during the early days of his ministry in Australia. He went to call on one of his elderly parishioners. Entering the room where the old man lay, he noticed a chair pulled up beside the man's bed. "I see that I am not your first visitor today," said Boreham. The old man then began to explain the presence of the empty chair. He said that when he was a small boy, he had difficulty praying. His pastor suggested that he overcome this difficulty by placing an empty chair in front of himself when he prayed, and by simply pretending that Jesus was sitting in that chair like an attentive friend. He said he had maintained that habit ever since. Boreham left the house a short while later. A few days later, however, then man's daughter came to tell him that he was dead. "I was out of the room only for a short time," said the daughter. "When I returned, he was gone. There was no change in him except I noticed that his hand was on the chair."
Unknown

Let us see God before man every day.
Robert Murray M'Cheyne

The holy heart can be hurt. But it answers injury with love and prayer and forgiveness.
W. E. McCumber

The devil enjoys hearing a prayer that is addressed to an audience.
Unknown

Do not work so hard for Christ that you have no strength to pray, for prayer requires strength.
J. Hudson Taylor

He prays well who is so absorbed with God that he does not know he is praying.
Francois de Sales

God never denied that soul anything that went as far as heaven to ask it.
John Trapp

Let me burn out for God. After all, whatever God may appoint, prayer is the great thing. Oh, that I may be a man of prayer!
Henry Martyn

The greatest good and the most profitable gain come when we are up against a blank wall. Then we learn to pray in plain language.
Arthur Lynip

Prayer is necessary because everything else is an illusion.
John Garvey

Prayer in the sense of petition, asking for things, is a small part of it; confession and penitence are its threshold, adoration its sanctuary, the presence and vision and enjoyment of God its bread and wine.
C. S. Lewis

The degree of our faith is the degree of our prayer.
The strength of our hope is the strength of our prayer.
The warmth of our charity is the warmth of our prayer.
Carlo Carretto

God insists that we ask, not because He needs to know our situation, but because we need the spiritual discipline of asking.
Catherine Marshall

A single grateful thought raised to heaven is the most perfect prayer.
Gotthold Ephraim Lessing

Do not let us fail one another in interest, care and practical help; but supremely we must not fail one another in prayer.
Michael Baughen

To live in prayer together is to walk in love together.
Margaret Moore Jacobs

If Christ Himself needed to retire from time to time to the mountain-top to pray, lesser men need not be ashamed to acknowledge that necessity.
B. H. Streeter

Prayer is aspiration. The self-satisfied disregard it. They who reach for higher things find it a necessity.

Prayer is a discipline. They who seek meaning and purpose in life discover it a wise teacher.

Prayer is an art. We perfect it through practice.

Gradually, the interval between prayer and deed diminishes- until, at last, all life becomes a sanctuary.

Alvin Fine

Pre-eminent, supreme among the helps to secret prayer I place, of course, the secret study of the holy written Word of God. Read it on your knees, at least on the knees of your spirit. Read it to reassure, to feed, to regulate, to kindle, to give to your secret prayer at once body and soul. Read it that you may hold faster your certainty of being heard. Read it that you may know with blessed definiteness whom you have believed, and what you have in Him, and how He is able to keep your deposit safe. Read it in the attitude of mind in which the apostles read it, in which the Lord read it. Read it, not seldom, to turn it at once into prayer.

H. C. G. Moule

Prayer of a soldier; "Oh, Lord, don't let nothin' get hold of me that you and me can't handle!"

Unknown

No man is greater than his prayer life. The pastor who is not praying is playing; the people who are not praying are straying. We have many organizers, but few agonizers; many players and payers, few pray-ers; many singers, few clingers; lots of pastors, few wrestlers; many fears, few tears; much fashion, little passion; many interferers, few intercessors; many writers, but few fighters. Failing here, we fail everywhere.

Leonard Ravenhill

I need the opportunity to free my mind of sorrow, personal concerns; to see my world through the mirrored reflection of holiness. I need a time of prayer to leap beyond what is limiting in me as a person, to rediscover what is important and what is trivial, to take counsel with what my tradition stresses as the living faith. I need prayer.

Albert Silverman

If only God would lean out of heaven and tell me [my children] are going to make it, I could relax. But God doesn't do that. He tells us to be the parents he has called us to be in his strength and promises to do his part. Driven to prayer (after discovering that manipulation didn't work), I began to realize I was only truly positive and confident when I'd been flat on my face before the Lord.

Jill Briscoe

The greatest element in life is not what occupies most of its time, else sleep would stand high in the scale. Nor is it what engrosses most of its thought, else money would be very high. The two or three hours of worship and preaching weekly has perhaps been the greatest signal influence on English life. Half an hour of prayer, morning or evening, every day, may be a greater element in shaping our course than all our conduct and all our thought.
P. T. Forsyth

God is perfect love and perfect wisdom. We do not pray in order to change His Will, but to bring our wills into harmony with His.
William Temple

My son, now will I teach thee the way of peace and inward liberty. Be desirous to do the will of another rather than thine own. Choose always to have less rather than more. Seek always the lowest place, and to be inferior to everyone. Wish always, and pray, that the will of God may be wholly fulfilled in thee.
Thomas Kempis

An enemy is a danger, but the danger is not what he can do to you. It is what he makes you do. If he fills you with envy, malice, hatred and all uncharitableness, he has done you real harm. But you can prevent that. Pray for him. If you say you cannot trust him, then watch and pray. But you cannot hate a man you pray for.
E. S. Waterhouse

The time of business does not differ from the time of prayer; and in the noise and clutter of my kitchen, while several persons are at the same time calling for different things, I possess God in as great tranquility as if I were upon my knees at the Blessed Sacrament.
Brother Lawrence

The Church has not yet touched the fringe of the possibilities of intercessory prayer. Her largest victories will be witnessed when individual Christians everywhere come to recognize their priesthood unto God and day by day give themselves onto prayer.
John Mott

God has one Son who lived without sin, but he has no Son who lived without prayer.
Unknown

Never give up praying until the answer comes.
George Muller

Jesus himself has shown us by his own example that prayer and fasting are the first and most effective weapons against the forces of evil.
John Paul II

Deepest communion with God is beyond words, on the other side of silence.
Madeleine L'Engle

God does not stand afar off as I struggle to speak. He cares enough to listen with more than casual attention. He translates my scrubby words and hears what is truly inside. He hears my sighs and uncertain gropings as fine prose.
Timothy Jones

If you can't pray a door open, don't pry it open.
Lyell Rader

Prayer is a choice. For us to pray to give thanks, or to voice our questions and doubts shows that we are choosing to leave an opening in our spirits. Without this opening, there is no vessel, no place into which God can breathe.
Joanna Laufer

We don't pray to get God's attention. We pray to turn our attention toward him.
Christopher Knippers

When you pray, you open yourself to the influence of the power which has revealed itself as love. The power gives you freedom and independence. Once touched by this power, you are no longer swayed back and forth by the countless opinions, ideas, and feelings which flow through you. You have found a center for your life that gives you a creative distance so that everything you see, hear, and feel can be tested against the source.
Henri Nouwen

Now, boys, remember one thing; do not make long prayers; always remember that the Lord knows something.
(A speaker addressing a graduating class at a theological seminary in Tennessee.)
Unknown

You have done everything you know to do to bring it to pass, and now it has brought you to your knees and you are desperate. You have finally arrived in the ultimate posture of worship- desperate despondency!
Tommy Tenney

Avail yourself of the greatest privilege [prayer] this side of heaven. Jesus Christ died to make this communion and communication with the Father possible.
Billy Graham

We have to pray with our eyes on God, not on the difficulties.
Oswald Chambers

The value of prayer is not that He will hear us…but that we will finally hear Him.
William McGill

Prayer is an end to isolation. It is living our daily life with someone; with Him who alone can deliver us from solitude.
Georges Lefevre

God's ultimate will is unchanging, but the way in which he chooses to realize this will is dependent on the prayers of his children. He wants us as covenant partners, not as automons or slaves.
Donald Bloesch

The essential truth is that discernment is a function of a loving, personal relationship to the Lord. It can normally be only as deep and as solid as that relationship itself. The true discerner must be a praying, loving person.
Unknown

I count all that part of my life lost which I spent not in communion with God or in doing good.
John Donne

Lord, the Scripture says: "There is a time for silence and a time for speech." Saviour, teach me the silence of humility, the silence of wisdom, the silence of love, the silence of perfection, the silence that speaks without words, the silence of faith. Lord, teach me to silence my own heart that I may listen to the gentle movement of the Holy Spirit within me and sense the depths which are of God.
Frankfurt prayer (Sixteenth century)

More prayer, more exercise of faith, more patient waiting, and the result will be blessing, abundant blessing. Thus I have found it many hundreds of times, and therefore I continually say to myself, "Hope thou in God."
George Mueller

Pride & Humility

It is only imperfection that complains of what is imperfect. The more perfect we are, the more gentle and quiet we become toward the defect of others.
Francois Fenelon

Let us be as watchful after the victory as before the battle.
Andrew Bonar

The man who is elated by success and cast down by failure is still a carnal man. At best his fruit will have a worm in it.
A. W. Tozer

Whenever our desire to be right overshadows our desire for another person's well-being, we are not living for Kingdom purposes.
Mary Albert Darling

A humble person can neither be put down nor exalted; he can neither be humiliated nor honored: he remains the same person under all circumstances.
Unknown

Spread abroad the name of Jesus in humility and with a meek heart; show him your feebleness, and he will become your strength.
Thomas Merton

Most people plot and plan themselves into mediocrity, while now and again somebody forgets himself into greatness.
E. Stanley Jones

Never be afraid of the world's censure; it's praise is much more to be dreaded.
C. H. Spurgeon

He has great tranquility of heart who cares neither for the praises nor the fault-finding of men. He will easily be content and pacified, whose conscience is pure. You are not holier if you are praised, nor the more worthless if you are found fault with.
Thomas Kempis

Every man carries the entire form of human condition.
Michel de Montaigne

What is humility? It is that habitual quality whereby we live in the truth of things: the truth that we are creatures and not the Creator; the truth that our life is a composite of good and evil, light and darkness; the truth that in our littleness we have been given extravagant dignity.
Robert F. Morneau

Be not angry that you cannot make others as you wish them to be since you cannot make yourself as you wish to be.
Thomas Kempis

Moses spent forty years thinking he was somebody; then he spent forty years on the backside of the desert realizing he was nobody; finally, he spent the last forty years of his life leaning what God can do with a nobody!
Dwight L. Moody

Nothing sets a person so much out of the devil's reach as humility.
Jonathan Edwards

God could not have chosen anyone less qualified, or more of a sinner, than myself. And so, for this wonderful work He intends to perform through us, He selected me- for God always chooses the weak and the absurd, and those who count for nothing.
Francis of Assisi

A humble heart is like a magnet that draws the favor of God toward us.
Jim Cymbala

We do not exist for ourselves.
Thomas Merton

When Jesus tells us to love our enemies, He Himself will give us the love with which to do it. We are neither factories nor reservoirs of His love, only channels. When we understand that, all excuse for pride is eliminated.
Corrie ten Boom

It is far more impressive when others discover your good qualities without your help.
Judith Martin

When we are humble enough to allow God to fill us with His love, a miracle happens.
Kim Moore

You who are letting miserable misunderstandings run on from year to year, meaning to clear them up some day; you who are keeping wretched quarrels alive because you cannot quite make up your minds that now is the day to sacrifice your pride and kill them; you who are letting your neighbor starve until you hear that he is dying of starvation or letting your friend's heart ache for a word of appreciation or sympathy, which you mean to give him some day; if you could only know and see and feel all of a sudden that time is short, how it would break the "spell." How you would go instantly and do the thing which you might never have another chance to do.
Phillips Brooks

A dear old friend of mine used to say with the truest Christian charity, when he heard any one being loudly condemned for some fault: "Ah! well, yes, it seems very bad to me, because it is not my way of sinning!"
Charles D. Williams

It is said an eastern monarch once charged his wise men to invent a sentence, to be ever in view, and which should be true and appropriate in all times and situations. They presented him with the words, "And this, too, shall pass away." How much it expresses! How chastening in the hour of pride! How consoling in the depths of affliction!
Abraham Lincoln

We need to arrange a servanthood conference, with workshops in love, forgiveness, feet-washing, cross bearing-in short, workshops in Christlikeness. God is not waiting for people to get big enough to use, but to get small enough in their own eyes for Him to entrust with His mission and Spirit. Christ cannot be represented by swaggering leaders who "lord it over" the flock of God. He cannot be represented by puffed-up laymen who nominate themselves as church bosses. He can be honestly manifested only in the lives of those who feel, as did Paul, that they are "less than the least of all the saints."
W. E. McCumber

He who is proud of his knowledge, has gout in the wrong end.
Thomas Adams

True humility is intelligent self respect which keeps us from thinking too highly or too meanly of ourselves. It makes us mindful of the nobility God meant us to have. Yet it makes us modest by reminding us how far we have come short of what we can be.
Ralph W. Sockman

It is from out of the depths of our humility that the height of our destiny looks grandest. Let me truly feel that in myself I am nothing, and at once, through every inlet of my soul. God comes in, and is everyone in me.
William Mountford

Humility is the altar upon which God wishes us to offer him sacrifices.
Francois de La Rochefoucauld

Let your old age be childlike, and your childhood like old age; that is, so that neither may your wisdom be with pride, nor your humility without wisdom.
Augustine of Hippo

It is amazing how strong we become when we begin to understand what weaklings we are!
Francois Fenelon

The meek man is not a human mouse afflicted with a sense of his own inferiority. Rather, he may be in his moral life as bold as a lion and as strong as Samson; but he has stopped being fooled about himself.
A. W. Tozer

It seemed to me that God had looked over the whole world to find a man who was weak enough to do His work, and when He at last found me, He said, "He is weak enough- he'll do." All God's giants have been weak men who did great things for God because they reckoned on His being with them.
J. Hudson Taylor (when someone complimented him on founding the China Inland Mission)

It's fun to believe in yourself, but don't be too easily convinced.
T. Harry Thompson

Not infrequently, we choose our goals to prove our importance.
Keith Huttenlocker

When a man forgets himself, he usually does something that everyone else remembers.
Unknown

What makes humility so desirable is the marvelous thing it does to us; it creates in us a capacity for the closest possible intimacy with God.
Monica Baldwin

Reflect that true humility consists to a great extent in being ready for what the Lord desires to do with you, and happy that He should do it, and in always considering yourselves unworthy to be called His servants.
Teresa of Avila

If you are humble, nothing will touch you, neither praise nor disgrace, because you know what you are.
Mother Teresa

My son, now will I teach thee the way of peace and inward liberty. Be desirous to do the will of another rather than thine own. Choose always to have less rather than more. Seek always the lowest place, and to be inferior to everyone. Wish always, and pray, that the will of God may be wholly fulfilled in thee.
Thomas Kempis

There is one vice of which no man in the world is free; which every one in the world loathes when he sees it in someone else; and of which hardly any people, except Christians ever imagine that they are guilty themselves....The essential vice, the utmost evil, is Pride. Unchastely, anger, greed, drunkenness, and all that, are mere fleabites in comparison: it was through Pride that the devil became the devil; Pride leads to every other vice: it is the complete anti-God state of mind...As long as you are proud you cannot know God. A proud man is always looking down on things and people; and, of course, as long as you are looking down, you cannot see something that is above you.
C. S. Lewis

Augustine says that we may, out of our dead sins, make stepping stones to rise to the heights of perfection. What did he mean by that? He meant that the memory of our falls may breed in us such a humility, such a distrust of self, such a constant clinging to Christ as we could never have had without the experience of our own weakness.
James Stalker

The first thing I ask is that people should not make use of my name, and should not call themselves Lutherans but Christians. What is Luther? The teaching is not mine. Nor was I crucified for anyone...How did I, poor stinking bag of maggots that I am, come to the point where people call the children of Christ by my evil name?
Martin Luther

Sabbath, Worship & Church

The morning is the gate of the day, and should be well guarded with prayer. It is one end of the thread on which the day's actions are strung, and should be well knotted with devotion. If we felt more the majesty of life we should be more careful of its mornings. He who rushes from his bed to his business and without worship is as foolish as though he had not put on his clothes, or washed his face, and as unwise as though he dashed into battle without arms or armor.
Charles Haddon Spurgeon

As the minister stepped up to the pulpit he discovered to his chagrin that he had forgotten his sermon notes. As it was too late to send someone for them, he turned to the congregation and said, by way of apology, that this morning he should have to depend upon the Lord for what he might say, but that for the evening service, he would be better prepared.
Unknown

If you will not worship God seven days a week, you do not worship him on one day a week.
A. W. Tozer

Every Sunday the ducks waddle out of their houses and waddle down Main Street to their church. They waddle into the sanctuary and squat in their proper pews. The duck choir waddles in and takes its place, then the duck minister comes forward and opens the duck Bible. He reads to them: "Ducks! God has given you wings! With wings you can fly! With wings you can mount up and soar like eagles. No walls can confine you! No fences can hold you! You have wings. God has given you wings and you can fly like birds!" All the ducks shouted, "Amen!" And they all waddled home.
Soren Kierkegaard

The whole world is nothing more than a singing and a dancing before the Holy One, blessed be He. Every Jew is a singer before Him, and every letter in the Torah is a musical note.
Nathan Naphtali

Make a plan now to keep a daily appointment with God. The enemy is going to tell you to set it aside, but you must carve out the time. If you're too busy to meet with the Lord, friend, then you are simply too busy.
Charles Swindoll

The story is told of a church that secured a new preacher, and the word spread around town about how well he preached. The church members were abuzz about what an improvement he was over their former preacher, and how much more attention they gave to his sermons. When the town cynic asked what made this new preacher so much better than his predecessor, he was told, "The old preacher told us that we're all sinners, and that if we didn't repent, we'd burn in hell forever!" This cynic then asked, "And what does this new one say?" The answer was, "That we're all sinners, and that if we don't repent, we'll burn in hell forever!" When the cynic responded that he didn't see any difference between the two of them, he was told, "This new preacher says it with tears in his eyes."
Tony Campolo

A Bible That Is Falling Apart Belongs To Someone Who Isn't
If You Want To Hear God Laugh, Tell Him Your Plans
Lent Is Spring Training For Christians
Now Open Between Easter And Christmas
Lost And Found Inside
Salvation Guaranteed, Or Your Sins Cheerfully Refunded!
Come Early To Get A Seat In Back
Happy Hour: Sundays At 10 A.M.
You think it's hot here?
If At First You Don't Succeed, Read The Instructions (The Bible!)
Ask About Our Pray-As-You-Go Plan
Have a God day!
Prepare For Your Finals! Read The Bible!
God Is. Any Questions?
Same Owner For 2,000 Years
The Little Book of Church Signs

Oh, what a blessing is Sunday, interposed between the waves of worldly business like the divine path of the Israelites through Jordan! There is nothing in which I would advise you to be more strictly conscientious than in keeping the Sabbath day holy.
William Wilberforce

One of the most refreshing daily exercises that you will ever participate in is the choice to spend time in worship. It is of vital importance that you understand that the time spent in sheer worship is going to enable you to withstand the storms of life.
Carol McLeod

I never knew how to worship until I knew how to love.
Henry Ward Beecher

I do not know of a denomination or local church in existence that has as its goal to teach its people to do everything Jesus said.
Dallas Willard

The whole duty and blessedness of waiting on God has its root in this, that He is such a blessed Being, full, to overflowing, of goodness and power and life and joy, that we, however wretched, cannot for any time come into contact with Him, without that life and power secretly, silently, beginning to enter into us and blessing us. God is Love! God's love is just His delight to impart Himself and His blessedness to His children. Come, and however feeble you feel, just wait in His presence. As a feeble invalid is brought out into the sunshine to let its warmth go through him, come with all that is dark and cold in you into the sunshine of God's holy, omnipotent love, and sit and wait there, with the one thought: Here I am, in the sunshine of His love. As the sun does its work in the weak one who seeks its rays, God will do His work in you.
Andrew Murray

When we stopped going to church and started being the church, something wonderful happened.
Twelve Tribes

Worship God in the difficult circumstances, and when He chooses, He will alter them in two seconds.
Oswald Chambers

Disregard the study of God, and you sentence yourself to stumble and blunder through life blindfolded.
J. I. Packer

We need to find God, and he can't be found in noise and restlessness. God is the friend of silence. See how nature- trees, flowers, grass- grows in silence; see the stars, the moon, and the sun, see how they move in silence. We need silence to be able to touch souls.
Mother Teresa

While it is a crucial mistake to assume that churches can be on an outward journey without being on an inward one, it is equally disastrous to assume that one can make the journey inward without taking the journey outward.
Elizabeth O'Connor

When a Christian shuns fellowship with other Christians, the devil smiles. When he stops studying the Bible, the devil laughs. When he stops praying, the devil shouts for joy.
Corrie Ten Boom

A world without a Sabbath would be like a man without a smile, like a summer without flowers, and like a homestead without a garden. It is the most joyous day of the whole week.
Henry Ward Beecher

What can God have that gives him greater satisfaction than that a thousand times a day all his creatures should thus pause to withdraw and worship him in the heart.
Brother Lawrence

To worship rightly is to love each other,
Each smile a hymn, each kindly deed a prayer.
John Greenleaf Whittier

A man who lived some six miles from the house of worship, complained to his pastor of the distance he had to go to attend public worship. "Never mind," said the minister, "remember every Sabbath you have the privilege of preaching a sermon six miles long- you preach the gospel to all the residents and people you pass."
Unknown

The phone rang in the office of a Washington D.C. church. The voice on the other end asked, "Will the President be in church Sunday morning?" The pastor quickly replied, "That I cannot promise, but I do know Jesus Christ will be here and that should be sufficient incentive for a reasonably large attendance."
Tony Bland

Read The Bible
It's User Friendly
Plus We Offer Tech
Support Here On
Sunday's At 10:30
On a church marquee

There is little good in filling churches with people who go out exactly the same as they came in; the call of the Church is not to fill churches but to fill heaven.
Andrew of Perugia

They crucified him with the criminals. Do you know what this implies? Don't be too surprised if I tell you that this was the first Christian fellowship, the first certain, indissoluble, and indestructible Christian community. Christian community is manifest wherever there is a group of people close to Jesus who are with him in such a way that they are directly and unambiguously affected by his promise and assurance. These may hear that everything he is, he is for them, and everything he does, he does for them. To live by this promise is to be a Christian community.
Karl Barth

There is a loyalty which turns into idolatry. The very thing which once freed us can turn into the very thing that enslaves us: a method of prayer, a technique of mediation, a way of expressing ourselves through art, music, writing or speaking, which was once the channel through which God reaches us, may have become the very thing which prevents our continued growth. We may confuse the channels of God with God himself!! This turns us into idolators of a certain system. We become fixed and petrified. It's natural to thrill at each new level of growth and feel that we've arrived. But God, the living God, keeps breaking our old molds; He constantly enlarges us, presenting new challenges and new sacraments.
Paul Tournier

Satan does not do his most subtle work in the saloon, but in the sanctuary.
Ralph Stoll

A church is not a Fortune 500 company. It's not simply another nonprofit organization, nor is it a social club. In fact, a healthy church is unlike any organization that man has ever devised, because man didn't devise it.
Mark Dever and Paul Alexander

Can I be a Christian without joining other Christians in the church? Yes, it is something like: being a soldier without an army, a seaman without a ship, a business man without a business, a tuba player without an orchestra, a football player without a team or a bee without a hive.
Mrs. William P. Jazen

Setting aside a day of rest is difficult. We are surrounded by too many things to do, too many places to go, and far too many distractions. What would it be like if we could ignore these distractions and spend an entire day every week with our family and friends, and our spiritual thoughts? An answer to this hypothetical question appears in the Talmud, which tells us that the world would be redeemed if everyone observed only two consecutive Sabbaths.
Robert Schoen

The Church has not yet touched the fringe of the possibilities of intercessory prayer. Her largest victories will be witnessed when individual Christians everywhere come to recognize their priesthood unto God and day by day give themselves onto prayer.
John Mott

A story is told about Daniel Webster. During his days in the city of Washington the great statesman attended worship regularly in a little rural church outside the city. Some of his colleagues were disturbed about it. They said it lacked prestige. And they asked him why he attended a little church in the sticks when he would be welcome in the more fashionable churches in Washington. Webster answered that when he attended church in Washington they preached to Daniel Webster, the statesman, but in the little church, they preached to Daniel Webster, the sinner.
Unknown

The regular worshipper enters a new world every day, a world which did not exist yesterday, a bright new world wherein the miraculous and the divine are within his grasp.
Reuben Katz

When a man told the clergyman he disapproved of organized religion, the latter assured him that his was the most disorganized one available.
Victor Solomon

Perhaps those who say they didn't get a thing out of the sermon didn't bring anything in which to take it home.
N. A. Prichard

Nobody worries about Christ as long as he can be kept shut up in churches. He is quite safe inside. But there is always trouble if you try and let him out.
G. A. Studdert Kennedy

The greatest element in life is not what occupies most of its time, else sleep would stand high in the scale. Nor is it what engrosses most of its thought, else money would be very high. The two or three hours of worship and preaching weekly has perhaps been the greatest signal influence on English life. Half an hour of prayer, morning or evening, every day, may be a greater element in shaping our course than all our conduct and all our thought.
P. T. Forsyth

If ever I had any doubts about the fundamental realities of religion, they could always be dispelled by one memory- the light upon my father's face as he came back from early communion.
Alfred Noyes

The church is the great lost and found department.
Robert Short

A layman visited a great city church during a business trip. After the service, he congratulated the minister on his service and sermon. "But," said the manufacturer, "if you were my salesman, I'd discharge you. You got my attention by your appearance, voice and manner; your prayer, reading and logical discourse aroused my interest; you warmed my heart with a desire for what you preached; and then- and then you stopped without asking me to do something about it. In business the important thing is to get them to sign on the dotted line."
James Duff

The church as a whole must be concerned with both evangelism and social action. It is not a case of either-or; it is both-and. Anything less is only a partial Gospel, not the whole counsel of God.
Robert De Haan

If the church were perfect, you could not belong.
Unknown

A rabbi whose congregation does not want to drive him out of town isn't a rabbi.
Talmudic saying

You have done everything you know to do to bring it to pass, and now it has brought you to your knees and you are desperate. You have finally arrived in the ultimate posture of worship- desperate despondency!
Tommy Tenney

If you give God a thimble, perhaps He will choose to fill it. If you give God a five-gallon bucket, perhaps He will choose to fill that. If you give Him a fifty-gallon drum, perhaps He will choose to do something extraordinary and fill even that. If God chooses to do a miracle, you'd better be ready for it. Don't buy a thimbleful of land. Buy a fifty-gallon drum.
(as told to Bill Hybels when visiting Robert Schuller to obtain his advice of the planning for Willow Creek church in Chicago)
Robert Schuller

Too many clergymen have become keepers of an aquarium instead of fishers of men- and often they are just swiping each other's fish.
Myron Augsburger

Do not let Sunday be taken from you. If your soul has no Sunday, it becomes an orphan.
Albert Schweitzer

Salvation

If ever you are tempted to say, "I wish someone were to die and leave me something in his will," allow me to tell you, "Someone has!"
David Shepherd

Mankind wants glory. We want health. We want wealth. We want happiness. We want all our felt needs met, all our little human itches scratched. We want a painless life. We want the crown without the cross. We want the gain without the pain. We want the words of Christ's salvation to be easy.
John MacArthur

Nothing marks so much the solid advancement of a soul, as the view of one's wretchedness without anxiety and without discouragement.
Francois Fenelon

Our salvation includes more than pardon from sin, deliverance from hell and a ticket to heaven. It includes all that we shall need on our journey.
Vance Havner

Ah! the bridge of grace will bear your weight, brother. Thousands of big sinners have gone across that bridge, yea, tens of thousands have gone over it. I can hear their trampings now as they traverse the great arches of the bridge of salvation. They come by their thousands, by their myriads; e'er since the day when Christ first entered into His glory, they come, and yet never a stone has sprung in that mighty bridge. Some have been the chief of sinners, and some have come at the very last of their days, but the arch has never yielded beneath their weight. I will go with them trusting to the same support; it will bear me over as it has borne them.
C. H. Spurgeon

The Hebrew evening/morning sequence conditions us to the rhythms of grace. We go to sleep, and God begins his work…We wake into a world we didn't make, into a salvation we didn't earn.
Eugene Peterson

The best way to prepare for the coming of Christ is never to forget the presence of Christ.
William Barclay

I can say that I never knew what joy was like until I gave up pursuing happiness, or cared to live until I chose to die. For these two discoveries I am beholden to Jesus.
Malcolm Muggeridge

Have peace in your heart, and thousands will be saved around you.
Seraphim of Sarov

The hope we have in Christ is an absolute certainty. We can be sure that the place Christ is preparing for us will be ready when we arrive, because with Him nothing is left to chance. Everything He promised He will deliver.
Billy Graham

If Jesus were born one thousand times in Bethlehem and not in me, then I would still be lost.
Corrie ten Boom

The Lord has made a promise **to** late repentance, but where has he made a promise **of** late repentance?
Thomas Brooks

How dangerous it is for our salvation, how unworthy of God and of ourselves, how pernicious even for the peace of our hearts, to want always to stay where we are! Our whole life was only given us to advance us by great strides toward our heavenly country.
Francois Fenelon

The gospel starts by teaching us that we, as creatures, are absolutely dependent on God, and that he, as Creator, has an absolute claim on us. Only when we have learned this can we see what sin is, and only when we see what sin is can we understand the good news of salvation from sin.
J. I. Packer

Godliness is a life-long business. The working out of the salvation that the Lord, himself, works in you is not a matter of certain hours, or of a limited period of life. Salvation is unfolded throughout our entire sojourn here.
Charles Spurgeon

May the strength of God pilot us.
May the power of God preserve us.
May the wisdom of God instruct us.
May the hand of God protect us.
May the way of God direct us.
May the shield of God defend us.
May the host of God guard us against the snares of evil and the temptations of the world.
May Christ be with us.
Christ before us.
Christ in us.
Christ over us.
May Thy salvation, O Lord, be always ours this day and forever more.
St. Patrick Breastplate

The following is a quotation from the words of Dr. W. B. Hinson, speaking from the pulpit a year after the commencement of the illness from which he ultimately died: "I remember a year ago when a man in this city said, 'You have got to go to your death.' I walked out to where I live, five miles out of this city, and I looked across at that mountain that I love, and I looked at the river in which I rejoice, and I looked at the stately trees that are always God's own poetry to my soul. Then in the evening I looked up into the great sky where God was lighting his lamps, and I said 'I may not see you many more times, but, Mountain, I shall be alive when you are gone; and, River, I shall be alive when you cease running toward the sea; and, Stars, I shall be alive when you have fallen from your sockets in the great down-pulling of the material universe!'" This is the confidence of one who knew the Saviour. Is it yours?
Advent Herald

The inn of a traveler on the way to Jerusalem.
Inscription on the grave of Dean Alford

No man ever enters heaven until he is first convinced that he deserves hell.
John Everett

We cannot resist the conviction that this world is for us only the porch of another and more magnificent temple of the Creator's majesty.
Frederick William Faber

Anyone can devise a plan by which good people may go to Heaven. Only God can devise a plan whereby sinners, who are His enemies, can go to Heaven.
Lewis Sperry Chafer

The battle- our battle- against every temptation that can ever try to take us on has already been won on that first Easter morning. All we're involved in is a mopping up operation.
Dale Evans Rogers

Christ would have lived, and taught, and preached, and prophesied, and wrought miracles in vain, if he had not crowned all by dying for our sins as our substitute! His death was our life. His death was the payment of our debt to God. Without his death we should have been of all creatures most miserable.
J. C. Ryle

If our greatest need had been information, God would have sent an educator. If our greatest need had been technology, God would have sent us a scientist. If our greatest need had been money, God would have sent us an economist. But since our greatest need was forgiveness, God sent us a Savior.
Roy Lessin

The founders of the world's religions say, "Do! Do! Do!" but Christ says, "Done! It is finished!"
Steve Kumar

Be aware of God's compassion, that it heals with oil and wine. Do not lose hope of salvation. Remember what is written- the one who falls shall rise again, and the one who turns away shall turn again; the wounded is healed; the one caught by wild beasts escapes; the one who confesses is not rejected. For the Lord does not want the sinner to die, but to return and live. There is still time for endurance, time for patience, time for healing, time for change. Have you fallen? Rise up, Have you sinned? Cease. Do not stand among sinners, but keep away from them. For when you turn back and weep, then you will be saved.
Basil the Great, in a letter to a monk who had sinned

There is nothing that is more dangerous to your own salvation, more unworthy of God and more harmful to your own happiness, than that you should be content to remain as you are.
Francois Fenelon

The greatest enemy to human souls is the self-righteous spirit which makes men look to themselves for salvation.
Charles Spurgeon

At a certain meeting two and a half people were converted to Christ. A friend asked if he meant two adults and a child. The facts were just the opposite two children and an adult. When a child is led to Christ, a whole life is saved!"
D .L. Moody

We know people who have been "converted" many times. Every time there is a church revival they go to the altar and get "saved." One minister told of a man in his congregation who had been "saved" seventeen times. During a revival meeting the evangelist made an altar call for all who wanted to be filled with the Spirit. The man who had been converted so often made his way toward the altar again. A woman from the congregation shouted, "Don't fill him, Lord. He leaks!" Those who become "unconverted" were never converted in the first place.
C. Sproul

We want gain without pain; we want the resurrection without going through the grave; we want life without experiencing death; we want a crown without going by way of the Cross. But in God's economy, the way up is down.
Nancy Leigh De Moss

Satan, Hell & Evil

Enemy-occupied territory- that is what the world is.
C. S. Lewis

We put ourselves there. The door to hell is locked from the inside.
James A. Pike

My main ambition in life is to be on the devil's most wanted list.
Leonard Ravenhill

No man can estimate what is really happening at the present. All we do know, and that to a large extent by direct experience, is that evil labors with vast power and perpetual success- in vain: preparing always only the soil for unexpected good to sprout in.
J. R. R. Tolkien

Between us and heaven or hell there is only life, which is the frailest thing in the world.
Blaise Pascal

Nothing sets a person so much out of the devil's reach as humility.
Jonathan Edwards

To give you an idea of the depth of Jesus' suffering, being abandoned by God is the definition of hell.
Tony Evans

Satan watcheth for those vessels that sail without a convoy.
George Swinnock

When the devil tries to remind you of your past, just turn around and remind him of his future.
Anonymous

When a Christian shuns fellowship with other Christians, the devil smiles. When he stops studying the Bible, the devil laughs. When he stops praying, the devil shouts for joy.
Corrie Ten Boom

I believe Satan to exist for two reasons: first, the Bible says so, and second, I've done business with him.
Dwight L. Moody

It is Satan's custom by small sins to draw us to greater, as the little sticks set the great ones on fire, and a wisp of straw kindles a block of wood.
Thomas Manton

I know well that when Christ is nearest, Satan is also busiest.
Robert Murray M'Cheyne

You are more evil than you have ever feared, and more loved than you have ever hoped.
Mark Driscoll

One phrase summarizes the horror of hell. "God isn't there."
Max Lucado

When flatterers meet, the devil goes to dinner.
John Ray

The devil, that old stager, who leads downward, perhaps, but fiddles all the way!
Robert Browning

God would never permit evil if he could not bring good out of evil.
Thomas Watson

The Devil will use our words and his dictionary.
Adrian Rogers

Three-hundred million years from now, the only thing that will matter is whether you're in Heaven or in Hell.
Mark Cahill

The devil enjoys hearing a prayer that is addressed to an audience.
Unknown

The devil shapes himself to the fashions of all men. If he meets with a proud man, or a prodigal man, then he makes himself a flatterer; if a covetous man, then he comes with a reward in his hand. He hath an apple for Eve, a grape for Noah, a change of raiment for Gehazi, a bag for Judas. He can dish out his meat for all palates; he hath a last to fit every shoe; he hath something to please all conditions.
William Jenkyn

God judged it better to bring good out of evil than to suffer no evil to exist.
Augustine of Hippo

When you steal a penny the devil makes a fortune.
Unknown

I think earth, if chosen instead of Heaven, will turn out to have been, all along, only a region in Hell; and earth, if put second to Heaven, to have been from the beginning a part of Heaven itself.
C. S. Lewis

Why should anyone be shattered by the thought of hell? It is not compulsory for anyone to go there.
Thomas Merton

When a man is getting better, he understands more and more clearly the evil that is still in him. When a man is getting worse, he understands his own badness less and less.
C. S. Lewis

When Walter Hooper reported to C. S. Lewis a gravestone that read, "Here lies an atheist all dressed up with no place to go," Lewis commented wryly, "I bet he wishes that were true."
Bert Ghezzi

Satan does not do his most subtle work in the saloon, but in the sanctuary.
Ralph Stoll

The Devil is a gentleman who never goes where he is not welcome.
John Lincoln

Nothing promotes the activity of the devil more than the Christian's proximity to God.
John Blanchard

Jesus himself has shown us by his own example that prayer and fasting are the first and most effective weapons against the forces of evil.
John Paul II

The Devil is a better theologian than any of us, yet is a Devil still.
A. W. Tozer

Whenever pain is so borne as to be prevented from breeding bitterness or any other evil fruit, a contribution is made to rescuing God's creation from the devil's grip.
Leonard Hodgson

Satan sometimes suggests that an offering will satisfy God, when in fact He is demanding our all.
Corrie ten Boom

Sin

God expects more failure from us than we do from ourselves because God knows who we are. We are not the righteous person who occasionally sins, we are the sinful person who occasionally- by God's grace- gets it right. When we start from this perspective we are released from the bondage of perfectionism and are able to forgive ourselves once and for all. We are to take our cue from him. We may be disappointed with ourselves but God is not. We may feel like condemning ourselves, but God does not.
James Bryan Smith

It is one thing for sin to live in us; it is another for us to live in sin.
John Murray

God sent me 1,000 hints that he didn't want me to keep doing what I was doing. But I didn't listen, so he set off a nuclear bomb.
Jack Abramoff

We put ourselves there. The door to hell is locked from the inside.
James A. Pike

Gossip is the art of confessing other people's sins.
Unknown

The story is told of a church that secured a new preacher, and the word spread around town about how well he preached. The church members were abuzz about what an improvement he was over their former preacher, and how much more attention they gave to his sermons. When the town cynic asked what made this new preacher so much better than his predecessor, he was told, "The old preacher told us that we're all sinners, and that if we didn't repent, we'd burn in hell forever!" This cynic then asked, "And what does this new one say?" The answer was, "That we're all sinners, and that if we don't repent, we'll burn in hell forever!" When the cynic responded that he didn't see any difference between the two of them, he was told, "This new preacher says it with tears in his eyes."
Tony Campolo

Sin cannot be reduced to manageable proportions.
Sinclair Ferguson

It would seem, after having been a Christian for almost 80 years, that I would no longer do ugly things that need forgiving. Yet I am constantly doing things to others that cause me to have to go back and ask their forgiveness. Sometimes these are things I actually do-other times they are simply attitudes I let creep in which break the circle of God's perfect love.
Corrie ten Boom

Creation had been given to men as a clean window through which the light of God could shine into men's souls. Sun and moon, night and day, rain, the sea, the crops, the flowering tree, all these things were transparent. They spoke to man not of themselves only but of Him who made them. Nature was symbolic. But the progressive degradation of man after the fall led the Gentiles further and further from this truth. Nature became opaque.
Thomas Merton

As the salt flavors every drop in the Atlantic, so does sin affect every atom of our nature.
Charles Spurgeon

We are not sinners because we sin; we sin because we are sinners.
R. C. Sproul

The confession of evil works is the first beginning of good works.
Augustine

The greatest wonder that I ever heard of is that God should ever justify me. I feel myself to be a lumpy of unworthiness, a mass of corruption, and a heap of sin apart from His almighty love. I know and am fully assured that I am justified by faith which is in Christ Jesus, and I am treated as if I had been perfectly just and made an heir of God and a joint-heir with Christ. And yet, by nature I must take my place among the most sinful. I, who am altogether undeserving, am treated as if I had been deserving. I am loved with as much love as if I had always been Godly, whereas before I was ungodly. Who can help being astonished at this? Gratitude for such favor stands dressed in robes of wonder.
Charles H. Spurgeon

Pray for a strong and lively sense of sin; the greater the sense of sin, the less sin.
Samuel Rutherford

Oh, how horrible our sins look when they are committed by someone else.
Charles Swindoll

We are all fallen creatures and all very hard to live with.
C. S. Lewis

To be sensible of our corruption and abhor our own transgressions is the first symptom of spiritual health.
J. C. Ryle

Ah! the bridge of grace will bear your weight, brother. Thousands of big sinners have gone across that bridge, yea, tens of thousands have gone over it. I can hear their trampings now as they traverse the great arches of the bridge of salvation. They come by their thousands, by their myriads; e'er since the day when Christ first entered into His glory, they come, and yet never a stone has sprung in that mighty bridge. Some have been the chief of sinners, and some have come at the very last of their days, but the arch has never yielded beneath their weight. I will go with them trusting to the same support; it will bear me over as it has borne them.
C. H. Spurgeon

Since 3600 BC the world has known only 292 years of peace. In that period, stretching more than 55 centuries, there have been an incredible 14,531 wars in which over 3.6 billion people have been killed.
John Ankerberg

Strange, though I am saved from sin, I am not saved from sinning.
Martin Luther

It is Satan's custom by small sins to draw us to greater, as the little sticks set the great ones on fire, and a wisp of straw kindles a block of wood.
Thomas Manton

We must be watchful, especially in the beginning of the temptation. The enemy is then more easily overcome, if he is not permitted in any wise to enter the door of our hearts, but is resisted without the gate at his first knock…First there comes to the mind a bare thought of evil, then a strong imagination thereof, afterward delight, and an evil motion, and then consent. And so little by little our wicked enemy gets complete entrance, because he is not resisted in the beginning. And the longer a man is slow to resist, so much the weaker does he become daily in himself, and the enemy stronger against him.
Thomas a Kempis

The saints are the sinners who keep on trying.
Robert Louis Stevenson

Some people confess a sin a thousand times, I tell them to confess it once, then thank God a thousand times for forgiving them.
Maurice Horn

Don't try to deal with sin, for you are sure to lose. Deal with Christ; let him deal with your sin and you are sure to win.
Arthur Elfstrand

We never pray for folks we gossip about, and we never gossip about the folk for whom we pray!
Leonard Ravenhill

A man's most glorious actions will at last be found to be but glorious sins, if he hath made himself, and not the glory of God, the end of those actions.
Thomas Brooks

The gospel starts by teaching us that we, as creatures, are absolutely dependent on God, and that he, as Creator, has an absolute claim on us. Only when we have learned this can we see what sin is, and only when we see what sin is can we understand the good news of salvation from sin.
J. I. Packer

When flatterers meet, the devil goes to dinner.
John Ray

A dear old friend of mine used to say with the truest Christian charity, when he heard any one being loudly condemned for some fault: "Ah! well, yes, it seems very bad to me, because it is not my way of sinning!"
Charles D. Williams

If envy was not such a tearing thing to feel it would be the most comic of sins. It is usually, if not always, based on a complete misunderstanding of another person's situation.
Monica Furlong

I don't just commit sin. Apart from God, I am sinful. My problem is not just what I do; it's who I am without His nature.
Beth Moore

I have heard thousands of confessions, but never one of covetousness.
Francis Xavier

Let a man go to a psychiatrist and what does he become? An adjusted sinner. Let a man go to a physician and what does he become? A healthy sinner. Let a man achieve wealth and what does he become? A wealthy sinner. Let a man join a church, sign a card, and turn over a new leaf and what does he become? A religious sinner. But let him go in sincere repentance and faith to the foot of Calvary's cross, and what does he become? A new creature in Jesus Christ, forgiven, reconciled, with meaning and purpose in his life and on the way to marvelous fulfillment in God's will.
Unknown

Sinners cannot find God for the same reason that criminals cannot find a policeman: They aren't looking!
Billy Sunday

To realize God's presence is the one sovereign remedy against temptation.
Francois Fenelon

Progress towards maturity is not to be measured by victory over the sins we are aware of, but by hatred of the sins which we had overlooked and which we now see all too clearly.
Arthur C. Custance

No man can break any of the Ten Commandments. He can only break himself against them.
G. K. Chesterton

What are our worst sins? They are chiefly our lost opportunities to grow in wisdom and in nobility of character. They lie in our failure to develop our fullest and best powers given to us by God. They are our missed marks:
The time we wasted.
The education we neglected.
The curiosity we stifled.
The adventures we by-passed.
The excitements of a child which we ignored.
The human relations we treated with indifference.
The entertainment we mistook for culture.
The freedom we left unsupported.
The causes that we scorned.
The books that we did not read.
The wonderful world that we did not penetrate.
Charles Shulman

The battle- our battle- against every temptation that can ever try to take us on has already been won on that first Easter morning. All we're involved in is a mopping up operation.
Dale Evans Rogers

We are as near to heaven as we are far from self, and far from the love of a sinful world.
Samuel Rutherford

Be aware of God's compassion, that it heals with oil and wine. Do not lose hope of salvation. Remember what is written-the one who falls shall rise again, and the one who turns away shall turn again; the wounded is healed; the one caught by wild beasts escapes; the one who confesses is not rejected. For the Lord does not want the sinner to die, but to return and live. There is still time for endurance, time for patience, time for healing, time for change. Have you fallen? Rise up, Have you sinned? Cease. Do not stand among sinners, but keep away from them. For when you turn back and weep, then you will be saved.
Basil the Great, in a letter to a monk who had sinned

Too many Christians envy the sinners their pleasure and the saints their joy, because they don't have either one.
Martin Luther

A story is told of old Thomas K. Beecher, who could not bear deceit in any form. Finding that a clock in his church was habitually too fast or too slow he hung a placard on the wall above it, reading in large letters: "DON'T BLAME MY HANDS- THE TROUBLE LIES DEEPER." That is where the trouble lies with us when our hands do wrong, or our feet, or our lips, or even our thoughts. The trouble lies so deep that only God's miracle power can deal with it. Sin indeed goes deep, but Christ goes deeper.
The Elim Evangel

Augustine says that we may, out of our dead sins, make stepping stones to rise to the heights of perfection. What did he mean by that? He meant that the memory of our falls may breed in us such a humility, such a distrust of self, such a constant clinging to Christ as we could never have had without the experience of our own weakness.
James Stalker

We can be assured that each step deeper into the Lord's Presence will reveal areas in our hearts which need to be cleansed. Do not be afraid. When the Spirit shows you areas of sin, it is not to condemn you, but to cleanse you.
Francis Frangipane

Strength

Will you be the rock that redirects the course of the river?
Claire Nuer

The love of Christ becomes the mightiest force in the world to the man who is yielded to it.
E. W. Kenyon

How often do we attempt work for God to the limit of our incompetency, rather than the limit of God's omnipotence?
J. Hudson Taylor

Courage comes and goes. Hold on for the next supply.
Thomas Merton

Very often what God first helps us towards is not the virtue itself but just this power of always trying again. For however important chastity (or courage, or truthfulness, or any other virtue) may be, this process trains us in habits of the soul which are more important still.
C. S. Lewis

Grace is not simply leniency when we have sinned. Grace is the enabling gift of God not to sin. Grace is power, not just pardon. Therefore the effort we make to obey God is not an effort done in our own strength, but in the strength which God supplies.
John Piper

Who is a wise man? -He who studies all the time.
Who is strong? -He who can limit himself.
Who is rich? -He who is happy with what he has.
The Talmud

When God is about to do something great, he starts with a difficulty. When he is about to do something truly magnificent, he starts with an impossibility.
Armin Gesswein

Courage doesn't always roar. Sometimes courage is the little voice at the end of the day that says, I'll try again tomorrow.
Unknown

When God wants to move a mountain, he does not take a bar of iron, but he takes a little worm. The fact is, we have too much strength. We are not weak enough. It is not our strength that we want. One drop of God's strength is worth more than all the world.
D. L. Moody

One with God is a majority.
Billy Graham

Have courage for the great sorrows of life and have patience for the small ones. Go to sleep in peace. God is awake.
Victor Hugo

Jesus Christ came into my prison cell last night, and every stone flashed like a ruby.
Samuel Rutherford

God has not promised skies always blue, flower-strewn pathways all our lives through;
God has not promised sun without rain, joy without sorrow, peace without pain.
But God has promised strength for the day,
rest for the labor, light for the way,
grace for the trials, help from above,
unfailing sympathy, undying love.
Annie Johnson Flint

Spread abroad the name of Jesus in humility and with a meek heart; show him your feebleness, and he will become your strength.
Thomas Merton

Trust in your Redeemer's strength… exercise what faith you have, and by and by He shall rise upon you with healing beneath His wings. Go from faith to faith and you shall receive blessing upon blessing.
Charles H. Spurgeon

We can be tired, weary and emotionally distraught, but after spending time alone with God, we find that He injects into our bodies energy, power and strength.
Charles Stanley

Faith gathers strength by waiting and praying.
E. M. Bounds

A man was carrying a heavy basket. His son asked to help him. The father cut a stick and placed it through the handle of the basket so that the end toward himself was very short; while the end toward the boy was three or four times as long. Each took hold of his end of the stick, and the basket was lifted and easily carried. The son was bearing the burden with the father, but he found his work easy and light because his father assumed the heavy end of the stick. Just so it is when we bear the yoke with Christ; He sees to it that the burden laid on us is light; He carries the heavy end.
John T. Faris

What are Christians put into the world for except to do the impossible in the strength of God?
S.C. Armstrong

Do not work so hard for Christ that you have no strength to pray, for prayer requires strength.
J. Hudson Taylor

I believe in the sun even when it isn't shining. I believe in love even when I am alone. I believe in God even when He is silent.
Jewish refugee, World War II, Poland

If only God would lean out of heaven and tell me [my children] are going to make it, I could relax. But God doesn't do that. He tells us to be the parents he has called us to be in his strength and promises to do his part. Driven to prayer (after discovering that manipulation didn't work), I began to realize I was only truly positive and confident when I'd been flat on my face before the Lord.
Jill Briscoe

In sorrow and suffering, go straight to God with confidence, and you will be strengthened, enlightened and instructed.
John of the Cross

Trying to do the Lord's work in your own strength is the most confusing, exhausting, and tedious of all work. But when you are filled with the Holy Spirit, then the ministry of Jesus just flows out of you.
Corrie Ten Boom

It is amazing how strong we become when we begin to understand what weaklings we are!
Francois Fenelon

The greatness of a man's power is the measure of his surrender.
William Booth

Thanksgiving & Gratitude

Why wait until the fourth Thursday in November? Why wait until the morning of December twenty-fifth? Thanksgiving to God should be an everyday affair. The time to be thankful is now!
Jim Gallery

A little boy kneeling by the side of the bed looked up to heaven and prayed, "And now, God, let me tell you about the things I'm not thankful for."
Unknown

Gratitude unlocks the fullness of life. It turns what we have into enough, and more. It turns denial into acceptance, chaos to order, confusion to clarity. It can turn a meal into a feast, a house into a home, a stranger into a friend. Gratitude makes sense of our past, brings peace for today, and creates a vision for tomorrow.
Melody Beattie

I can seldom read scripture now without tears of joy and gratitude.
Hudson Taylor

Thanksgiving is a time of quiet reflection upon the past and an annual reminder that God has, again, been ever so faithful.
Chuck Swindoll

Best of all is it to preserve everything in a pure, still heart, and let there be for every pulse a thanksgiving, and for every breath a song.
Konrad von Gesner

Every little blessing is far too precious to ever forget to say "thank you!"
Laura Regis

We cannot explain why these little signs mean so much to us. But the fact is that a word of thanks for some small thing can transform our day.
Jeanne Reidy

A spirit of thankfulness is one of the most distinctive marks of a Christian whose heart is attuned to the Lord. Thank God in the midst of trials and every persecution.
Billy Graham

We must find time to stop and thank the people who make a difference in our lives.
Dan Zadra

Thanksgiving is good but thanks-living is better.
Matthew Henry

We give thanks this morning for the incredible beauty of this day, for the magnificence of life, and for our own individual potential still untapped. As we reflect on these blessings, we praise God for the good signs in our own lives- good signs of the past and good signs ahead.
Richard G. Capen, Jr.

It is generally true that all that is required to make men unmindful of what they owe to God for any blessing, is, that they should receive that blessing often and regularly.
Richard Whately

Joy untouched by thankfulness is always suspect.
Theodor Haecker

The phone rang. It was my friend Annette. She had been going through a rough time. "I feel so alone," she said. "I've even lost God and don't know how to find him." I'd felt the same way once, and told Annette how making a gratitude list had helped. "Write down the numbers one through fifty down the side of a piece of paper," I explained. "Then go back and count the things you're thankful for. And remember, it's not the things you're supposed to be thankful for, but the things you really are thankful for." "Okay then, I'll give it a try," Annette said, hanging up. Not long after, the phone rang again. It was Annette. "I found him!" she exclaimed joyfully.
Lora Clark

When it comes to life, the critical thing is whether you take things for granted or take them with gratitude.
Gilbert Keith Chesterton

Life itself, every bit of health that we enjoy, every hour of liberty and free enjoyment, the ability to see, to hear, to speak, to think, and to imagine- all this comes from the hand of God. We show our gratitude by giving back to Him a part of that which He has given to us.
Billy Graham

Think of 5 things you are grateful for today...Now how do you feel?
Tim Sanders

Reflect upon your present blessings, of which every man has many; not on your past misfortunes, of which all men have some.
Charles Dickens

Jesus, please teach me to appreciate what I have before time forces me to appreciate what I had.
Susan L. Lenzkes

God has two dwellings – one in heaven and the other in a thankful heart.
Izaar Walton

Some people confess a sin a thousand times, I tell them to confess it once, then thank God a thousand times for forgiving them.
Maurice Horn

Peace is seeing a sunrise or a sunset and knowing whom to thank.
Unknown

God is pleased with no music below so much as with the thanksgiving songs of relieved widows and supported orphans; of rejoicing, comforted, and thankful persons.
Jeremy Taylor

If anyone would tell you the shortest, surest way to happiness and all perfection, he must tell you to make it a rule to yourself to thank and praise God for everything that happens to you. For it is certain that whatever happens to you, if you thank and praise God for it, you turn it into a blessing.
William Law

There is power in gratitude to heal us spiritually, emotionally, and relationally.
Kerry & Chris Shook

I thank Thee first because I was never robbed before; second, because although they took my purse they did not take my life; third, although they took my all, it was not much; and fourth, because it was I who was robbed and not I who robbed.
Henry Matthey, on the night he was robbed, he prayed this prayer

O, heavenly Father: we thank thee for food and remember the hungry.
We thank thee for health and remember the sick.
We thank thee for friends and remember the friendless.
We thank thee for freedom and remember the enslaved.
May these remembrances stir us to service,
That thy gifts to us may be used for others.
Amen.
Pauline Phillips

We can thank God for everything good, and all the rest we don't comprehend yet.
Kristin Armstrong

If I were to wake up one morning and find I was an atheist with my faith in God completely gone, I think I would miss almost more than anything else having someone to thank…I can hardly conceive what it would be like never, never being able to say in a moment of exhilaration or of unexpected happiness or of rescue from deep distress, "O God, you're good to me!"
David Read

Aren't you glad that God doesn't give you only that which you remember to thank him for?
Max Lacado

If any one would tell you the surest, shortest way to all happiness and all perfection, he must tell you to make it a rule to yourself, to thank God for every thing that happens to you.
William Law

A life in thankfulness releases the glory of God.
Bengt Sundberg

I thank Thee, Lord, for blessings, big and small; For spring's warm glow and songbird's welcome call; For autumn's hue and winter's white snow shawl.
I thank Thee for the harvest rich with grain; For tall trees and the quiet shadowed lane; For rushing stream, for birds that love to fly; My country's land, the mountains and the plain.
I thank Thee for each sunset in the sky, For sleepy nights, the bed in which I lie; A life of truth and peace; a woman's hand, Her hand in mine unit the day I die.
I thank Thee, Lord, for all these things above; But most of all I thank Thee for Thy love.
Ralph Gaither (written while a POW in North Vietnam)

Have you ever stopped to be thankful just for yourself?
Bill Pearce

A single grateful thought raised to heaven is the most perfect prayer.
Gotthold Ephraim Lessing

Dear GOD:
I want to thank You for what you have already done.
I am not going to wait until I see results or receive rewards; I am thanking you right now.
I am not going to wait until I feel better or things look better; I am thanking you right now.
I am not going to wait until people say they are sorry or until they stop talking about me; I am thanking you right now.
I am not going to wait until the pain in my body disappears; I am thanking you right now.
I am not going to wait until my financial situation improves; I am going to thank you right now.
I am not going to wait until the children are asleep and the house is quiet; I am going to thank you right now.
I am not going to wait until I get promoted at work or until I get the job; I am going to thank you right now.
I am not going to wait until I understand every experience in my life that has caused me pain or grief; I am thanking you right now.
I am not going to wait until the journey gets easier or the challenges are removed; I am thanking you right now.
I am thanking you because I am alive. I am thanking you because I made it through the day's difficulties. I am thanking you because I have walked around the obstacles…I am thanking you because I have the ability and the opportunity to do more and do better.
I'm thanking you because FATHER, YOU haven't given up on me.
Unknown

Gratitude is the most fruitful way of deepening your consciousness that you are not an "accident," but a divine choice.
Henri J. Nouwen

The great painter boasted that he mixed all his colours with brains, and the great saint may be said to mix all his thoughts with thanks.
G. K. Chesterton

One of life's gifts is that each of us, no matter how tired and downtrodden, finds reasons for thankfulness.
J. Robert Maskin

Is not sight a jewel? Is not hearing a treasure? Is not speech a glory? O my Lord pardon my ingratitude, and pity my dullness who am not sensible of these gifts.
Thomas Traherne

Oh teach me, Lord, to treasure much
The simple things of life- the touch
Of wind and snow, of rain and sun;
And when the hours of work are done,
The quietness of rest, the fair
And healing sustenance of prayer.
And, Lord of living, help me keep
A shining, singing gladness deep
Within for blessings yet to be
Through all eternity.
Unknown

The man who forgets to be thankful has fallen asleep in life.
Robert Louis Stevenson

MONTHLY STATEMENT (If God Should Bill Us)
Due to God, your Father in Heaven and Round About- For Services rendered during one month.
30 days of care and supervision, air, light, sunshine, and rain.
240 hours of restful recreative sleep.
720 hours of physical upkeep of heart, lungs, senses, digestion, locomotion.
90 very satisfying meals.
1 competent mind to analyze and judge, a memory to retain, a will to act.
A family that loves you, rejoices and sorrows with you.
A host of friends who believe in you and overlook your oddities and mistakes.
Neighbors, near and far, who band together to build a better community.
Skies and seasons that bring beauty and grandeur, parks and gardens.
A church that is free and strong, affording you worship, guidance, solace and fellowship.
Love from a God of justice, compassion and forgiveness, whose plans and purposes were spelled out by His Son, and whose Spirit abides with you.
Unknown

For the ability to be of service to a fellow creature, we ought to give thanks, not demand it.
W. J. Cameron

He enjoys much who is thankful for little.
Thomas Secker

Happiness is itself a kind of gratitude.
Unknown

In the morning hours of a new day we take a moment to give thought to what this day may mean for us. What is a day in a person's life? Isn't it the most precious treasure that can be given to us? If we were denied this day in which to live, you know full well, all of our possessions would mean nothing, our fondest hopes and plans would be of no avail. First and foremost, therefore, is the gift of a new day, one more day of life. Therefore, let us begin the day properly. Let us thank God for this wonderful gift.

Let us resolve not to waste one hour of it. Let us resolve to share happiness with those who are closest to us- our family; our neighbors; our associates. This is the greater meaning of the verse we read in the Holy Bible: "So teach us to number our days that we may get us a heart of wisdom."
Morris Goldstein

Gratitude to God makes even a temporal blessing a taste of heaven.
William Romaine

Wisdom & Truth

Do not seek to plunge into the sea of knowledge all at once, but go there by way of the many streams that flow into it, since it is wiser to reach the more difficult things by way of the less difficult... I charge you to be slow to speak and slow to frequent places where men talk. Embrace cleanness of conscience. Be constant in prayer. Love to dwell in your inner room if you would penetrate into the inner room of your Beloved. Be courteous to everyone. Do not look too deeply into the deeds of others. Do not be overly familiar with anyone, for too great a familiarity breeds contempt and offers an occasion for being distracted from study. Do not in any way wish to pry into the words and deeds of worldly people. Flee from useless conversations. Do not forget to imitate the ways of the saints and holy people. Do not feel obligated to listen to what everyone says, but commit to memory anything good that you might hear others say... By these steps you will bring forth useful branches and fruits in the vineyard of the Lord of Sabaoth while life is in you. If you walk this way, you may obtain all that you desire.
Thomas Aquinas

Wisdom, the wisdom of God, is not something that is acquired by man, but something that is bestowed by God upon his elect. It is a divine endownment and not a human acquisition.
Spiros Zodhiates

We are the most appealing to others, and happiest within, when we are completely ourselves.
Luci Swindoll

People who make decisions based merely on what seems most advisable to them will inevitably choose something inferior to God's best. Jesus, the ultimate model for the Christian life, did not rely on His own best thinking, but depended completely on His heavenly Father for wisdom in everything.
Henry Blackaby

I wake up early in the morning to do my dreaming- at four o'clock, 'cause I'm not a big sleeper. I think of God as a farmer throwing out nuggets of wisdom and inspiration first thing. I get out there and pick 'em up before everyone else. In the wee hours, the world is quiet and I can really listen to God.
Dolly Parton

We regret losing a purse full of money, but a good thought which has come to us, which we've heard or read, a thought which we should have remembered and applied to our life, which could have improved the world- we lose this thought and promptly forget about it, and we do not regret it, though it is more precious than millions.
Leo Tolstoy

Let me learn by paradox that the way down is up, that to be low is to be high… that to have nothing is to possess all, that to bear the cross is to wear the crown… that the valley is the place of vision.
The Valley of Vision: A Collection of Puritan Prayers

Men take more pains to mask than mend.
Benjamin Franklin

The three essential rules when speaking of others are: Is it true? Is it kind? Is it necessary?
Unknown

There is not greatness where there is not simplicity, goodness and truth.
Leo Tolstoy

A wise man once said, "Whatever came to me, I looked on as God's gift for some special purpose. If it was a difficulty, I knew He gave it to me to struggle with, to strengthen my mind and my faith." That idea has sweetened and helped me all of my life.
Unknown

Life provides losses and heartbreak. But the greatest tragedy is to have the experience and miss the meaning. I am determined not to miss that meaning.
Robin Roberts

Get your friends to tell you your faults, or better still, welcome an enemy who will watch you keenly and sting you savagely. What a blessing such an irritating citric will be to a wise man, what an intolerable nuisance to a fool!
Charles Haddon Spurgeon

It has come to pass that man's knowledge has surpassed his wisdom. He is afraid of what he knows.
Guy D. Newman

A man stopped every morning to set his watch by the clock on the local bank. One day the banker stepped outside to ask him why. "Well," said the man, "I am the man who sounds the noon siren and I want to be sure it is the correct time." "That's strange," said the banker, "I set this clock by that siren each day."
Unknown

All too often modern man becomes the plaything of his circumstances because he no longer has any leisure time; he doesn't know how to provide himself with the leisure he needs to stop to take a good look at himself.
Michel Quoist

"Be yourself" is about the worst advice you could give some people.
Unknown

To be really truthful, we have to do more than stop lying. Really, most of the work is positively learning how to speak the whole truth in love.
Tim Stafford

Mark it down. God never turns away the honest seeker. Go to God with your questions. You may not find all the answers, but in finding God, you known the One who does.
Max Lucado

Today I bent the truth to be kind, and I have no regret, for I am far surer of what is kind than I am of what is true.
Robert Brault

Who is a wise man? -He who studies all the time.
Who is strong? -He who can limit himself.
Who is rich? -He who is happy with what he has.
The Talmud

An honest man with an open Bible and a pad and pencil is sure to find out what is wrong with him very quickly.
A. W. Tozer

In obedience to discernment, more discernment will come. We need to be attentive and alert in order to hear and understand God's call and then act, knowing that God blesses even our mistakes.
Unknown

When I was young, I was sure of everything. In a few years, having been mistaken a thousand times, I was not half so sure of most things as I was before. At present, I am hardly sure of anything but what God has revealed to man.
John Wesley

A wise man will make haste to forgive, because he knows the true value of time.
Samuel Johnson

A God you understood would be less than yourself.
Flannery O'Connor

Men occasionally stumble over the truth, but most of them pick themselves up and hurry on as if nothing happened.
Winston Churchill

Every day that you attempt to see things as they are in truth is a supremely successful day.
Vernon Howard

Truth is the most powerful force on earth because it cannot be changed.
Mike Murdock

Nobody ever outgrows Scripture; the Book widens and deepens with our years.
Charles Spurgeon

Truth may walk through the world unarmed.
Bedouin

A religion that is small enough for our understanding would not be big enough for our needs.
Corrie ten Boom

When I was young, I was sure of everything. In a few years, having been mistaken a thousand times, I was not half so sure of most things as I was before. At present, I am hardly sure of anything but what God has revealed to man.
John Wesley

Truthfulness is much more than the absence of lies. It is genuine communication of minds and hearts. Real truthfulness reflects the character of God, who is always exactly what He says he is, and who speaks painful but joyful truth, never any small talk to our hearts. Think of Jesus: ever kind, but relentlessly truthful.
Tim Stafford

The Lord has taught us that nobody can know God unless God teaches him.
Irenaeus

Of all kinds of knowledge that we can ever obtain, the knowledge of God and the knowledge of ourselves are the most important.
Jonathan Edwards

It is said an eastern monarch once charged his wise men to invent a sentence, to be ever in view, and which should be true and appropriate in all times and situations. They presented him with the words, "And this, too, shall pass away." How much it expresses! How chastening in the hour of pride! How consoling in the depths of affliction!
Abraham Lincoln

If envy was not such a tearing thing to feel it would be the most comic of sins. It is usually, if not always, based on a complete misunderstanding of another person's situation.
Monica Furlong

The older I get, the surer I am that I'm not running the show.
Leonard Cohen

Every man is a fool for at least five minutes every day. Wisdom consists in not exceeding that limit.
Elbert Hubbard

Let your old age be childlike, and your childhood like old age; that is, so that neither may your wisdom be with pride, nor your humility without wisdom.
Augustine of Hippo

When filled with holy truth the mind rests.
C. H. Spurgeon

A loving heart is the truest wisdom.
Charles Dickens

A wise man is never less alone than when he is alone.
Jonathan Swift

Almost all men are affected with the disease of desiring to obtain useless knowledge.
John Calvin

We grasp for truth and lose it till it comes to us by love.
Madeleine L'Engle

One can never wrestle enough with God if one does so out of pure regard for the truth. Christ likes us to prefer truth to him because, before being Christ, he is truth. If one turns aside from him to go toward the truth, one will not go far before falling into his arms.
Simone Weil

Progress towards maturity is not to be measured by victory over the sins we are aware of, but by hatred of the sins which we had overlooked and which we now see all too clearly.
Arthur C. Custance

Knowledge is limitless. Therefore, there is a minuscule difference between those who know a lot and those who know very little.
Leo Tolstoy

To profit from good advice requires more wisdom than to give it.
Unknown

His words are the essence of truth…Jesus never uttered opinions. He never guessed; He knew, and He knows.
A. W. Tozer

We occasionally stumble over the truth, but most of us pick ourselves up and hurry on as if nothing happened.
Unknown

Men tell you the facts, but God will tell you the truth!
Unknown

When a true thought enters any man's mind, be he saint or sinner, it must of necessity be God's thought, for God is the origin of all true thoughts and things. That is why many real truths are spoken and written by persons other than Christians.
A. W. Tozer

The most certain sign of wisdom is a continual cheerfulness.
Michel De Montaigne

Each day just ask Jesus to go with you and listen to his counsel. Ask for discernment and wisdom and The God of all will grant you these things for he has promised to answer whatever you ask if you ask for something which is in his will for you.
The only time it won't go well with you, if the Lord wants you somewhere else.
Unknown

There is only one theology, but there are many theologians.
Athenagoras I

There is no need to look anywhere else for truth which we can easily obtain from the church. The apostles have, as it were, deposited this truth in all its fullness in this depository, so that whoever wants to may draw from this water of life. This is the gate of life; all others are thieves and robbers.
Irenaeus

Whenever two people meet there are really six people present. There is each man as he sees himself, each as the other person sees him, and each man as he really is.
William James

I am greater than the stars for I know that they are up there and they do not know that I am down here.
William Temple

Half the work that is done in this world is to make things appear what they are not.
Ellas Beadle

God, give us grace to accept with serenity the things that cannot be changed, courage to change the things which should be changed, and the wisdom to distinguish the one from the other.
Reinhold Niebuhr

God is perfect love and perfect wisdom. We do not pray in order to change His Will, but to bring our wills into harmony with His.
William Temple

About The Authors

Over these past fifteen years of ministry, we have found it helpful to compile a list of those individuals whose writings we have chosen to share.

This list is organized according to the life-lines of those authors, beginning in the earliest history of our Christian Church, and leading up to our most recent Christian contributors.

While this list is by no means exhaustive in who we have represented over the years, we believe this table of many of the most frequently shared will perhaps aid us all in "framing" where and when many of these important and profound thoughts have been generated.

AUTHOR	VOCATION	LIFE DATE
	2nd Century	
Irenaeus	French bishop, Christian writer	175-195
	4th Century	
Jerome	Latin Bible translator and Biblical scholar	345-419
John Chrysostom	Early church father and Christian philosopher	347-407
Augustine of Hippo	Algerian, Bishop of Hippo, early Christian church father, thinker	354-430
	7th Century	
Isaac the Syrian	Syrian bishop, theologian, author	613-700
	11th Century	
Bernard of Clairvaux	Christian teacher of medieval Christianity	1090-1153
	12th Century	
Francis of Assisi	Italian Catholic friar & preacher	1181-1226
	13th Century	
Thomas Aquinas	Italian theologian and philosopher	1225-1274
Meister Eckhart	German mystical theologian	1260-1328
	14th Century	
Johannes Tauler	German mystic, Catholic preacher, theologian	1300-1361
Julian of Norwich	English anchoress, Christian mystic, author	1342-1416
Thomas a Kempis	German spiritual writer	1380-1471
	15th Century	
Martin Luther	German monk, professor of theology	1483-1546
William Tyndale	English biblical translator and martyr	1495-1536
	16th Century	
John Calvin	French Protestant reformer	1509-1564
Teresa of Avila	Spanish Carmelite mystic and reformer	1515-1582
Lancelot Andrewes	Theologian, one of creators of King James version	1555-1626
Francis de Sales	French Roman Catholic bishop and spiritual writer	1567-1622
George Herbert	English poet and hymn writer and Anglican priest	1593-1633

AUTHOR	VOCATION	LIFE DATE
17th Century		
Samuel Rutherford	Scottish Presbyterian theologian	1600-1661
Brother Lawrence	Carmelite mystic, French monk/cook	1611-1691
Richard Baxter	English preacher	1615-1691
Blaise Pascal	French mathematician, scientist, and religious writer	1623-1662
John Bunyan	English preacher and author	1628-1688
John Locke	English philosopher	1632-1704
Isaac Newton	English mathematician and Christian thinker	1642-1727
Francois Fenelon	French mystic and archbishop of Cambrai	1651-1715
Matthew Henry	English Presbyterian minister, commentary author	1662-1714
Isaac Watts	English clergyman, poet and hymn writer	1674-1748
William Law	Anglican spiritual writer	1686-1761
18th Century		
Jonathan Edwards	American theologian, missionary	1703-1758
John Wesley	Founder of Methodism	1703-1791
Samuel Johnson	English author, devout Anglican	1709-1784
George Whitefield	English clergyman and evangelist	1714-1770
Johann Wolfgang von Goethe	German poet, scientist, philosopher	1749-1832
William Wilberforce	English abolitionist and philanthropist	1759-1833
Charles Finney	Presbyterian minister	1792-1875
Henry Law	Anglican dean and evangelical writer	1797-1844
19th Century		
Horace Bushnell	American Congregational theologian	1802-1876
Robert Browning	English poet	1812-1889
Robert Murray McCheyne	Scottish minister and writer	1813-1843
Soren Kierkegaard	Danish religious philosopher, writer	1813-1855
Henry Ward Beecher	American congregational minister	1813-1887
J. B. Stoney	Christian author	1814-1897

AUTHOR	VOCATION	LIFE DATE
J. C. Ryle	Evangelical parish priest, author	1816-1900
Henry David Thoreau	American essayist and poet	1817-1862
Florence Nightingale	Reformer of hospital nursing	1820-1910
George MacDonald	Scottish minister and writer	1824-1905
Leo Tolstoy	Russian novelist and social reformer	1828-1910
Lewis Carroll	English author & Anglican deacon	1832-1898
James Hudson Taylor	Missionary	1832-1905
Hannah Whitall Smith	American Author	1832-1911
Charles Haddon Spurgeon	English Baptist preacher	1834-1892
Phillips Brooks	American preacher	1835-1893
D. L. Moody	American evangelist	1837-1899
F. B. Meyer	Evangelical Baptist minister	1847-1929
Robert Louis Stevenson	Scottish novelist, brought up in religious home	1850-1894
William Ralph Inge	English academic, writer and theologian	1860-1954
Alfred North Whitehead	English philosopher	1861-1947
Billy Sunday	American evangelist	1862-1935
George Washington Carver	American scientist and educator	1864-1943
Andre Gide	French author, humanist, moralist, champion of poor	1869-1951
Oswald Chambers	Scottish evangelist and devotional writer	1874-1917
Gilbert Keith Chesterton	English writer and Christian apologist	1874-1936
Evelyn Underhill	English mystical writer	1875-1941
Albert Schweitzer	German theologian, medial missionary	1875-1965
Harry Emerson Fosdick	American liberal Protestant minister	1878-1969
E. Stanley Jones	Missionary to India, author	1884-1973
Paul Tillich	German-born American theologian and philosopher	1886-1965

AUTHOR	VOCATION	LIFE DATE
Reinhold Niebuhr	American theologian	1892-1971
Pearl S. Buck	American author	1892-1973
Corrie Ten Boom	Dutch evangelist and author	1892-1983
Fulton Sheen	American Roman Catholic bishop and broadcaster	1895-1979
Norman Vincent Peale	American minister and author	1896-1993
A. W. Tozer	American Methodist pastor and author	1897-1963
C. S. Lewis	Theologian, writer, Christian apologist	1898-1963
Martin Lloyd-Jones	Welsh pastor and author	1899-1981
20th Century		
Elton Trueblood	Quaker philosopher and theologian	1900-1994
Vance Havner	American devotional writer	1901-1986
Watchman Nee	Chinese home church leader, author, jailed 20 years	1903-1972
Clare Boothe Luce	American playwright, legislator, and diplomat	1903-1987
Dietrich Bonhoeffer	Theologian	1906-1945
William Barclay	Scottish biblical scholar	1907-1978
Alan Redpath	Evangelist and Bible teacher	1907-1989
Leonard Ravenhill	English Christian evangelist & author	1907-1994
Simone Weil	French philosopher, converted to Catholicism, writer	1909-1943
Mother Teresa	Albanian missionary to India	1910-1997
Francis Schaeffer	Presbyterian minister, author	1912-1984
Thomas Merton	American Trappist monk, Catholic author, and poet	1915-1968
Richard Halverson	Presbyterian minister and chaplain of U.S. Senate	1916-1995
Lewis Smedes	American professor, author	1921-
Henri Nouwen	Dutch spiritual writer, Catholic priest, theologian	1932-1997
Dallas Willard	American spiritual philosopher	1935-2013
Billy Graham	Christian evangelist	1918-
Charles Swindoll	American preacher, author	1924-
Frederick Buechner	American spiritual writer, Presbyterian minister	1926-

AUTHOR	VOCATION	LIFE DATE
J. I. Packer	Evangelical priest, author	1926-
Elisabeth Elliot	Belgium missionary, writer, and radio show host	1927-
Warren Wiersbe	American pastor, author	1929-
James Dobson	Evangelical leader, author	1936-
John MacArthur	American pastor, author	1939-
Bruce Wilkinson	American evangelist	1940-
Richard Foster	American author	1942-
Ravi Zacharias	India apologist, author	1946-
Philip Yancey	American journalist, author	1948-
Bill Hybels	Evangelical leader, pastor, author	1952-
Max Lucado	Pastor, author	1955-
Beth Moore	Author	1957-

There's More!

If you enjoyed this book, you might also enjoy these other books by Eric Elder Ministries, including:

- *Two Weeks With God*
- *What God Says About Sex*
- *Exodus: Lessons In Freedom*
- *Jesus: Lessons In Love*
- *Acts: Lessons In Faith*
- *Nehemiah: Lessons In Rebuilding*
- *Ephesians: Lessons In Grace*
- *Israel: Lessons From The Holy Land*
- *Israel For Kids: Lessons From The Holy Land*
- *The Top 20 Passages In The Bible*
- *Loving Thoughts On Death And Dying*
- *Our Favorite Christian Quotations*
- *Romans: Lessons In Renewing Your Mind*
- *St. Nicholas: The Believer*
- *San Nicolás: El Creyente (Spanish Edition of St. Nicholas)*
- *Making The Most Of The Darkness*
- *15 Tips For A Stronger Marriage*
- *A Personal Journal With 101 Quotes On Prayer*
- *A Personal Journal With 101 Quotes On Love*
- and *A Personal Journal With 101 Quotes On Faith*

To order or learn more, please visit:

www.InspiringBooks.com

www.ingramcontent.com/pod-product-compliance
Lightning Source LLC
Chambersburg PA
CBHW082352270326
41935CB00013B/1597